Technology, Education—Connections
The TEC Series

Series Editor: Marcia C. Linn
Advisory Board: Robert Bjork, Chris Dede,
Carol Lee, Jim Minstrell, Jonathan Osborne, Mitch Resnick

Video Games and Learning:
Teaching and Participatory Culture in the Digital Age
Kurt Squire

Teaching and Learning in Public:
Professional Development Through Shared Inquiry
Stephanie Sisk-Hilton

Rethinking Education in the Age of Technology:
The Digital Revolution and Schooling in America
Allan Collins and Richard Halverson

The Computer Clubhouse:
Constructionism and Creativity in Youth Communities
Yasmin B. Kafai, Kylie A. Peppler, and Robbin N. Chapman, Editors

WISE Science: Web-Based Inquiry in the Classroom
James D. Slotta and Marcia C. Linn

Creating and Sustaining Online Professional Learning Communities
Joni K. Falk and Brian Drayton, Editors

Designing Coherent Science Education:
Implications for Curriculum, Instruction, and Policy
Yael Kali, Marcia C. Linn, and Jo Ellen Roseman, Editors

Data-Driven School Improvement:
Linking Data and Learning
Ellen B. Mandinach and Margaret Honey, Editors

Electric Worlds in the Classroom:
Teaching and Learning with Role-Based Computer Games
Brian M. Slator and Associates

Meaningful Learning Using Technology:
What Educators Need to Know and Do
Elizabeth A. Ashburn and Robert E. Floden, Editors

Using Technology Wisely:
The Keys to Success in Schools
Harold Wenglinsky

VIDEO GAMES
AND LEARNING

Teaching and Participatory Culture
in the Digital Age

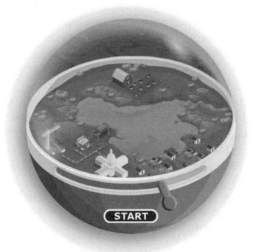

Kurt Squire
Foreword by James Paul Gee
Featuring contributions by Henry Jenkins

Teachers College, Columbia University
New York and London

Published by Teachers College Press, 1234 Amsterdam Avenue, New York, NY 10027

Library of Congress Cataloging-in-Publication Data

Squire, Kurt.
  Video games and learning : teaching and participatory culture in the digital age / Kurt Squire ; foreword by James Paul Gee ; featuring contributions by Henry Jenkins.
      p. cm. -- (Technology, education--connections : the TEC series)
  Includes bibliographical references and index.
  ISBN 978-0-8077-5198-5 (pbk. : alk. paper) -- ISBN 978-0-8077-5199-2 (hardcover : alk. paper)
    1. Video games--Study and teaching. 2. Video games and children. 3. Education--Effect of technological innovations on. 4. Computer-assisted instruction--United States. I. Jenkins, Henry, 1958- II. Title.
    GV1469.3.S76 2011
    794.8'2071--dc23   2011017769

ISBN 978-0-8077-5198-5 (paper)
ISBN 978-0-8077-5199-2 (cloth)

Printed on acid-free paper
Manufactured in the United States of America

18 17 16 15 14 13 12 11   8 7 6 5 4 3 2 1

Contents

Foreword *by James Paul Gee*   ix

Preface   xi

Acknowledgments   xv

Chapter 1.
Possible Worlds: Why Study Video Games? Aren't They a Waste of Time?   1

     Designing Experience, or That Evasive "Fun Factor"   5

     Social Gaming: Possible Identities   10

     Possible Cultures   12

     Digital Media and Learning   14

     Theory and Practice   15

     Feature: *The Most Fun You Can Have with
Model Railroads Without Sniffing Glue*   17

Chapter 2.
Ideological Worlds: What Makes a "Good" Educational Game?   19

     Interest-Driven Learning   19

     Worlds with Bias   22

     Civilization as a Geographical Model   26

     Ideological Worlds as Frameworks for Thinking   28

     Meaning-Making in Ideological Worlds   30

     Participation in Ideological Worlds   31

     Theory and Practice   35

     Feature: *Cooperative Game Play*   38

Chapter 3.
Teaching with Games: Learning Through Play   **40**

    Before-School Corpse Retrievals   40

    From Players to Designers   43

    Interest-Driven Learning   46

    Open Access   48

    The Montessori System: Following the Needs of the Child   48

    Toward Game-Based Pedagogies   57

    Theory and Practice   59

Chapter 4.
Community Organizing for Participatory Learning   **61**

    Creating a Community to Learn With   62

    Inside Online Affinity Spaces   69

    Education in a Digital Age: Participatory Education   71

    Learning Through Participation   71

    Theory and Practice   75

Chapter 5.
Games-to-Teach: Designing Games for Learning   **77**

    Broadening the Discussion of Education and Games   77

    Games, Popular Media, Science, and Learning   79

    Creating a Research Agenda for Games and Education   80

    Designing Games for Learning   85

    Building an Educational Game from Scratch   90

    Inventing New Genres: *Environmental Detectives*   99

    Theory and Practice   104

    Feature: *Learning to Be a Full-Spectrum Warrior*   107

Chapter 6.
Games in Classrooms: Replaying History   **109**

    Teaching World History   109

    Introducing *Civ3*   113

    Failure, Trade Offs, and Just-in-Time Lectures   116

    "This Game Isn't So Bad": Frustration, Failure, and Appropriation   117

    The Emergence of a Game-Playing Culture   118

Recursive Play   122

What Students Learned   127

Civilization Camp: Developing Expert Gamers   128

Creating a New Gaming Culture   129

Developing Gaming Expertise   129

Theory and Practice   138

Chapter 7.
The Aesthetics of Play   **140**

Games, Learning, Society: Building a Program   141

The Aesthetics of Game-Based Learning   142

Aesthetics of Being *Viewtiful Joe*   145

Apolyton University: Trajectories of Participation   150

During-Action Reports: Cognitive Artifacts That Organize Practice 152

Design Thinking   155

Designing *Civ4*   159

Toward an Aesthetics of Game-Based Learning   160

Theory and Practice   161

Feature: *I Love Rock 'n' Roll*   164

Chapter 8.
Design Literacy: Productive Play   **165**

Developing Game Expertise   166

Developing Game Fluency   168

Games as Occasions of Theory Building and Testing   169

Competition and Learning   170

Organizing by Competitions   172

Trajectories of Participation   176

Centers of Expertise   177

What Learning Occurred? A Community Well Played   177

Theory and Practice   180

Chapter 9.
Games Go to School: Situated Learning, Adaptable Curricula   **182**

Place-Based Gaming   185

Place-Based Learning   188

Learning Through Design, or How to Design an Educational Game   189

From Game Designer to Community Organizer   192

Community Organizing as Curriculum   194

Ramping Up   196

Situating Learning at South Beach   198

Scientific Citizenship   207

Scaling   210

Theory and Practice   211

Chapter 10.
The Future of Games for Learning   **213**

Creating Education Media   213

Independent Games   214

Informal Learning Contexts   220

Scientific Citizenship   221

Example: *Citizen Science*   222

Mobile Media   224

Creating the Future of Educational Technology   227

Coda: On Researching the Effectiveness of Educational Interventions   **228**

Gold Standard Research   228

"Science" Fetish   230

Health Care Envy   232

References   **235**

Index   **241**

About the Author   **253**

Foreword

In the past few years, the field of games and learning has taken off like a rocket. Kurt Squire is one of the main people who helped design the rocket, and his powers as a gamer-generation scholar have been a large part of why the rocket is on track for a very successful flight. In this book we get to share in Kurt's journey as a gamer, a teacher, and a scholar. We see the three roles come together, each one deeply informing the other.

Kurt is a true enthusiast for games, gaming, and gamers. But, as an educator, he is not just pushing games. He is pushing a much stronger "drug," one that can, in the right conditions, become addictive to humans: deep and challenging learning. Although one would never know it from school, for us humans, learning is a source of pleasure as deep and instinctive as sex and food. That is why good scientists, good gamers, and good fan fiction writers never stop learning, growing, and challenging their current level of mastery.

There is a saying that it takes 10,000 hours of practice to be an expert at anything. But have you ever wondered what motivates people to put in those hours? It isn't money, since most scientists, gamers, and fan fiction writers don't make much money. And people readily become experts at things for which they earn no money, like designing houses in *The Sims* or engaging in citizen science. What motivates them is pure pleasure, the pleasure of "flow," the zone we humans enter when we engage with highly motivating challenges that feel tough but doable.

Games today encourage a form of learning that Kurt wants to see spread. This form of learning can most certainly be done with games, but it can be done in other ways as well. This sort of learning has been given many different names: "gamelike learning," "well-mentored problem-based learning," "well-designed learning experiences," and others.

In the jargon of educational research, this type of learning is sometimes called "situated, embodied, problem-based learning." It is *problem based* because it is focused on learners being able to use information, facts, and formulas to solve problems, not just to pass paper-and-pencil tests of fact retention. It is *situated* because the problems are placed in actual contexts where their solutions can be tested against feedback from the real world or a virtual world meant to model aspects of the real world. It is *embodied* because the learners do things and do not just think things. They use their minds, bodies, and smart tools. Games are a very good platform for such learning. They hold out even greater progress in the future. But there are other platforms.

Good video games are nothing but well-designed problem-solving spaces with copious feedback, good mentoring from the game's design and associated fan communities, and a "win state." Actually (though no one should tell gamers this), having a win state and way stations—"levels"—on the way to it is just a form of "assessment."

However, good games—and good game scholars like Kurt—know that even games do not teach with the game alone. They teach through good design and through associated interest- and passion-driven groups of fans on the Internet who reflect on, critique, explicate, study, and design and redesign aspects of their favorite games. In these groups, people of different ages and degrees of expertise mentor each other and set shared and high standards.

The field of "games and learning" has, thus, inspired a new foundation for the learning sciences generally. But this makes the whole thing sound boring, certainly more boring than playing a good game. But here is where Kurt can help. He has written a book that is deep, complex, and challenging, but you will never know it, since you will have so much fun reading it. Just like a good game.

—James Paul Gee
Mary Lou Fulton Presidential Professor of Literacy Studies
Arizona State University

Preface

I was born in 1972. That's the same year that *Pong* came out for the Odyssey. So I grew up with video games. I was in that first wave of kids that made Atari a household name. In the 1990s, I was among those jumping on the Internet to play First-Person Shooters (FPSs) and Multi-User Dungeons (MUDs), eventually coming back to consoles.

Today, my relationship with games is continuing to change as I play them with my kids. As I introduce my 3-year-old to *Super Mario Galaxies*, I see him awaken with wonder as he leaps with gravity-defying bounds and confronts the evil Bowser. He nimbly navigates his iPad, jumping between games, television shows, and creative applications without hesitating. Games have crossed generations. They have taken their place alongside books and television as media integrated into the fabric of our lives, and every indication is that they will continue to grow and evolve with us.

We've both grown some in the past 40 years. Video games are maturing, expanding, diversifying, and exerting influence across entertainment, business, and, increasingly, education. This book explicitly explores this last idea—the idea that if games are here to stay, what can and should be their impact on learning and education?

This book attempts to understand what properties make a good educational game, and then to judiciously and creatively apply those ideas to the design of learning environments. It's not just any old kind of game that can teach; there are specific properties of "educational" games that make them important for engagement and learning.

There's no one formula for creating an educational book (what a concept!) or an educational film. Likewise, there is no one way to create educational games. In fact, as educators and designers, we are not really good at it yet, but we're starting to get there.

Whether or not we, as a society, pursue the enterprise of educational video games isn't the entire question, though. Video games already enable people to build civilizations, run virtual businesses, or lead organizations of real people. We need to understand the impact of these experiences and the pressures they put back on institutions like schools.

This book is organized around my own experiences as a gamer, a researcher, and an educator, which I use to illuminate and theorize about the evolution of the field of games and learning. I tell stories that don't usually make it into the average research article on educational gaming. If you want to read the analysis of methods and extensive citations of previous literature that do delve into this area, check out the full reference list at the back of the book.

I've also attempted to analyze games in depth without losing readers who might be unfamiliar with particular titles such as *World of Warcraft* or *Civilization*. I've relegated the most arcane discussions of gaming minutiae to footnotes. I also trust that readers know how to Google unfamiliar terms (such as allusions to *Barrens chat*) and to skip past sections that are not interesting to them. Featured games and gaming phenomenon are also reviewed in sidebars throughout the chapters and in featured mini-essays between the chapters. Many of these quick takes on popular games are excerpted from columns published on Joystick101.org or in *Computer Games* magazine (some cowritten with Henry Jenkins). They are meant to pique your interest to play and to be provocative rather than conclusive.

Often, scientists and educational leaders charge that we need evidence that video games work for learning. I would certainly agree with that statement, although for me the trick is defining what we really mean by *evidence*, *video games*, and *learning*. At the moment, education is largely gripped by physics envy, or, more appropriately, health care envy (see pp. 232–234), which is driving the discourse of educational research. In contrast, evidence (if you believe your textbooks) is something brought to bear in an argument. Good evidence, then, is something that can be brought to bear on an issue (rather than output from a particular research method). No one research method should rule them all.

We need to operationalize what we mean by *video games* and *learning*. Although there's a crop of good educational games on the market (see *GameStar Mechanic*, *PeaceMakers*, *Resilient Planet*, *Cosmos Chaos*, and *DimenxianM*), most published studies have examined media that *don't* embody most of the unique features of these games (see Mayer & Johnson, 2010; Randel, Morris, Wetzel, & Whitehill, 1992). Further, the kinds of learning goals (decoding of written text, memorizing terms, performance of mathematical operations, identifying correct multiple-choice responses) that many "educational" games strive to promote may not align with contemporary educational goals and may also be seen as distracting from the more important problems facing educators.

As a result, we risk having *a lot* of evidence developed through very precise methods that isn't useful or appropriate for making claims on video games and learning. Evidence generated by questionable games or games not well aligned with the learning goals we would like to see isn't good evidence at all. To take a really mundane (yet plausible) example, we don't need a highly controlled experiment testing whether playing *Oregon Trail* increases students' memorization of factual U.S. history. *Oregon Trail* (as good as it was at the time, and it's still better than many games) doesn't employ many of the features of contemporary games, and few people would argue that a failure to memorize U.S. history factoids is the pressing problem of the 21st century. In fact, the bigger problem is an overemphasis on such memorization at the expense of understanding larger concepts (see Wineburg, 2000).

We *do* need, however, research that carefully identifies the aspects of games that make them good learning environments, such as how they operate as social systems that enable people to develop identities as designers of systems and producers of knowledge (see chapters 4, 8, and 9). As we develop better understandings of how game-based learning operates, we may want to compare game-based pedagogies to other pedagogies. In general, the field has relatively poor methods for comparing educational programs (such as the reading program Success for All) longitudinally, because of complicating issues such as local control of education, students' autonomy, accounting for unintended consequences of educational interventions, and teachers' professional autonomy in choosing teaching goals and methods.

So, what *do* we know from good research on good games? Although there are many good literature reviews of games that dig into the details of very specific design features (see Gredler, 2004; Rieber, 2005), this book focuses on creating a vision of digital games and learning that draws on critical analyses of games, naturalistic research of game communities, descriptions of design research, and empirical studies of learning through games. Oddly, the researchers in these communities often don't talk to one another (game people think educators are lame, and educators think that game people are hyperviolent misogynists destroying all that is good in the world). Yet, at a minimum, educators researching and designing games for learning should understand something about the medium. Perhaps educators will try a few of the teaching ideas interspersed throughout this book or, better yet, become inspired to apply these ideas in new ways within their practice.

My hope is that educators will at least skim the sections on game criticism and that game designers will review the sections on teaching. This easily could have been (and, indeed, at times was) three separate books on designing educational games, teaching with games, and mobile media and education. In an age in which we are rethinking the book, I've experimented with sidebars, footnotes, and other design elements to give a flavor of the interconnectedness of these issues in the field. More related content, expanded essays, and academic articles are available at kurtsquire.info/.

Acknowledgments

This book couldn't have been written without the help of many, many people. First, I'd like to thank James Paul Gee for suggestions on organizing the book, critical feedback during its editing, and mentoring throughout my career. Hopefully, Jim, it's come a long way since the "glorious mess" that you so graciously waded through. Likewise, Henry Jenkins contributed to more than just the essays in the book; I hope the reader will also see some of his thinking in my writing.

The book couldn't have gone long before sharing the work of my wife Constance Steinkuehler. As with any better half, she has contributed so much to this intellectual work that I don't know where her ideas end and mine begin. The book would never have been completed if she didn't pick up the slack in our house created by writing this book.

This book never would have happened if it weren't for Meg Lemke's infinite patience in suffering through multiple long-winded drafts and her faith that this project could become a reality. For the early chapters, I am indebted to teachers like James Douglas, Janet Kretschmer, Nancy Wells, Dawn Bullen, and Ann Jurisson, who helped develop whatever instincts I have for education, as did Chris Wolfe and everyone at Western College.

I'm deeply indebted to Sasha Barab for his guidance in my dissertation and for sharing his understanding of sociocultural learning theory, which constitutes the middle chapters. He created a supportive community of stellar graduate students, which I'm still trying to recreate to this day. Likewise, thanks to Tony Betrus and Edd Schneider for paving the way to study games at Indiana and to Elizabeth Boling and Bob Appelman for supporting Jon Goodwin and me in creating Joystick101.org.

It feels like a stretch to say that I wrote the last half of the book myself, as it was a collaborative work conducted across many teams. The work of the Games-to-Teach Project was a collaboration among Alex Chisholm, Henry Jenkins, Eric Klopfer, and myself, along with 20 or so students. None of the work on mobile media would be possible without Eric Klopfer's generosity and intellect.

None of the *Civ* work could have happened without Levi Giovanetto, Ben DeVane, and Shree Durga, who ran the project, shared their insights, and co-authored versions of these chapters that appeared in journals. I also want to thank the teachers at the MATCH school who facilitated that work and Geraldine Haas who assisted in that data collection and provided support during that phase of my research.

This *Civ* research and the subsequent research on mobile media were funded by the MacArthur Foundation, and I'd like to thank Connie Yowell for her support. This research was also supported by the Department of Education STAR Schools program, and I'm indebted to Chris Dede, Eric Klopfer, and program officer Brian Lekander. In addition, I'd like to thank Elizabeth VanderPutten at the National Science Foundation for funding the extension of this work in *Citizen Science* and for taking a risk on my collaboration with Filament Games. Matt Gaydos, lead designer of *Citizen Science,* has been driving much of the conversation around assessment and pedagogy that appears in the later chapters. Finally, Dan Norton and Dan White at Filament have been not only great collaborators, but also great friends throughout this journey, and I look forward to working on the next chapters together.

A special thanks goes out to all of the graduate students who conducted this research and who were the fuel for this research engine. I've learned more from you all than you ever could from me, and I'm indebted to each of you for investing yourselves in these projects. A special thanks goes to Mingfong Jan for being the glue running the mobile media project, a generous spirit, and wonderful photographer whose work added so much to this book. Similarly, Ben DeVane was constantly shuffled across projects and provided an intellectual glue tying them together. The chapters on mobile media are really the work, not of me, but of a team including Mingfong Jan, Ben DeVane, Jim Mathews, John Martin, Chris Holden, and Mark Wagler. My thinking on community organizing and place-based learning is really the result of conversations with Mark and Jim. I hope that I can give back to them a fraction of what they've given me, and that these chapters live up to the educational values they embody.

Finally, I'd like to thank my colleagues at the Wisconsin Institutes for Discovery. Rich Halverson helped set up this book and has been a tireless advocate for this project, as well as a wonderful collaborator. Likewise, I need to thank Susan Millar and Sangtae Kim for having confidence to embark on this next chapter of trying to improve public understanding of science through games. The best is still yet to come.

VIDEO GAMES
AND LEARNING

Teaching and Participatory Culture
in the Digital Age

CHAPTER 1

Possible Worlds: Why Study Video Games? Aren't They a Waste of Time?

"Come on, class. Please tell me that *someone* read the chapter."

I looked nervously around the room. "Please don't call on me," I thought. Of course we hadn't read it. Why Jim Douglas, my high school history teacher, even entertained the idea that we might have read it was beyond me. Douglas taught with the Socratic method and expected us to read the *entire* chapter before we started each new unit. Later, I thrived under this teaching style—because he assumed *we* were responsible for our own learning.

"So none of you can explain the causal factors behind Spanish colonization?" (Long pause). "Does anyone at least know what ships they had?"

We were getting nervous. Douglas's policy was that if "there was nothing left to discuss" then we would take the test, which would mean that we would all fail.

I tried to picture what a Spanish ship looked like. An image of a galleon popped into my head. I raised my hand.

"They had galleons."

"Very good, Mr. Squire. They had galleons. Now why would they have galleons?"

"For carrying gold."

"Yes, for carrying gold." Not Alistair Cooke, but we were getting somewhere.

"Yes, that's right . . . for gold. And they had war galleons to protect the galleons carrying the gold. These had a lot of guns." I was warming up. "The French mostly had *barques*. The Dutch, *fluyts*. The English, merchantmen. If you saw a *pinnace*, that was French, Dutch, maybe even a pirate."

Douglas was surprised, if not impressed. I wasn't known for "reading ahead."

But I was rolling. "The Dutch—they were mostly traders. They didn't have much territory, although Curacao was a great trading base." As I rambled on about the Caribbean, my friend Jason shot me an incredulous look as if to say, "Where in the hell are you getting this . . . is it a joke?"

It was, in fact, the result of my spending way too much time playing *Sid Meier's Pirates!* on my Commodore 64. *Pirates!* is an action-role-playing game, in which you are . . . well . . . a pirate (see Figure 1.1). I first played it in 1987, but *Pirates!* has been updated and re-released several times (including for the Nintendo Wii in 2010).

Here's the gist of it: You are a pirate in one of five time periods (between 1520 and 1700). The Han Solo of the high seas, you swashbuckle through the Spanish Main representing the French, Dutch, Spanish, or English. In addition to engaging in sword fights and ship battles, you trade and smuggle to create a privateering empire. *Pirates!* is open ended; the "story" is the one *you* create. There are few instructions, few quests, and no set narrative. No two games are exactly alike.

As a (potentially) educational game, *Pirates!* works because it is incredibly specific. Each city fluctuates in size, power, or nationality according to the time period, so players get to see how the Caribbean evolved. In the late 1500s, the Spanish dominate, meaning that if you're playing as the Dutch (my favorite) you're vastly outnumbered. But there is untold opportunity if you become friendly with the French and English, learn where their ports are, and plunder the Spanish (see Figure 1.1).

How the game unfolds is up to you. When I played as the Dutch, a favorite ploy at the end of my career was to capture a town and make it Dutch. I'd earn a title from the governor, then sail out and re-attack the *same* city, only this time making it French. This earned a huge land gift from the French, but ticked off the Dutch. I'd do this a few more times until the Dutch caught on and no longer welcomed me on

Figure 1.1.
Sid Meier's Pirates!

Dutch soil. But I kept my land—and infamous reputation—created by my piratey behavior. The underlying rules *encouraged* you to think like a pirate.

Players learn as much about Caribbean geography and history as they learn about swordplay. You're immersed in this world during the game, so you *have* to learn how the various types of sailors, nations, and geography affect your plans. For example, early on in the game, most players want to sack Panama because it's incredibly wealthy. But, if you try this, you'll quickly learn that it's also well defended and removed from the Spanish Main, which means you're going to need hundreds of sailors to even have a chance. You can't build a crew like that overnight. First, you need to build notoriety by attacking smaller ports and building a crew, and then you have to get them all to Panama before they mutiny. I vividly remember taking a wrong turn into the Gulf of Mexico and almost losing my ship because I didn't know my basic geography.

Learning geography through playing a game such as *Pirates!* is a commonplace experience for my generation. In fact, Levi Giovanetto and I recently surveyed University of Wisconsin–Madison undergraduates and found that most of the students had played *SimCity* and almost *everyone* had played *Oregon Trail*. The majority of the students felt these games helped them in school. The gaming generation is growing up, and they show no signs of giving up their gaming. When parents play Nintendo Wii with their kids and video game conferences include panels such as "I'm Getting Old: When Life Cuts into Gaming," you know it's not just teenage fantasy anymore. (See Not Your Big Brother's Games sidebar.)

Not Your Big Brother's Games

Many educators believe that the most popular video games have violent themes, and it just isn't true. WiiFit has sold as much or more than every version of every *Halo* game ever made. Every year, the list of the most popular games includes titles such as *The Sims* as well as music games, sports games, and racing games. But even that doesn't capture the diversity of games.

Take, for example, *Harvest Moon*: a farming-simulation game in which the player runs a family farm. The player has to tend the crops, raise livestock, befriend townspeople, and get married (if you want). Hundreds of thousands of people love this game.

Harvest Moon isn't alone. Other wildly successful non-violent, non-sexual games include *Rock Band* (in which you are a musician), *Nintendogs* (in which you raise a pet), and *Brain Age* (in which you try to increase mental agility by doing quizzes and puzzles).

Yet probably because of the size and cultural influence of the baby boom generation, video games are regarded by many as a fringe medium, and some still argue that games are trivial. This position is baffling, given the social, economic, and cultural impact of games. Games *already* operate as a medium for learning, whether or not we design educational games. Millions of people have learned some history from *Pirates!* and have explored the basic concepts of urban planning from *SimCity*. As Stephen Johnson (2005) popularly argued, even when games aren't "educational," the intellectual play of video games is productive in its own right. Video games are all about problem solving. Just as we recognize chess as a complex game and use it for studying the mind (think of how we program computers to play chess against chess masters), video games enable us to study how people who are spread across thousands of miles collaborate in real time to solve problems in games such as *World of Warcraft* (see *World of Warcraft* sidebar).

Video games now include a diverse range of experiences, from music simulation to multiplayer role-playing games with new models of distributed leadership (see Steinkuehler, 2006).

For educators, the questions are practical as well as philosophical. How does playing a historical game shape our thoughts about history? Can games be used for learning? If games do become widespread, what does this mean for the future of schools?

World of Warcraft

World of Warcraft, or *WoW*, is one of the most influential video games ever produced (with around 12 million sales). In this well-designed, massively multiplayer game, players create characters and interact in a virtual world that is populated by participants from all parts of the world. Players explore this world as they complete quests, form groups to take down bosses, join guilds (more permanent social groups) to meet friends, and compete in skill-based tournaments.

As an example of its cultural impact, consider the following scenario. One player, Ben Schultz, created a character named Leeroy Jenkins and filmed a video of Leeroy eschewing all social norms and running straight into a battle while his teammates were busy strategizing and calculating the odds of success. The video went viral (i.e., was widely viewed and distributed among people on the Internet) and became so widely known that it was referenced in *South Park* and Leeroy became the answer to a *Jeopardy* question.

Will Wright, designer of *SimCity*, *The Sims*, and *Spore* and one of the most important creative geniuses of our time, explained the educational potential of the medium: "Start with systems," Will said. "Games teach about systems in ways that no other medium can."

Will was right. *Pirates!* isn't about teaching declarative facts such as "the Spanish conquistadors colonized the Americas for gold." *Pirates!* puts the player in a *micro-world* of the ancient Caribbean in which they experience it as a system. Through cycles of action and feedback, players learn some facts (e.g., galleons are for carrying plunder), but, more importantly, they learn the *rules* underlying that world, the relationships of these rules, and the emergent properties of the system (e.g., to start a raid on Panama you must have a string of friendly ports, a fleet of galleons, and a lot of luck). James Paul Gee (2005) argues that what gamers learn is *embodied empathy for a complex system*. Video game players develop a feel or intuition of how systems work.

This *systemic* thinking is valuable because it helps people solve problems holistically, rather than focusing on single-cause solutions. Video game players learn that if you change one variable, for instance, the type of ships available, it affects the entire system (e.g., the placement of cities). Systemic thinking isn't valued much inside schools today (particularly because it isn't captured well by standardized tests), but this type of thinking is important everywhere outside school, from ecology to engineering to politics. If video games can support systemic thinking in these areas, they could be powerful educational tools indeed.

So far we've focused on the intellectual aspects of gaming, but isn't that missing the point? The allure of video games for education is that students learn while being thoroughly engaged in play. Might we design similar learning environments for schools?

DESIGNING EXPERIENCE, OR THAT EVASIVE "FUN FACTOR"

One response might be, "Of course *Pirates!* is fun. You get to be a pirate." It's true that learning history is more fun when you approach it as a pirate. But is that a bad thing? Why not learn academic content by playing interesting roles, such as learning history by becoming a privateer or studying science as a forensic investigator?

Studying video games in depth teaches us that a game isn't automatically fun just because it's about pirates. Every year many games are released in which players are pirates, soldiers, or other interesting characters, but the games aren't very good and don't sell well. The difference between good and bad games is more in the polished game experience than in the content. The textbook example of this is *Diner Dash*, the game about being a waitress (see *Diner Dash* sidebar and Figure 1.2).

> ## Diner Dash
>
> *Diner Dash* illustrates how good games can arise from boring content. *Diner Dash* is a real-time strategy game that "found" the game in balancing a section of tables (seating patrons, taking orders, delivering food in a timely fashion, and getting the check out fast). The designers added the story of a waitress thumbing her nose at her corporate job and struggling to start her own business. *Diner Dash* was one of the most compelling games that year.
>
> How is it that a game like *Diner Dash* is fun (despite the lack of sex and violence), whereas others with sexier, more interesting premises are not? There are many answers. Good games are cleverly designed. They involve hours of play-testing. The player's experience is sculpted so that it feels like a warm hug. Let's return to *Pirates!* to see how it works.

An Orchestration of Time

When *Pirates!* is compared with other pirate games, the prevalence of overlapping short-, medium-, and long-range goals stands out. From the moment you pick up the box, the long-term goals (plunder cities, win fame and fortune) are enticingly communicated. Short-term goals are presented by the game system. Vulnerable merchantmen ships sail past. Unguarded cities lay ahead. These potential goals "pull" players toward their long-term destiny of reaching infamy.

Figure 1.2.
Diner Dash

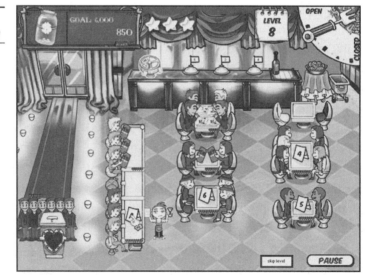

To see how well *Pirates!* is designed, try playing it with a stopwatch. Short-term goals (restock supplies, sail to the next harbor, battle) take between 45 seconds and 2 minutes. Completing a short-term goal (such as restocking a ship) should not take an hour.[1] In contrast, *Sea Dogs* has fully 3-D cities. What could be wrong with that? It's a feature players clamored for. While it's visually interesting, the 3-D design means that it takes 5 to 10 minutes to do simple housekeeping tasks in port, such as restocking supplies. Many critics panned it for being a pirate game in which you "spend your time walking around town." We can infer a design rule from this comparison: "Make short-term goals doable in a short amount of time." Interestingly, *Pirates!* and *World of Warcraft* can both be divvied up into short-term goals of 60 to 90 seconds, medium-range goals of 45 to 60 minutes), and long-term goals of 3 to 4 hours. *World of Warcraft* battles take 45 to 60 seconds, hunts (3 or 4 overlapping quests) take just under an hour, and raids go on for 3 to 4 hours, including preparation and debriefing.[2]

Overlapping Goals

A second design rule is to provide *overlapping goals*. When a *Pirates!* player sails into town for the first time, the governor instructs him or her to visit a neighboring city and receive a reward. So now the player has a long-term goal (earn fame and riches) and two short-term goals (attack a ship and visit a neighboring port). The short-term goals compete with one another, which gives the player an interesting choice: Do I attack that ship on the horizon, or do I sail to the next port?

But it gets better. As the player sets sail, he or she might also see an enemy town that is ripe for the picking. Attacking this port becomes a new medium-range goal. *Pirates!* constantly presents players with these overlapping goals. The importance of *clearly* communicating such goals can't be understated. Video games do a lot of work to make these goals compelling to players. These goals *seduce* players into pursuing them. As video game designers, it's always shocking just how much you have to lead players by the nose.

---

1. Interestingly, ship battles in the original *Pirates!* often went on longer, but in subsequent versions, designers used tricks to shorten them.

2. In fact, instances (typical five-person group activities) were designed to take 2 to 3 hours in earlier versions of the game, but when you had a bad group of players, your whole evening could be ruined. So Blizzard trimmed down group hunts to about an hour. Now, an instance is just one part of a gaming evening. A potential downside is that this design decreases players' commitment to the group. If you have a bad group, you don't have to learn how to fix it; you just move on. Raids (the longer activities, with a constant set of members) still recruit such group commitment.

As we design learning environments, video games teach us to ask: What goals do I offer players (or learners)? Will relatively trivial goals be attained quickly? Are they clear and overlapping so that my players feel compelled to continue? Does my environment constantly advertise new, seductive things to do? Is the game designed to produce emotionally satisfying experiences?

Anyone can theorize about design for learning, but good games *execute* these goals. We often think that this is because entertainment games have huge budgets, yet this isn't always the case. Many wonderful, small-budget entertainment games like *Flower* or *World of Goo* put their educational brethren to shame. Good game developers tweak games for months or years after many educational developers would have already shipped their educational game. Famously, Blizzard won't ship a game "until it's done," even if that means extra years of development and testing.

Throughout this book, I analyze both entertainment and educational games. This method is similar to what Doug Church calls *formal abstract design tools*. Church, a veteran game designer (now at Electronic Arts [EA]), uses concepts such as overlapping goals or power-up curves (the rate at which players gain new skills) to understand game design. Church invented these terms to help game designers learn from games across genres and to teach them to look beneath the surface of game features and toward interacting systems.

This spirit of studying one another's games—and then "stealing" features that work—is one reason that the games industry has grown and improved so rapidly. Commercial game designers play one another's games *all the time*. If there's a feature that works in one game, it will be adopted by others in the next product cycle. Ideas jump across games at a dizzying pace that puts academic "knowledge dissemination" to shame. Educational technologists rarely make their work available for others to critique, let alone build on.

Possibility Spaces

But video games aren't just about polished experiences; they can be more deeply transformative experiences in which we can do new things and become new kinds of people. Game designer Raph Koster (2004) talks about this in cognitive terms in his *Theory of Fun for Game Design*; games are fun because they provide new problems to solve. We stop playing when we get bored—when all the learning is done. We might contrast these open possibilities with closed ones. Games (or careers) with developmental paths that lead nowhere are like dead-end jobs. In *Civilization*, it's knowing how your game will end before you even start. In *World of Warcraft*, it's that moment when players say, "So I get better gear to do bigger battles to get bigger gear. What's the point of this again?" It's being able to predict every move in a game before it happens. Good games (think of classic nonvideo games, such as chess or basketball) refresh themselves, offering new lessons the more that we play.

Games like *Pirates!* or *Civilization* advertise these possibilities well, but there is nothing like a multiplayer game to amplify these possibilities. Multiplayer games continuously refresh themselves as we learn to be different kinds of people in social groups. Consider the first time a newcomer walks into a city in *WoW*. The experience is one giant exposure after another to interesting "possibilities." New players see a variety of characters riding outlandish-looking mounts. They see curious flying contraptions, rogues bouncing up and down, or goblins selling their wares. This is to say nothing of the chat channels, which now brim with esoteric conversations. Each element points to potential futures for the player.

This struck me the first time I saw a tauren druid decked out in the Cenarion Rainment, the "tier 1 dungeon set" (see Figure 1.3). Simply the existence of a gear set made out of tree branches inexplicably delighted me. What were those things? How do you get them? Do they have special powers? And what shoes do you wear with those?

Opening Social Horizons

These moments open horizons or players. Curiosities are piqued, desires are stoked, and feelings of wonder are stimulated. For a brief moment, anything is possible. When I saw that druid, I wanted to become a powerful, nature-channeling, bad-ass cow too. I imagined slaying monsters, saving friends, and emerging with cool-looking tree-branch shoulders that symbolized my exploits.

**Figure 1.3.
Tauren Druid with
Leafy Shoulders
(Cenarion Spaulders)
in *World of Warcraft***

In essence, people's characters *themselves* are walking billboards for the game's possibilities. Each glowing sword, flame-hooved horse, or YouTube video of a hilarious prank advertises new possibilities. A key *WoW* design decision may be *not* starting newbies in large, populated cities but instead waiting until they had experienced core game systems, such as combat, quests, and grouping, before lifting the veil and showing the game's depth. This moment happens around the 4- to 6-hour mark, which is about the time that a nonhardcore player would be just about ready to put the game down after a night or weekend of playing. Only then do the designers go for the kill and get you hooked.

I can still recall my inaugural voyage into Ironforge. My first character was a night elf, so it was a hike. Trekking through swamplands and snowy mountains, I saw crocodiles, gnomes, dwarves—outlandish creatures nothing like the denizens of my forest home. I struggled to navigate the crowded thoroughfares until a friend logged in and offered to show me around. He pointed out the giant cauldrons of Ironforge, with its blacksmiths and their clients in their crazy helmets, fancy pants, and glowing swords. He showed me trainers, vendors, and the Auction House where players buy and sell stuff, much like an "in-game eBay." He told me to make friends with a crafter to help with my gear.[3] He believed that a shrewd trader could make more money buying and selling goods than hunting, but it required dedication and an in-depth knowledge of *WoW*'s markets.

SOCIAL GAMING: POSSIBLE IDENTITIES

Games' possibility spaces are deeply social, even in single player games. I first learned to play *Civilization* by having a college roommate show me the basics. On consoles, kids show off games such as *Madden* (see *Madden* sidebar) or *Ico* (see Stevens, Satwicz, & McCarthy, 2008) to peers crowded behind them on the couch.

As studies of game players in their natural habitats (inasmuch as they exist) reveal, gaming is a deeply social activity for most players. Research shows that it is often players, not designers, who publicize possibilities through sharing stories, formal and informal apprenticing, and group activities (Steinkuehler, 2006).

Massively multiplayer games enable people to play together and collaborate in activities to achieve mutually desirable goals, and this intensifies learning. Massively multiplayer games researcher Constance Steinkuehler (my wife, who will be cited

---

3. *WoW* has changed over the years to require less social interdependence. Now, you can get goods through the Auction House or by making random requests in town, making it less personal and social. Stop me before I long for the days of crafting in *Star Wars Galaxies*.

throughout this book, as I've learned a lot from her) shows how even mundane activities such as a group hunt have instruction embedded within them. That Ironforge tour I described earlier may seem pedestrian, but my friend was showing me how to read the environment. He showed me what was worth noticing and what wasn't, what practices made up the world, and what kind of a character I could become.

Madden

Many games—not just strategy games—recruit systemic thinking. Sports games such as *Madden* are classic examples. Play a lot of *Madden*, and you will see patterns in how games unfold. I learned to "see" soccer games by playing *FIFA* with my brother (who was good enough at soccer to explain what parts were realistic and which parts weren't).

I was surprised to learn that pro players play video games to learn, too. When asked what helped him make the transition between basketball and football, Antonio Gates, an All-Pro NFL tight end, told *Sports Illustrated* (Silver, 2004):

> You know what helped? Playing *Madden*. I was always the Chargers. After I got here, I'd play the game and notice things about the defenses. I started recognizing formations in the [video] game, then I'd get to practice and see them there [in actual practice].

Lauren Silberman (2009) studied athletes and video games and found that players ranging from the University of Wisconsin baseball team to the Boston Red Sox use them as visualization tools. It helps them see the playbook, identify patterns, or generally just keep their heads in the game on off days.

This mentoring is routine in collaborative gaming. Anyone who has run an endgame group in a *WoW* instance (a dungeon that takes 2 to 4 hours to complete) should understand this. Let's say I'm a newbie "tank," which means my job is to absorb damage so that the healers and damage dealers in my group can do *their* jobs without dying. As we prepare for the battle, someone will ask, "OK, who has been here before?" Players fess up about who knows what battles. Because some monsters are "chained" together (pull one and they all come after you), there are strategies for me, as the tank, to keep the monsters focused on me and for damage dealers to "control" monsters by putting them to sleep or freezing them and so on. The approach is contingent on group makeup, meaning different constellations of players use different strategies.

As the group members negotiate, they're debating not just procedures, but also the goals of the activity itself. Will the group play as efficiently as possible? Or is there room for experimentation and error? Whereas some people value quick achievement, others (like me) enjoy the unexpected. I'm not happy unless everyone is operating right at the edge of his or her competence, and I like to court danger with taunts on occasion. (I'm not sure whether it's always appreciated).

We see these values negotiated most often when the group confronts failure. Is it OK to occasionally make a mistake, especially if it means a better experience, or should every battle be methodically planned? Games let us play with different value systems (which is more difficult to do in our real lives at home or at work). In the simplest of situations, players' activities are coordinated in ways that shape knowledge, skills, values, and even identities.

This form of learning—having people (including novices and experts) engaged in joint problem solving—is considered by learning theorists such as Annemarie Palincsar and Ann Brown (1984) to be perhaps the "best" form of learning. Yet it is rarely utilized in schools, which focus on individual work and are segregated by skill level. Typically in each class, there is one "expert" (the teacher), whose job it is to impart knowledge to the students, who are supposed to diligently work on their own learning. Educators have tried a variety of peer-to-peer approaches with good success, particularly when they leverage the diversity of abilities that exist in class (no matter how much we may try to track students). My own teaching experiences have been in multiage classrooms, so this idea of segregating people by ability has always seemed a little odd to me (see Chapter 3). Games excel at promoting different levels of expertise, and educators might embrace, rather than apologize for, this capacity.

POSSIBLE CULTURES

Thus, to understand how games operate, we need to look beyond the game itself and toward the broader cultural contexts in which it is situated. In many game communities, players themselves become the content, making them emblematic of *participatory* media culture. When my friend showed me around Ironforge, he was a central part of my game experience. This is also true of game communities around single-player games (see Chapter 7), particularly within the resource sites created for the games.

Online communities are also an integral part of massively multiplayer games such as *WoW*. The *WoW* community has actively cataloged every monster, item, and so on, to the point that the game is basically mapped out. Plunk the name of any item into Google (or better yet, thottbot.com or wowiki.com, the *WoW*-specific information databases) and you will find everything you need to know about the item's origin, attributes, and value.[4] The current site du jour is Elitist Jerks, a guild site visited by people from around the world for its quality resources and discussion. As designers respond to this increasingly savvy player base, they ramp up the game's complexity so that the game and players literally co-evolve. In fact, game designer Soren Johnson (in press) has argued that *WoW* is one big evolutionary struggle between players and designers toward creating a complex, fair, and balanced game system.

Let's compare this open, participatory culture to the environment of most schools. Gamers are surrounded by walk-throughs, guides, even videos explaining and demonstrating almost every nuance of the game. If, for example, a player wants to become a good tank, he or she can find forum threads, spreadsheets, and guides explaining gear, strategy, or how to deal with annoying damage dealers who don't do their jobs. In educational terms, there are examples, nonexamples, and worked problems for players to analyze to improve their performance. It's as if students had access, not only to the teacher's notes, but also to the guidebook, the Cliff notes, and experts in the field in question. Schools, in contrast, segregate learners by ability level and erect strong barriers between classrooms and authentic communities of practice.

But games aren't just open environments; they are carefully crafted learning experiences. Take the trajectory of how players learn about gear in *WoW*. The player's first task is to choose the "right" type of equipment after completing a quest. For example, do I choose cloth or leather? This is really a faux choice; there is one correct answer (whichever type your class wears). But seeing the items "previews" statistics that will soon matter. Next, players find new items in the world and must compare them to learn more about item attributes. Is the new item I found better than what I have? Again, this decision is straightforward, as there is only one variable initially (armor points). Soon enough, players must compare items in detail. I recently decided which of the two items in Figure 1.4 I should get for tanking. Even seasoned *WoW* players might have a hard time discerning the difference between them.[5]

---

4. If a *WoW* player asks a question in general chat, such as "Where do I get the Cenarion Shoulders?" the response is usually "thottbot" or "wowiki," meaning, go look up the information yourself rather than clog the chat channel with simple requests for information that anyone could find on the web. The logic of this system valuing self-directed learning is contrary to the values reflected in the design of our schools.

5. The answer is: "It depends." The general consensus is that the trollwoven spaulders are better tanking gear than hateful spaulders because the trollwoven spaulders enable better damage-dealing, which is good for "holding aggro" (keeping the monsters aggressive toward you and not your party). Critical strikes are useful in generating threat, and the trollwoven include almost twice the attack power, even if you add a gem for agility

Figure 1.4. Comparing Two Types of Leather Shoulder Pads in *World of Warcraft*.

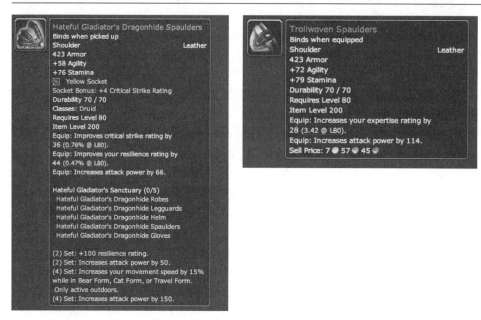

DIGITAL MEDIA AND LEARNING

Although games are a vivid example of participatory culture (especially when compared with broadcast media), a profound shift is occurring across media and institutions. Digital development and production tools such as GarageBand, iMovie, and YouTube are reshaping music and video. Blogs like *Daily Kos* are reshaping public discourse. The list goes on. These media present opportunities for ordinary people to follow a passion, develop expertise in a particular domain, and then reach a global audience through online publishing (for a thorough description, see Jenkins, 2006, or Black, 2008). What games do is guide and scaffold this trajectory.

Ironically, we can point to examples across almost every aspect of life where this takes place *except* for formal schooling. While schools remain static, *learning* is changing; every day, millions of people log on to *Daily Kos* to learn about politics or join a Flickr group to hone their photography skills. Researchers such as Doug

---

on the hateful spaulders. Plus, the extra expertise (with a weapon) provided by the trollwoven spaulders is important because it helps negate your opponents' chance to parry or dodge your attacks. As you can see, both items are viable, but when you get into optimizing gear, the trollwoven spaulders will make a bigger difference when multiplied across 16 items.

Levin and Sousan Arafeh (2002) have found that kids' Internet use shows that when they want to learn something personally meaningful, they look online. Online learning is personally meaningful, tailored to their interests and ability level, and provides immediate feedback.

In many respects, the promise of video games is about realizing age-old visions of education proposed by Maria Montessori or John Dewey. However, digital media make new things possible—such as leading a *Civilization* game or collaborating in real time with people around the world. We need to rethink what we want out of education in the digital age.

THEORY AND PRACTICE

Returning to our question, "Why study video games?" we have four responses:

1. People are developing academic interests and learning academic content through games, regardless of whether or not we design them for education. Players learn the basic facts of their games (the names of pieces, the maps, the terms), but, more important, they learn the emergent properties of the game as a system. How learners interpret game experiences and relate them to other aspects of life is explored further in chapter 7.
2. Games are deeply engaging for those who play them, and we can study games' educational design principles, such as orchestrating time, providing overlapping goals, constructing open-ended problems, and maintaining open social horizons. Even if we don't bring a game into every classroom, we can incorporate these principles in our instruction.
3. Third, games are emblematic of a broader shift toward participatory culture and suggest ways of structuring participatory educational experiences. Gaming communities push players from consumption to production. This is a useful model for educators (see chapters 4 and 7).
4. Finally, and most important for me, games, when they work, are aesthetically enlivening experiences, worthy of study in and of themselves as part of human experience. In my mind, this property should make them intriguing to anyone responsible for designing experiences for others. However, the moral imperative to study enlivening experiences is especially true for educators, who are responsible for shaping the daily lives of children attending school out of compulsion. Any time that we turn a child off to learning rather than awakening their intellectual curiosity, we've failed. In

fact, in a digital, participatory age, awakening students' interests and curiosity
and empowering them to pursue them may be what constitutes a "basic"
education.

This first chapter tried to make the case for studying games as an important
site of learning. The next chapter digs deeper and asks, "What should a good educational game look like?"

THE MOST FUN YOU CAN HAVE WITH MODEL RAILROADS WITHOUT SNIFFING GLUE

"Mostly sunny with a 25% chance of . . ." the morning DJ cut off as my roommate hit snooze. It was 6:00 a.m., which meant that I'd played *Railroad Tycoon II* (1998) for nearly 7 hours. "I'll quit just as soon as I connect Chicago and New York . . ."

A Digital Model Railroad

Railroad Tycoon II (*RT2*), the sequel to Sid Meier's 1990 *Railroad Tycoon*, is a linked series of scenarios such as connecting New York to Chicago, building the first transcontinental railroad, creating the Orient Express, and so on. Scenarios become campaigns, which, like military campaigns, allow you to build a company through time, so that *RT2* feels somewhat like a role-playing game (RPG). Trains get faster. Production and technology become more complex. As in *SimCity,* you need money to build in *RT2,* so much of the game is strategic expansion, linking up profitable routes, managing your company's stocks and bonds, and, of course, running the trains on time. You can also build new maps, create scenarios, or play online.

RT2 is not only a powerful railroad simulation but a formidable financial one as well. You can participate in all the financial wheeling and dealing of the Guilded Age and progressive era: Create shell companies and float yourself a loan from the main company; drive the stock of your primary company into the dirt and then buy it back, build it up, and flip your stock for profit. Some players forsake the railroad building altogether and make it a financial game of buying and selling companies. In short, you can do everything except create the savings and loan crisis (or more recently WorldCom). In fact, you could probably do that too in the right scenario.

Powerful Simulation Editor + Railroad Enthusiasts = Geek Heaven

"Railroad buffs have definitely loved *RT2*. Some folks complained about the speed of the game when they had 1,400 trains running simultaneously," noted Phil Steinmeyer, head designer of *RT2*. Wait, 1,400 trains? At one time? My all-night scenario topped out at about 15 trains. Who is building 1,400 trains?

To find out, I investigated fan sites such as the Indianapolis Depot, which has historical trains, custom maps, and new scenarios ranging from Santa Claus's railroad to historical routes in India. I talked to the head conductor Wabash Banks, who described *RT2* as an extension of his long-standing interest in railroads. Many railroad buffs are enthusiastic supporters of the game for its factual accuracy and underlying models.

RT2 works because it is *more* than a digital train set; it simulates railroad baroning, which extends the concept of model railroads by enabling players to do the following:

- Adopt a unique perspective (a baron), control financial variables, and interact with geography in a way that is inaccessible with a model railroad.
- See how a system behaves over time. Digital simulations are good at compressing or stretching time. *RT2* squeezes a decade of railroading into 90 minutes.
- Explore "what if" scenarios. There is no one way to beat the game. Players solve problems instead of guessing the designers' intentions.
- Learn the properties of the simulation through increasingly complex scenarios. No newbie player could play *RT2*'s financial game right away, but the mission structure walks players through different game systems.
- Design their own interactive content for other players. It's like players creating tools for other players to create their own railroads.

In fact, watching your trains run *is* a little like building a model railroad. Set it up, sit back, and watch your trains take folks from San Francisco to Atlanta. Without the sticky glue.

CHAPTER 2

Ideological Worlds: What Makes a "Good" Educational Game?

Chapter 1 argued for studying games as a new site for learning. This chapter asks, *What makes a good educational game?* And it builds on Chapter 1 by using game series such as *Civilization*, *SimCity*, and *The Sims* to discuss important educational issues such as oversimplification or bias. We often see games' educational value as being in their realism or complexity, but good games find "the game in the content." They inspire interest, creativity, and social interaction. Later on in this book, we'll explore how to design such games.

INTEREST-DRIVEN LEARNING

"I'm tired. I'm heading home," David said. It was still early, maybe midnight. I asked what was up. "Oh, nothing . . . We were out late last night. Maybe I'll just pack it in."

"That's cool . . . See you back at the place," I said. What I was really thinking was: If I waited a few minutes, I could sneak out of the party and squeeze in a few turns of *Civilization* on the house computer while he slept and my housemates "Smurf" and "J-Man" remained at the party. You see, there was only one computer for the four of us, and Smurf owned it. Ever since he'd installed *Civilization*, negotiating "*Civ* time" was an issue. Multiple *Civ*-addicted college students sharing one computer is a bad, bad scenario.

I don't know why I didn't see it coming. When I escaped home, I wasn't greeted by an unoccupied computer but instead by David, who was knee deep in fighting the Aztecs.

"What are you doing!?" I asked.

"What are *you* doing!?" he challenged back.

"I guess we're geeks," I conceded. Rather than fight, we agreed to take turns before Smurf got home.

Soon enough, an angry Smurf charged through the door. "You guys just left me there. Get off my computer. Go to bed!"

We sloughed off to the living room and fired up Tecmo Bowl. It *was* kind of mean—and awfully dorky—for us to abandon friends at a party for a computer game. After a few minutes, though, we realized he was a little *too* angry. We peeked back into Smurf's room, only to see him playing *Civilization*.

It's hard to capture how groundbreaking the first *Civilization* game was when it was released in 1991. In *Civilization*, players choose a civilization (Egyptian, Russian, Iroquois, American, German, etc.) to lead for 6,000 years (if successful). Through military might, cultural domination, diplomatic victory, or, my favorite way, a "space race victory," the goal is to be the first civilization to colonize a planet in the Alpha Centauri System.

The game is enormous. Starting in 4000 BC, players begin with just a settler, which is used to start a city (and hence a civilization). From there, players choose which technologies (such as the wheel or pottery) to research, add more settlers to improve the land (once the appropriate technologies are discovered), and build city improvements (such as temples or granaries). Part of why *Civilization* works is that you start small: a settler and a small plot of land. Each game evolves through your choices regarding which technologies to pursue, how to balance military strength versus infrastructure (a classic "guns vs. butter" problem), how to expand, and whether to go to war to protect your interests. My favorite part is building wonders of the world (such as the Colossus or the Great Wall of China). All the while, players compete with computer-controlled civilizations for these scarce resources. For a kid who cut his teeth on *Pac-Man*, *Bard's Tale*, and *Pirates!*, *Civilization* was a revelation.

Civ tied together themes from geography, economics, politics, and history, enabling me to identify holes in my understanding, such as, "What was happening in sub-Saharan Africa during the Roman Empire?" These connective questions come naturally to a *Civ* player but are rarely interrogated when topics are presented separately in school. At the time, I was an undergraduate studying social studies education in the Western College Program at Miami University. Between my teacher James Douglas's class and Sid Meier's games, I developed an interest in history and education.[1]

---

1. My *Pirates!* episode got me off to a good start with Mr. Douglas. I was such a dork that in my senior year I became a teaching assistant for his AP history class so that I could observe his teaching methods. For example, when someone asked, "Can I go to the bathroom?" he would say, "You're 17 years old. Don't you feel demeaned asking permission to do what any 4-year-old can do on her own?" This bathroom example illustrates how our system fails to give freedom and demand responsibility from students. Many other educators make similar observations; one of my favorites is Ted Sizer's (2004) *Horace's Compromise*.

SimCity

I could have opened this chapter by discussing late-night *SimCity* sessions. Some evil colleague installed *SimCity* in our Mac lab at college, and it sucked away hours of our lives.

    Civilization built on these compelling facets of simulation games but added a competitive dimension. In *SimCity*, you compete with the game model itself, trying to build your city according to whatever goals you choose. One common goal is to build an ecofriendly city. As players attempt to build public transportation or parks, they might run low on cash. To raise cash via property taxes, they might create a new subdivision. This new subdivision might create a mini-increase in crime if it is not properly policed, so more money is needed . . . and so the game continues. In many respects, the joy of *SimCity* is monitoring the "artificial life" of your creation as it grows and evolves over time.

My first academic exploration of games came in Computers and Cognition, a course taught by Christopher Wolfe (who became my advisor). We played *Smithville*, *Hidden Agenda*, *SimAnt*, *SimEarth*, *SimCity*, and *Net Trek* (awesome), read theories of hypertext, and discussed constructionist learning theory (Wolfe, 1995). Constructionism, associated with Seymour Papert (1981), is the idea that we learn best through constructing understandings through personally meaningful projects. I still recall my first assignment for Dr. Wolfe, which was to build a class hypercard stack on constructivism. Each of us took a subtopic (a nice, parsimonious assignment, I'd say) and then built our own group project. My friend David Simutis and I made an enormous hypercard stack called "The Hitchhiker's Guide to Western," which lived on the group's computers for years after we graduated. We read newsgroups such as alt.barney.dinosaur.die.die.die. We got email accounts and signed up for the grunge-L list. As J. C. Herz (1995) documented in *Surfing on the Internet*, we contemplated life in a world in which people might access—and contribute to!—whatever information they wanted from their desktop.

The field of digital media and learning formed because my generation played games and experienced participatory culture as *students*. We remember discovering the Internet and realizing that it changed everything (even if we didn't quite know how). Not everyone gamed 12 hours a day or even owned their own computer, but almost everyone played educational games, tried programming games in BASIC, and authored content on the web. There's a saying that we study the technologies we grew up with because they shape our basic experiences and expectations. Today's graduate students are gaming and Internet kids, and tomorrow's may be the mobile generation.

This story is an example of interest-driven learning. Playing *Pirates!* led to my interest in history and my identity as someone who was interested in education. Next, I found a mentor who nurtured that interest and suggested ways I might extend it. From there, I discovered *Civilization* and further delved into this interest. I was lucky enough to pursue these interests in both courses and graduate seminars and through my apprenticeship at the McGuffey Foundation School (discussed in Chapter 5).

So for many from my generation, the question "Can you learn with games?" is moot. The real questions are "*How* do we make *good* learning games?" and "Can games help transform education?"

WORLDS WITH BIAS

Video games are unique in that they are participatory. Games are complex systems that invite us to *play* with them. They are dynamic in that they unfold over time; most games evolve in response to our choices. Many games that are of interest to educators are *simulations*. They aren't *perfect* simulations, and it's not always clear what they are a simulation of, but very often they try to create some *experience* for the player. The real learning occurs through the transformations we have through playing and then engaging in related practices (viewing gaming forums, playing with friends, and so on). Let's return to *Civilization* as an example.

Educators often raise two issues with *Civilization*: "Who designs it (and do they know anything about history)?" and "The game is overly simplified and distorts reality."

Who Designs It?

This answer is straightforward: game designers. They are entertainers above all else. Firaxis, the makers of *Civilization*, are not professional historians, scholars, or educators. Game developers such as Sid Meier and Will Wright are classic Renaissance (mostly) men; they direct the programming, graphic design, and sound effects on many games, working with teams of developers. Sid Meier, the creative genius behind *Civilization*, builds historical games (*Civ, Pirates!*, and *Railroad Tycoon*), military strategy games (*F-15 Strike Eagle, Silent Service*), and whimsical games (*Sid Meier's SimGolf*). He also plays the piano—and particularly enjoys Bach—and sings in his church choir. Subsequent *Civ* designers share this breadth of interests. Brian Reynolds, lead designer of *Civ2*, studied philosophy at Berkeley. Jeff Briggs, lead designer of *Civ3*, has a PhD in music composition and is a history buff. Soren Johnson, lead designer of *Civ4*, has a BA in history and a master's in computer science from Stanford.

Civilization's designers iterate on its flaws over time. For example, *Civ3* didn't handle slavery, religion, or disease especially well. No one wanted to touch slavery for the obvious reasons, and it seemed similarly impossible to do religion without offending somebody.[2] It's also not fun to have 95% of your civilization die from diseases that are out of your control. In *Civ4*, designers included slavery as a labor system and religion as a tool for generating happiness and making money. The slave trade, which was so important to colonialism, still isn't realistically represented, nor are diseases.

Civilization's designers readily acknowledge its simplifications. Some ideas (such as the importance of raising sheep for wool) are excluded to keep the number of resources manageable. Others are simplified so that players can see the effects of their actions. If the model gets too complex, you can't observe the consequences, and then it is not entertaining or educational. Many educators make this mistake (let's include everything so that it's realistic), which makes a model less useful for learning. We don't want a 1:1 map of the world; we want a model to illustrate ideas. This is why many science researchers use simplified models.

One way that designers address these imperfections is by shipping the game with robust editing tools. If you don't like the stock game rules, change them yourself! People add resources like wool, create their own civilizations, or build "total conversion" mods, turning the game into a *Lord of the Rings* map, for example. Some even use *Civ*'s tools for historical modeling.

Inaccuracies and Simplifications

This main lesson—*models have to be simplified if they are to be understood*—is important for both game design and for educators. Many scientists distinguish between two kinds of models: *idea* models, which illustrate key concepts (such as predator-prey relationships) and *predictive* models, which predict events.[3] No one would argue that *Civilization* is a good predictive model; global leaders shouldn't make policy decisions based on playing *Civ*.

However, Civ does enable players to see history and geopolitics from different perspectives. For example, try to wage a military-cultural war against a far-off civilization with ancient traditions and see how far you get. Or play a closed, theocratic government and watch as your economy stagnates. In fact, theocratic civilizations almost

---

2. A notable exception is *Sid Meier's Alpha Centauri*, designed by Brian Reynolds. Brian's interest in philosophy comes through as players choose among different cultural values in deciding how to colonize outer space. Here, science fiction provided a convenient cover for exploring cultural and philosophical issues.

3. Although there are technical differences between models and simulations (models are static; simulations, dynamic), I use the terms interchangeably here.

always have little scientific advancement and often end up going to war to defend their interests. One big idea in *Civ* is that new technologies enable you to use *new* resources, creating economic benefits for advanced nations. Civilizations that invest in technologies reap the benefits; iron isn't valuable until you discover ironworking. Today, new resources may become valuable as we discover nanotech or turbine technologies.

These relationships aren't scripted into the game; they are patterns that can be observed after repeated game play. You may learn them not from programming the game but instead by studying the emergent properties of the model. The learning is addictive. Of course, we want students to test these inferences on other representations of history. We want conversations between historical observations and game play, something that games invite and sustain and which can be scaffolded in classroom discussion.

Bias in Games

As you read that last section, hopefully you thought, "But isn't that model biased?" The answer is, "Of course!" In fact, this bias is its biggest strength. First, remember that all representations of history are imperfect. Simplification is at the heart of historical interpretation; books include some facts and leave out others, while films tell stories from particular perspectives. Games happen to frame history according to certain variables (and not others).

History is simplified in even more subtle ways. Historians always choose a starting date and an ending date to their stories; if you were to move those dates forward or back a few years, the story would change. Same goes for geographic boundaries. As my history professor Alan Karras taught, U.S. history looks different when it's not divided by the familiar periods (colonial history, Civil War, and so on) because the time period you choose to study leads historical accounts toward "inevitable" events (see also Karras & McNeill, 1992). Similarly, the history of European colonization looks different when the Caribbean is included. Many historians cross such traditional boundaries to find fresh insights.

During my brief graduate career in history, I was shocked by how many books there are on any topic. I had to read over 50 books on the history of the American South for just two courses, and even then, professors said I was only just getting a flavor for the topic. Any serious historian would read hundreds more. The same is true of political figures; think of how many Lincoln biographies there are. You can only "grok" a topic after looking at many accounts of a phenomenon.

So all representations have their slant, but games uniquely *force* players to confront many of these assumptions directly. The most obvious example in *Civ* is how it models foreign relations. In *Civ* (as in life) more advanced civilizations strong-arm less-developed civilizations into sharing precious resources, giving access to military space, or joining in foreign conflicts. They might give away technologies or food in return for a friendly United Nations vote. Every player knows this (and often curses it). It's impossible to play *Civ* without picking up on this bias, although to what extent the player relates this to U.S. policy depends on the context (including their preexisting beliefs and purpose for playing).

Seeing a game unfold also reveals what is missing from a game. In realistic maps, Native American civilizations will develop large, advanced settlements. With no diseases such as smallpox to wipe them out, they stay populated, which changes history dramatically. How players interpret these causes (and decide to pursue the questions that arise) depends on players' goals, knowledge, and the gaming context. When I teach with *Civilization*, I use this missing feature as a teachable moment to discuss the size of Native American civilizations (which most people underestimate) and the importance of diseases. When *Civ* play is framed as a colonial simulation, students often make interesting observations:

1. "Old world" civilizations can become part of a vast trading network spanning from China to Egypt to England. This network trades technology, resources, and economic goods, not to mention diseases, so that they advance more quickly than the Americas or sub-Saharan Africa.
2. The "new world" doesn't have elephants, camels, or horses. This means that there is no natural "cavalry unit" and spells big trouble should armed conflict arise.
3. Native American civilizations are much larger than students ever realized.

How *Civilization*'s model is biased is the subject of academic debate. I'd say that there are at least four groups of bias:

1. *Bias toward management.* This one is kind of obvious (and was first raised by Friedman, 1999). Because *Civilization* is a *game* in which players affect the world, a well-managed civilization does "better" than a poorly managed one. There are good arguments on either side of this issue, but suffice it to say that the bias is there.[4] What meanings players actually make of the bias is a different

---

4. For an analysis of values in the fate of civilizations, see Jared Diamond's (2004) *Collapse*, a book that argues that many civilizations have failed because they destroyed their local ecology. Other world histories (including Diamond's *Guns, Germs, and Steel*, 1999) frame history largely as the result of conditions that civilizations are placed in. Within Diamond's work, this apparent contradiction is largely a matter of time and geographical scale; in the short term, relatively isolated societies make decisions that lead them to flourish or decline. Over millennia and across broad regions (e.g., an entire continent) these differences tend to wash out.

question altogether. The drive to see the world in terms of management may be an inherent bias resulting from playing games, just as the narrative structure of books may invite us to see the world in terms of simple, linear causality and watching films may lead us to emphasize the importance of personal narratives.

2. *Progress and science*. The standard rules of games are biased toward scientific progress being good. New discoveries make things *better*. The story of most *Civilization* games is that new technological discoveries provide advantages over other civilizations. There is little opportunity to ask if this really is progress. It's an interesting question because in "real history" less-advanced civilizations that adopt new technologies tend to get attacked or assimilated. After all, there aren't many hunter-gatherers running around.

3. *Critical-Marxist orientation to power and conflict*. Despite the many "critical" reads of *Civilization* as being biased toward Western notions of progress (see Schut, 2007), there is an undercurrent of power coming from material goods and the use of such power by governments to obtain and secure resources. If a civilization controls resources but has inadequate military, economic, religious, or diplomatic power, it will be attacked, which is not exactly how manifest destiny was taught in my textbook.

4. *Geographical materialist theory of history*. From an educational perspective, the most interesting bias of *Civilization* is that everything emanates from geographical positioning. For example, start a civilization in the Nile Valley, and it will grow fast and then suffer from diseases. If they survive, the Egyptians must confront the Babylonians to the east and the Greeks to the north, which requires military spending. Expanding south on the Nile toward Kenya means assimilating or conquering African tribes and obtaining horses and bronze. If the Egyptians *don't* obtain horses and bronze, they stand little chance against Greek hoplites and Roman legionnaires. Almost every game played on this scenario unfolds similarly, and players start to infer rules for how history plays out on broad time scales.

Because these biases reveal themselves to the player (who is often yelling, "This is unfair! I hate the Greeks!"), most players learn them.

CIVILIZATION AS A GEOGRAPHICAL MODEL

Once you accept that bias is inherent in the game, *Civilization* is good for thinking about how geography and broad policy decisions (such as guns vs. butter) have an impact on history. To explain, examine figures 2.2 and 2.3 from *Civ3*. Figure 2.2

Figure 2.2.
***Civ3* World Map**

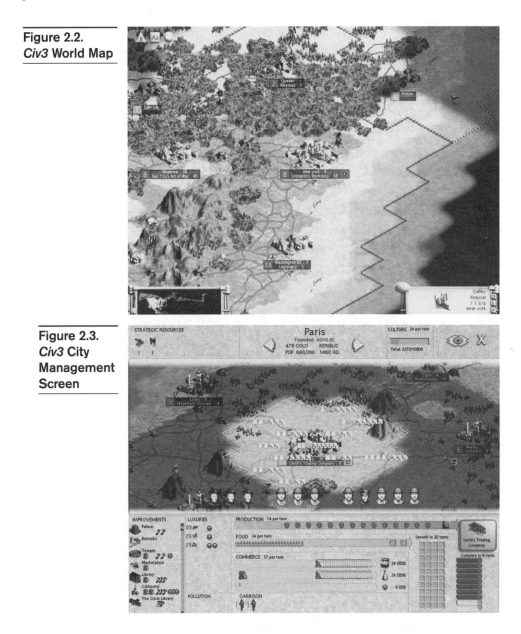

Figure 2.3.
***Civ3* City Management Screen**

shows the map players see most of the time. The map shows physical geography, natural resources, political geography, and human modifications to the environment, such as cities, roads, farms, and railroads. (Incidentally, teachers love that playing *Civ* involves staring at maps all day. As one student put it, "*Civ* is a boring 'natural resource' diagram from your textbook come to life.") Figure 2.2 shows how these resources are gathered and manipulated via cities.

Geography undergirds game play as players study the map to infer the *strategic* implications of these elements. It matters, for example, that the Nile is long and snaking and that there are horses, bronze, and gold to the south, because it affects how cities form. The Sahara Desert also serves as a natural border constraining westward expansion. These lessons correspond to middle school world geography standards.

So the game comes down to one's ability to gather resources, to amplify them by building structures, and then to make strategic decisions on how to maximize them. For example, if one is on an island, then your number-one goal should be to pursue fishing and sailing technologies (much like the Phoenicians). Conversely, the Persians sit at the crossroads of Asia and Europe and thus are well positioned to control trade routes, so your first job is to build your military to counteract threats from neighboring civilizations.

Remarkably, many historical phenomena are simulated "well enough" through these variables. To be sure, *Civ* contains some 10,000 concepts that make even the most advanced educational software look embarrassingly simple. Yet the foundations of *Civ* are straightforward, which Chris Crawford (2003) has argued is at the core of its appeal. A simplified, elegant model is easier for people to understand and much more useful than a "perfect" model that is too complex.

Getting an ideal model "right" so that it is both fun to play and generates insights is the key for both research and education. Idea simulations such as the Lotka-Volterra equations (the basis for many predator-prey models) do not model entire ecosystems. Lotka-Volterra doesn't *predict* what happens to a deer population if a particular policy toward wolves is adopted in Yellowstone National Park, for example. Rather, it shows patterns over time and highlights nonintuitive relationships. Lotka-Volterra shows how an imbalanced system eventually results in the predators themselves dying. First, the predators kill off the prey. With no prey left, the predators eventually starve. After the predators die from a lack of food, the prey rebounds. Now, there's an overabundance of prey, which enables the predator to rebound, and the whole thing repeats itself. (Google it, play with some of the models, and you'll see.)

So, asking whether or not *Civilization* is "accurate" misses the point. My argument is that *Civ* (1) provides a framework tying together world geopolitical history; (2) gives fluency with a model that is useful for analyzing world history on broad time scales; and (3) inspires revisiting, tinkering, and socializing. These same factors make good success criteria for games more generally.

IDEOLOGICAL WORLDS AS FRAMEWORKS FOR THINKING

Games are "ideological worlds" in that they instantiate ideas through implicit rule sets and systems (rather than by telling stories). The word *ideological* tries to capture that they are built according to theories of how the world operates (implicitly or explicitly). Every game makes value judgments about what is and is not important. I prefer the word *world* to *system* because games are not (usually) abstracted rule systems but worlds rich with representations. These representations might be of cities, resources, and armies, such as in *Civilization*, or automobiles, city streets, and their denizens, such as in *Grand Theft Auto*. Although it's useful to look at games as systems, the term *system* shortchanges the role of graphics and sound in how players infer meaning from games. Visual representations are a critical part of meaning-making.

Games and Simulations

Games differ from simulations in that they give roles, goals, and agency; elicit fantasies (including transgressive play); and design experiences to manage complexity and learning. Dan Norton (2008) sums it up well with the phrase "roles and goals." In the case of *Civ*, your role is a leader, somewhere between a dictator, a president, and God. This trade off between realism (what role do you play in *Civ*?) and engagement (it's fun to test out your ideas without annual elections) is part of the allure of games. The Senate in *Civ2*, for example, intervenes on military decisions. Players can avoid this by overthrowing their government and installing a fascist state before going to war. Current versions still penalize players for unpopular wars, but more coherently.

Game designers often say, "It's OK to sacrifice realistic *roles* if they support players in pursuing meaningful goals." Critics may argue that these simplifications are dangerous, but none of the hundreds of *Civ* players I've interviewed (some even as young as 8 years old) have ever confused their role with that of the president or emperor (see Chapters 6 and 8). This fictional conceit loses realism, but buys the ability to affect multiple levels of a system. As an educator, I tend to start with authentic experiences (such as being a scientist), which is fine, but also precludes many interesting roles (such as a time traveller).

The latter part of the equation is *goals*. Games entice players into developing goals. Players' goals are a property of neither the player nor the game, but are a coupling of the possibilities of the game space and the player's desires. *Civilization* has the capacity for players to do many things, ranging from leading a peaceful global society to waging religious wars to wiping civilizations off the map. Yet players do things all the time that the designers didn't anticipate. Thus, even though *Civilization* isn't a perfect simulation, its value is in its gameness.

This distinction between games as rule-based systems versus worlds mirrors the "narratology versus ludology" debate that once defined game studies as a field. The debate, in essence, is whether to study games as *media* or *play*. Study them as media, and we are inclined to see them in the context of the history of media, which includes books, film, TV, radio, and so on. Study them as play, and they are situated in the tradition of toys, hobbies, board games, and sport.

Games are both media *and* play. They allow us to play with representations, such as when we play being a gang member who wears a Hawaiian shirt and drives a pink Cadillac in *Grand Theft Auto: San Andreas,* and to test the rule systems of those representations, such as taking that getup into rival-gang territory.

No one game captures everything perfectly, so ideally we want multiple frameworks for thinking about any topic. Students should experience a variety of theories of history. For example, *Civilization* deals with history at such broad time scales that "great people" are unimportant. Students might imagine how *Civ* would be different with a "great man" theory of history (see Chapter 6).

MEANING-MAKING IN IDEOLOGICAL WORLDS

How do we make meaning within ideological worlds? Within game contexts, at least two qualities are important: (1) the learning cycle of a player developing goals, reading the game space for information, taking action in the game world, and then reading games for feedback; and (2) the social experience of participating in particular game communities, which is where much of the reflection, interpretation, and media production occurs as interpretations are debated and legitimized.

Meaning-making within games is a deeply *productive* act. Players formulate goals, develop plans and strategies to reach those goals, and read the game space to understand what happens—all within a broader social context. Learning has been thought of as an active process for a long time, and if there is one message coming out of the learning sciences over the past 30 years, it is that learners are active meaning makers who *create* knowledge from experiences. However, learning through game play is about creating knowledge in a way that challenges even our most "student-centered" notions of learning.

Meaning-making is related to particular goals. When first playing *Civ,* you start with a vague goal, which for me was "play Smurf's cool game." What made it cool, from a distance, was its complexity and ability to grip my friend for hours at a time. Next, I was taken by the ability to "replay" history. Could I play as a Native American tribe and fend off Europeans? From there, I developed more specific goals (if I "discovered" Europe, maybe I could strike peaceful diplomatic agreements and protect myself). Moving forward, I developed more sophisticated strategies (grow quickly and research naval technologies). Every student I have studied has his or her own trajectory (explored further in Chapter 8). For some, an interest in ancient Rome translates to a focus on achieving great wonders, which leads to understanding cultural and economic variables. Others take to naval warfare, which might lead to learning about Vikings.

This process is deeply *productive* in that players constantly construct goals, strategies, and theories about the game system. You can see the products of these strategies on screen, in how cities grow, how trade routes are constructed, and how military defense systems are built. But there is also the theory production in the player's mind. As designers of educational games, we want to align this theorizing with socially valued forms of thinking, whether it is thinking like a citizen scientist or like an engineer.

Michael Nitsche (2008) provides a useful way to navigate these planes of gaming. The first plane is the game as it is encoded in the box. The second plane is the game that unfolds on screen. There is no "game" without the player. The third plane is the game being played in the player's mind. Will Wright (quoted in Pearce, 2001) argues that from the moment the player looks at the box, he or she is constructing a model of the game. Game play for Wright is simply the process of developing deeper understandings of that model. Understanding this mental plane is critical for understanding *The Sims* (see *The Sims* sidebar). I might, for example, play a game based on my family. The people on screen aren't "my family," but in my mind, I am playing my family. The fourth plane is the action occurring in real space (the mouse clicks and so on). This is the "button mashing" plane; those who claim that games are just button mashing are focusing on this interaction (but not really understanding it). The fifth plane is the social plane. This plane is gaming in its social context, which might involve performative dimensions (as in *Rock Band*) or competitive play.

PARTICIPATION IN IDEOLOGICAL WORLDS

So far, we've focused on games as interactions between humans and computers (largely planes 1–4), but this fifth social plane may be most important for learning, and we need to unpack how it drives advanced game play. Consider how *The Sims* encourages people to be not just *consumers* but *producers* of content (something studied in more depth by James Paul Gee and Elizabeth Hayes, 2010). When I first reviewed *The Sims* back in 2000, I was amazed at how Wright and his team did not include every person, family, or piece of furniture imaginable in the game, but instead gave *players* the ability to produce and distribute content. Essentially, the team put players to work for them in *creating* game content. *Spore*, the design game in which players design cells, organisms, tribes, civilizations, and planets, takes this strategy even further, as the creatures, vehicles, buildings, and cities that players create through play become the content of others' games. A key to *The Sims* wild success, I think, is that it didn't try to be all games to all people; rather, it gave players the tools by which they could make unique game experiences that they wanted to play (like having the band the Damned move into their neighborhood and pee on their floor, which happened to me).

The Sims

The Sims, the household simulation game designed by Will Wright and his Maxis team, is a touchstone example for educators. Proving that popular games don't need to be violent, *The Sims* is the top-selling PC game of all time. It's now a multibillion-dollar franchise and has sold over 125 million titles.

Few things are more fascinating than watching and experimenting with people. Many *Sims* players start by modeling their real-life household to see what happens. I was shocked to learn that, according to *The Sims*, my life would be better if (1) I ate breakfast with my family (meeting my social, nutritional, and comfort needs as well as improving my relationships), and (2) I bought a good couch (meeting my needs for more social interaction, comfort, and fun, as well as providing space for relationship building, even while reading books). All kinds of people came to visit when I had a good couch.

Wright (quoted in Pearson, 2001) reports that most players use *The Sims* as an interactive storytelling machine. Maxis provides tools so that players can easily take pictures and post their stories online. Still, playing *The Sims* can be quite transgressive. Sending a housewife in need of social interaction next door to talk to an attractive neighbor feels infinitely more transgressive to me than shooting aliens in *Doom*.

So what is *The Sims*, really? A quick answer is an interactive digital dollhouse with built-in shopping, storybook making, and scrapbooking. Critics note a strong materialist bias underlying *The Sims*, in that better couches, for example, tend to make people happier. The game pokes fun at this bias. For example, the advertising copy for a table available for purchase in the game reads, "This end table will improve your life!" This can lead to some confusion about when *The Sims* is serious and when it is satire. It also raises the possibility that there is a strong materialist bias in the world. Wright (quoted in Pearce, 2001) claims that the game is about several things, including the tension between pursuing material goods in order to make our lives better and the tendency for those material possessions to own us, rather than the other way around.

The Sims isn't the only game that supports player creativity. For years, games have shipped with modification, or "modding," tools that players use to generate content. What Maxis did was make the line between consumers and producers *fluid*, so that players could *very easily* create and upload their own characters, houses, and furniture to *The Sims* website. For Wright, creating a "smooth ramp between consumer and producer" is paramount. In an interview with Celia Pearce (2001), he says,

> I think there are going to be certain types of new media where this is the natural form of interaction. With something like *The Sims*, it's meant to be a very smooth ramp. I buy this game and it might be a while before I tune into the web button, but it's real easy and so I don't really have to go out of my way to share my experience. As opposed to somebody who's doing a home page, where they have to actually figure out how to deal with their ISP. Or the film thing, where in fact, I have to actually pull out my camera and start doing work to make the film.

To put this quote in perspective, think of how, in 2000, few people (especially nongamers) would have signed up for a game and gone online to download content made by strangers. One might also ask, in turn, how many would have felt comfortable creating content. That's what *The Sims* did.

The Sims excelled in making this ramp from consumer to producer "smooth," to use Will Wright's term. There are simple and obvious ways that one can begin producing content, starting with uploading one's *Sims* characters. Next, one might use the game as a story-creating engine by using the "scrapbook" feature. Wright reports that for many people, advanced game play consists largely of using the game as a storytelling engine, and there are wide reports of this feature being used for family therapy.[5] At the highest levels, players might actually create custom characters and furniture for *The Sims* and earn real world cash from other players.

This *fluidity* of production found in *The Sims* can also be found in entirely different games, such as *World of Warcraft*. In *WoW*, players begin participation in amateur production by downloading user-generated add-ons that are required to participate in high-end gaming practices. As Steinkuehler and Johnson (2009) argue, they begin customizing the user interface and, in some cases, even developing their own mods and add-ons. In both games, there is a trajectory of experience that starts with *using* user-generated content and grows into *contributing* user-generated content.

---

5. There is even an article titled "How to Use *The Sims* for Family Counseling" on eHow.com (http://www.ehow.com/how_4611836_learn-couples-counseling-*Sims*.html).

Across our studies of games and game players, our research team has found a general trajectory of experience (see Figure 2.4). Players begin as "n00bs" with little experience. First, they develop basic knowledge and experience with important game functions. But with a game like *Civilization*, that's simply achieving competency—becoming a basic-level gamer with perhaps 40 or 50 hours under one's belt. Past this point, the player begins developing exploits for gaming the system—simple solution paths that work across almost every situation. In *Civ*, for years this was "leave 2 phalanx in every city." A good game avoids these optimal solution paths, giving players many interesting decisions to make (see Balancing sidebar).

Gaming forums are the Wild, Wild West where this intellectual work happens (for examples of how this works in *WoW*, see Steinkuehler & Chmiel, 2006). In these forums, players post data from their games and examine others' data. They collectively analyze data across games and propose rule changes. As players gather superior strategies (collections of moves and approaches), they change the broader rule systems. Eventually, players create their own "mods," which are versions of the game with different rules. In *Civ*, this process is pretty clean-cut. Players build mods such as "Give peace a chance," which prohibits players from going to war, and then official expansion packs and future versions of the game include scenarios based on these mods. In this way, the fan community functions as an unofficial research and development lab.

**Figure 2.4.
Trajectories of
Participation
in Gaming
Communiites**

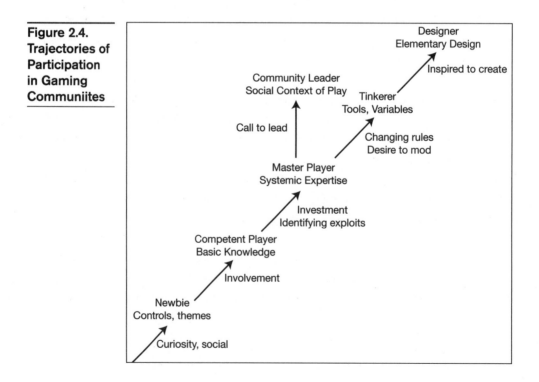

Balancing

Avoiding these optimal solution paths is also called balancing. To understand the difficulty of creating such well-balanced systems, consider something like *World of Warcraft*. Here's a game that is played worldwide by over 10 million people, many of whom spend extensive time examining systems, looking for exploits, and sharing them on sites such as Elitist Jerks.

Raph Koster, a lead game designer, artfully described the epic battle between players and designers in massively multiplayer games—one that designers are destined to lose. He frames players' pattern-seeking behavior in evolutionary terms, arguing that those who do not learn to see through the optimal solution paths of today's world (such as eliminating credit card debt) are in deep trouble indeed.

Blizzard has been able to achieve optimal balance in *WoW* because they've had nearly a decade to perfect it. If a system isn't working, they change it. Then they change it again. And again. It would be great if designers of educational systems had a similar design-user feedback-redesign loop. Sadly, we don't, and most educational games yield experiences that are good for learning some basic descriptive knowledge and manipulations, but not much else.

The participatory structure of game communities enables such remarkable learning to occur. However, we can't simply design games, stick them into classrooms, and then expect students to begin rewriting their textbooks. The school-based culture of passive knowledge reception (as opposed to production) needs to change. Such a change would require revolutionizing across the entire education system—from the professional development of teachers (who *themselves* are treated as recipients, not producers, of knowledge) to the assessment system.

THEORY AND PRACTICE

This chapter started with the question "What makes a good educational game?" One response might be "something that represents the domain accurately or recapitulates professional practices." But such approaches that privilege authenticity may also miss educationally beneficial opportunities that are newly available with digital media, such as leading a civilization for 6,000 years or traveling through time. Let's take the findings from the Chapter 1 and turn them into criteria for good educational games:

- *Good educational games employ academic knowledge as a tool for achieving goals.* Recall how in *Pirates!* geography is a tool for success. In games, players employ knowledge and understandings as tools for action.
- *Good educational games lend themselves to systemic understandings.* Games appear to be particularly good for immersing learners within systems and enabling them to explore the emergent properties of systems. Other media and curricular strategies may be better suited toward other goals.
- *Good educational games employ sophisticated game design techniques* (e.g., orchestrations of time, overlapping goal structures) to provide a polished experience.
- *Good educational games offer multiple ways of playing them, so that players can experiment with a variety of identities in a group.* Good games let reluctant kids lead, encourage advanced students to help others, or engender friendships among isolated students. If games are ultimately participatory, good educational games might encourage *learners* to set up and negotiate these social structures *themselves* as a part of game play.
- *Good educational games pique players' interests.* In fact, authenticity or realism may be *less* important than raising interest in terms in academic subjects, in terms of designing and selecting games for learning. Students can critique games as historical interpretations or, in some cases, play with systems and then build their own mods of the game. These approaches position students as critical consumers and producers, rather than passive recipients.
- *Good educational games are ideological worlds that instantiate particular ways of viewing and valuing the world.* Good games don't shroud these biases, but engage the player in a critical conversation about the world. In the case of *Civilization*, its material-geographic bias may be its biggest strength as it pushes the player to think about the causes of colonization. Educators may be better off choosing a game with a strong point of view and encouraging students to deconstruct it than choosing one that claims neutrality.
- *Good games are social, in that they encourage social interaction of different forms and lead to productive practices (fan communities, fan fiction, machinima).* Educators might inject games with social dynamics that encourage reflection, argumentation, and discussion. Some mechanics, such as supporting the development of expertise in different areas, lead naturally to peer-to-peer learning, apprenticeship, and production. As designers, we need to look for ways to encourage such discussion by creating memorable moments, differential access to information, or differentiated expertise.

- *Good games inspire creativity and smooth ramps to usher players from users to producers.* Examples of such games might be science games in which people design bridges, robots, or buildings (examples of such games are *Pontifex, Mind Rover,* and *World of Goo*; see Chapter 8) and historical games in which people role-play in creative ways and write about their experiences as a form of historical interpretation (as in *Revolution*; see Chapter 5).

The next chapter turns our focus to the social organization of game communities, providing a preview into how learning might be organized in the digital age.

COOPERATIVE GAME PLAY

by Kurt Squire and Henry Jenkins

Gamers are growing up. What do aging gamers want? One theory is that gamers want to socialize. Picture this: A 32-year-old gamer comes home from work. After dinner, his or her child is in bed, leaving an hour, at best a few hours, for gaming before the next morning. Marathon game sessions are out of the question. The desire to spend time with loved ones is paramount, and unless our gaming hero wants to create domestic turbulence, he or she had better not commandeer the home entertainment system.

Cooperative game play is one way out. Co-op modes allow multiple players to collaborate against common challenges. However, co-op modes have been an add-on rather than a core game play feature.

Square-Enix's *Final Fantasy: Crystal Chronicles* is one of the first games designed to be co-op first, single player second. In *Crystal Chronicles*, up to four players must organize tactical decisions, share inventory, and rely on one another's strengths. When a Game Boy Advance (GBA) is connected to the GameCube, each player gets a private screen and controller, giving him or her access to different information. The information on the GBA is meant to be private: Nobody really wants to see other players' inventories splattered across the TV screen.

As *Crystal Chronicles* players will attest, when a player has private information that he or she needs to share, the game suddenly becomes a stimulus for communication outside the TV screen. The talk around the game is a continuous flurry of tactical discussion. Furthermore, synchronized attacks create special bonuses, so the room quickly fills with chants of "Three, two, one, go!"

Teams that fail to coordinate are quickly decimated. This concept of mutually dependent fortunes—"If you die, I die"—makes *Crystal Chronicles* more compelling than preceding games in which a teammate's death relegated that player to a virtual penalty box from which he or she had to watch his or her teammates clear enemies alone.

Cooperative game play that combines differentiated access to information and co-dependent goals has applications far greater than entertainment games. In education, for example, we know that having novices and experts work together in concert on problems is among the most powerful forms of learning. Eric Klopfer and colleagues at the Massachusetts Institute of Technology have been applying this principle toward educational ends through augmented reality games.

In a game called *Mystery at the Museum*, which is played at the Boston Museum of Science, teens and parents play in pairs as a detective, technologist, or scientist on a mission to solve a museum theft. Students and parents constitute a team, and each member gets different information based on his or her role. Parents and children report that the game provides new opportunities for them to work and play together. As one parent put it, "I can't remember the last time I talked to my [14-year-old] son for this long without fighting."

CHAPTER 3

Teaching with Games: Learning Through Play

Hopefully, I've persuaded you that we can learn from games and that they represent new additions to our intellectual repertoire. But educators might reasonably ask:

- Can we ever put such games into classrooms?
- Don't games that require hours to learn and involve overt competition go against the grain of school?
- How would a games-based curriculum look?

This chapter draws on experiences teaching with games and aligned pedagogies in alternative environments to sketch out a vision of what such a system might look like. For those educators who are still skeptical of games, this discussion may challenge assumptions about schooling and learning.

BEFORE-SCHOOL CORPSE RETRIEVALS

"What in the hell were you doing back there, Kurt?"

"Yeah, what was up with that? Please tell me you got my corpse." A third kid pushed the first two aside. We barely fit in the narrow hallway of McGuffey Foundation School and this was becoming a scene.

"Whatever, man. I don't care. Did you get my stuff back?" A chorus of kids chimed in. "Yeah, c'mon, did you get it?" I was backed up against the wall, accosted by a pack of angry 5th graders. It was 8:30 a.m.

Before school on that cold winter morning, I had been online MUDding (MUD is text-based, online cooperative gaming—a precursor to *WoW*) with these same kids on a game called *Avatar*. I had led them into an area slightly above our levels.

Of course, I got us all killed. Now, in today's gaming world, this wouldn't be such a big deal. People die all the time. But, back in 1995 in *Avatar* (as in most early MUDs), the death penalties were severe. First, you lost 50% of the experience you had gained toward the next level. Imagine putting in 22 hours toward a level only to die and lose 11 hours of work. Cruel by today's standards, but normal for the time.

It gets worse. When you were resurrected, you came back to life naked. Completely naked. No swords, shields, helmet, underwear . . . nothing. (OK, you had underwear in our family-friendly MUD). If you ran back to your corpse within the hour, you could "loot yourself" and get back your stuff. But if you took longer than an hour, it was gone to the ether, forever.

Doing corpse retrievals was, as you might imagine, tricky business. First, you had to remember where you were in this twisty passage of text. There were no maps unless you made them yourself. Everyone I knew kept notes next to their computers saying stuff like "L, L, F, F, F, R, F, F, F, L" to remind themselves that, in order to get to the town of Midgaard from Nom (a popular starting position), you would go left, left, then forward three times, turn right, go forward three more times, and then turn left . . . or some such thing. This was only for unusual places; even my 5th graders had memorized basic paths such as how to get to town.

Even if you found your corpse, you had to avoid getting killed by aggressive monsters. Fortunately, you could "flee" (by typing /flee), which would send you to a random room, but this was dangerous because you might run into another monster. Losing all your stuff (which happened at least once to everyone) meant rebuilding a character from scratch. The most heartbreaking losses were special items, such as a locket from an evil witch gained with a friend in a meaningful battle. Almost every gamer keeps at least a few of these things on them, even though inventory space is notoriously limited, a phenomenon researched by some of these same kids, 15 years later (see Zimmerman, Squire, Steinkuehler, & Dikkers, 2009).

So this is all to say that dying was a really bad thing.

But it was especially bad if you had to catch a bus to school in 5 minutes. Parents generally did not understand the importance of corpse retrievals.

In this case, the guy who got them killed was their teacher. Panic ensued.

"We're screwed!" one yelled at me.

"I have to catch the bus!" another added.

"Kurt! *You* can be late!" one finally realized. The next few minutes involved a group of 9-year-olds trying to convince me to take one on the chin while they raced for the bus.

I stayed on, clock ticking, got their stuff, and sped off to try to make first hour. Driving to school, I nervously tried to concoct a reason for my tardiness. Because we team-taught classes, it wouldn't be the end of the world if I were late. As I attempted to sneak in through the back door, the always cheerful Liz Woedl called out from her room, "Nice of you to join us, Kurt!" I was busted.

After class, and after I was accosted by the aggressive mob, Janet Kretschmer, the principal, found me.

"So, did you get everything taken care of?"

"Umm . . . yeah . . . so you . . ." I wasn't sure how to play this one.

"Oh, yes, I heard. What on Earth were you doing taking kids to the Temple of Zin *before school*?" She had a point. *That* was the irresponsible part. Janet was generally on top of things.

My principal (maybe the only one in the United States at the time) not only played *Avatar* but was an immortal there.

In fact, it was through Janet that I first learned about *Avatar* (which at the time was called *Farside*). Janet (as she brilliantly recounts in *Darii, the Godmother*, n.d.) started MUDding when she heard her kids discussing "rings of holding," Ciquala swords, and other arcane trivia. She soon learned that her kids were going home every day, logging on to the Internet (which in 1994 was unusual), and playing MUDs. After confiscating a note saying "4e 5s 16w," she decided to log on herself to see what it was about.

It wasn't long before she, too, was hooked. Here, beneath the rest of the world's radar, was a virtual world of mysterious places, people, and things. For a newbie, it can take hours to even figure out who was "real," who was controlled by the computer, or what this even was.

Soon Janet had multiple characters and was approached to become an administrator within the community (essentially giving her the keys to the place). She checked in on players and resolved disputes. In addition to becoming an "immortal" (the highest possible level), she later contributed to several major designs. For example, the angel system enabled level-50 players to morph into angels, giving up their celestial bodies (and goods) to become permanent helpers who specialized in doing nice things such as corpse runs for newbies.

In fact, I recently had the wonderful experience of orchestrating a reunion between Janet, a few of those 5th graders (who are now entering graduate school), and myself. I asked Janet, "What on Earth got you to MUD?" She retold how it was actually the kids who invited her in (a testament to their relationship), adding, "That was part of why it succeeded. They invited me into their play space. But it enabled me to be there and accessible to them. I could keep a watchful eye without necessarily intruding. They knew they could find me if they ran into trouble."

Eric, one of the 5th graders, smiled and nodded: "Yeah—that's one of the things I appreciated. You weren't butting in, but you were always there if we needed it. If things got a little out of control—and they sometimes did—you would help straighten it out."

Janet wanted *someone* to keep an eye on these guys. Eric confirmed that their parents had no idea what they were doing—or that it was even technically possible. Janet could have just told their parents (and in fact she did). But had she attempted to shut down their fun, they would have simply moved on to another game, and this time not invited the adults. Playing along with them (albeit at a distance) allowed her to gain unique access to their lives. In short, she was doing a version of what Jane Jacobs (1961) described in *The Death and Life of Great American Cities* as the "watchful eye," but for the digital age.

As teachers, we used gaming as a way to connect with students. We noted if a student was keeping odd hours. We checked if a student was notably irritable or despondent. On a simpler level, it let us just talk. Video gaming is a lot like shooting baskets in that you can focus on one activity and use the interstitial times for conversation.

Sometimes gaming was the only thread left for us to connect to students. As an example, Janet tells a story about becoming an immortal after one student used foul language on a public, "family" channel (a banishable offense). This transgression resulted in our *entire* local service provider (the only one in the region) being banned from the game. This would be like an entire town losing its access to *World of Warcraft* forever. You don't want to know the vengeance the other kids were plotting.

The culprit was dealing with a lot of home issues and was lashing out all over the place. He already wasn't very popular, and if other kids had gotten a hold of him, things could have gone really badly. Janet used it as a teachable moment with the boy, and eventually she got hold of Snikt, the designer/owner of the MUD, on the phone and fixed the situation.

FROM PLAYERS TO DESIGNERS

What was innovative about the games of that period (and this is still true today for games that allow mods) was that immortals like Janet created entirely new content. Janet, for example, created a "MUD School" to teach players how to play. Any player—even kids—could invent new creatures and author new areas or suggest changes to the underlying rule structure or administrative policies.

This trajectory from user to designer is both remarkable and typical of the online games from this period. In my mind, it still is an educational promise of games:

How can we take newbies and turn them into content *producers*? How can we make them authors in a domain where they create the *content*, the *rules* by which it governs, and the social systems that encompass it? In short, this trajectory is going from being a game *player* to being a game *designer* and *community organizer* (see Figure 2.4). In education, we might want students to design games about things other than orcs and elves, but we would love for them to develop this kind of deep knowledge, systemic understandings, communication skills, and leadership and responsibility over their social organizations.

In fact, *many* of our 20-odd kids who played *Avatar* produced content or became immortals. Two 5th graders (Eric Weiner and Nate Berger) wrote an area based on the Hundred Acre Wood (from *Winnie-the-Pooh*). This area, which was nearly 50 pages long, included maps, room and area descriptions, action-and-response triggers, and monsters and their items (including statistics). They turned it in as a writing assignment and got feedback. Other kids wrote fan fiction.

Skeptics might counter, "Yes, but what were they *learning*?" The most obvious benchmark of learning was spelling. Every student who played *Avatar* showed a marked improvement in spelling. This may be surprising, but not if you are familiar with most 5th-grade boys' spelling. In order to be understood by the machine or the people grouping with you, you had to at least approximate the English language.

What the kids remember most was the chance to be taken seriously by adults as competent peers and the experience of writing something played by thousands of people from around the world (including many in their school). Because they gamed before school, these kids often grouped with Europeans, which was important if you were a 5th grader from Oxford, Ohio. As one student described to me, "There was something really cool about having a computer programmer from the Netherlands mailing you pictures of his cat. Sounds kind of strange now, but it meant something at the time."

Nate used this experience of writing his 100-Acre Wood as the basis for his entrance essay into Dartmouth's creative writing program. For Nate, the experience was about becoming an author. He learned (1) that writing a novel-length project could be satisfying, (2) what it's like to undertake a project in which the results aren't known ahead of time, and (3) what it's like to collaborate. He now described writing "100-Acre Wood" as a lesson in debunking the lonely-writer assertion—that writers must slave away at a masterpiece that is unveiled to the public at the end of a lonely process. Writing "100-Acre Wood" taught him that writing could be collaborative.

Literacy scholars such as James Paul Gee might describe this as learning to think of writing as *design* (see New London Group, 2000). These students were learning to work with a symbol system. In this case, the symbol system was mostly verbal language arranged in database format, but it also included maps and numerical values. Writing "100-Acre Wood" went beyond impressing the teacher and getting an A on the assignment. These students were using language to create specific effects in audiences—laughter, fright, surprise, and so on. Finally, these students were learning to position themselves as authors in terms of the MUD community as they made bids to become immortals.

For education, *Avatar* provides an incredibly powerful lesson: Learners should have clearly visible opportunities to become *leaders*, *teachers*, or *authors* in the domains they are studying. It should be clearly communicated what players must do to become experts, and they should have opportunities to interact with such experts regularly. By contrast, school functions to isolate students by age ability, filters all information through the teacher, and features few opportunities to interact with experts, much less *become* one.

To get a sense of how such a digital, participatory literacy might "transfer," it's worth sharing what Nate and Eric did next. As a gag (and a gift to their principal), they recruited me in a secret plan: They wanted to write a MUD area based on their school, and it would be called Operation Jelly-Filled Doughnuts so we could discuss it openly without being detected. Over the next several weeks, they turned McGuffey Foundation School into a MUD dungeon. Schoolrooms and corners of the playground became "rooms." Kids, parents, and teachers became monsters, each with unique abilities and items. For example, in her classroom, Sue (our science teachers) had a replica NASA spacesuit that became a highly valued set of armor that gave players extra intelligence, charisma, and mana (points for spell casting).

All teachers were boss monsters with signature moves. One teacher had an icy stare that would freeze you; another had a lecture spell that would put you to sleep. Nate's beloved Pittsburgh Pirates pump hat gave bonuses to agility, I believe, but took away a few points of charisma (a subject of much debate). Eric and Nate wanted to model how one of them got run over by a pack of 5-year-olds after the bell rang for recess, so the kindergartners were a roving mob of weak, low-level creatures that did immense damage.

My favorite example was the "teacher's red pen," the area's highest level weapon. There was a low-level chance that teachers would drop a teacher's red pen, which did decent damage but, more important, cast a whole series of "debuffs" (spells that make you weaker or less intelligent). In the presence of the almighty teacher's red pen, everyone loses his or her cool, modeling how being graded can negatively affect self-confidence.

INTEREST-DRIVEN LEARNING

It's essential to remember that these weren't kids let loose on the Internet who magically ended up writing game areas. They had a strong support network that nurtured and guided their interest. Like most stories of this sort, it starts at home. Both Eric and Nate had computers in the home and parents who cultivated their enthusiasm, although much of their gaming took place at the library. For kicks, I followed them after school once to see how they pulled off their gaming. In addition to being informative and entertaining, it shed light on how millions of youth today play *Runescape*. They started at Kmart, where they stocked up on candy and ran errands for their parents to provide cover. Next, they went to the public library for its free broadband. Before long, a librarian found them, so they moved to the college library. Gaming was banned there, but they discovered a way to hack in. On most days they could sneak in 2–3 hours of broadband gaming, which in the days of 2,400-baud modems was a big deal.

At school, they had a master teacher, Janet, who understood the research on kids' reading: Interest-driven learning can be a powerful motivator. When passionate about a topic, students will willingly read and write texts that are far more complicated than texts about topics they are not passionate about (Steinkuehler, Compton-Lilly, & King, (2010).

Identifying students' passions and using them as a vehicle for relating academic content is something the skilled teachers at McGuffey encouraged me to do regardless of technology. One student, Jason, refused to complete assignments or even to respond to adults. After becoming friends with Jason through gaming, I discovered his real passion in life was raising Great Pyrenees dogs. He loved learning about how Great Pyrenees protected herds from predators or how the breed evolved.[1] If you got Jason talking about Great Pyrenees, not only would he open up, but he wouldn't *stop* talking. I researched the breed so I could engage in conversation with him (I was raising Lucy, my own Chow-Lab-mix puppy at the time). From there,

---

1. This is, in fact, really cool stuff. Jason taught me how Great Pyrenees were bred to basically look like gigantic 200-lb. sheep. They live among the sheep, peacefully, until a bear or wolf comes along, at which point the dog lunges for the predator's throat and the predator learns that these dogs are not big sheep at all. Jason told me about this after two of his dogs took out coyotes the night before. I didn't believe him (and because this was the early days of the Internet, it took a while to decisively settle the debate). However, he was right. After that, whenever possible I channeled Jason's interests in Great Pyrenees to advance his learning. I think a key was that I took an interest in Jason's hobbies and was willing to learn from him.

we forged a friendship that enabled me to work with Jason on academic matters, either by relating things to his interest or just by calling upon the goodwill we had developed.

Some (see National Endowment for the Arts, 2004) discount appealing to learners as pandering or fear that seductive educational materials will dampen students' desire to learn for learning's sake. We need to remember that educators don't simply want learning for learning's sake; we want students to learn what *we want them to learn* and then *respond* as if it's for learning's own sake. Jason didn't hate *all* kinds of learning; he simply disliked what he *had* to do in school. He loved learning about Great Pyrenees for learning's own sake. How do we create a coupling between the students' interests and academically valued ones? Sometimes we avoid the reality that there *is* a degree of indoctrination involved in trying to get kids to care about the same kinds of things "we" do. Maybe one reason that my relationship with Jason worked is that he *also* succeeded in getting *me* to care about the things he does.

Although this principle (learning is most powerful when it is driven by passion) is not new, many digital media researchers believe that it is increasingly relevant to the future of education, given the explosion of digital media. Kids have so much media—from podcasts to video games—vying for their attention that they are forced to choose to focus on their passions. As the sportswriter Bill Simmons is fond of pointing out, when people like me grew up, we had three or four TV stations to choose from, plus whatever books our parents owned. Something as simple as my favorite baseball team playing on TV against the Kansas City Royals was gripping because the Royals have a (live!) fountain in Kaufmann Stadium.

In contrast, today's baseball fans can watch almost all of their hometown games on basic-cable TV, join free fantasy baseball leagues, receive live updates of the day's games, listen to any major league game on their phones for $10 a year, and even watch live games on their iPhones. Or, they can become creators and start blogs or participate in fan forums.

Media researcher Mimi Ito and her colleagues (2008) conducted an intensive 3-year study of youth engaging in such media practices and concluded that the process goes something like this: Youth begin by *hanging out* in places of interest to them (such as MUDs, Internet forums, or after-school settings). They start *messing around* with media (such as writing their own MUD areas on the back of their notebooks or editing their own videos). After messing around for a while, they start *geeking out* on specific practices. They hang out on forums, start their own film production companies, or join a MUD development team. This trajectory captures pretty well what happened to Nate and Eric.

OPEN ACCESS

Interest-driven communities like MUDs, sports fan pages, or fan fiction communities all share a second quality usually not found in schools: They have *open access* and enable newcomers to interact with experts on a regular basis. When forming a group to go hunting in the MUD universe, no one cared that Eric and Nate were in 5th grade. People did care if they couldn't do their job, which included spelling reasonably well. Further, the mechanisms for advancement were transparent and well articulated.

When many teachers encounter these ideas, their first reaction is that "it will never work with real kids in schools." They raise legitimate concerns: How do you manage a classroom of 25 kids each doing separate things? What do you do with the kid who never develops an interest in math, writing, or other academic subjects? How do you get kids to do the very hard work involved in producing something of quality?

Indeed, there are whole communities of educators who have been exploring these issues. Art educators are one group who often use design-oriented pedagogies in studio-type learning environments to capitalize on and extend students' interest. Schools such as McGuffey have developed similar pedagogies while also dealing with the realities of "normal" student-teacher ratios. We will provide case studies of whole-classroom and whole-school participation in later chapters, but first let's consider an entire system of educators across the world teaching similarly with deep ties to gaming.

THE MONTESSORI SYSTEM: FOLLOWING THE NEEDS OF THE CHILD

If I told you there was a school district that produced the founders of Google and Amazon.com; Will Wright, the creator of the most profitable video game franchise *The Sims*; P Diddy, one of the most successful hip-hop artists and entrepreneurs of all time; and Katherine Graham, the Pulitzer Prize–winning journalist and editor of the *Washington Post*, as well as Jacqueline Bouvier Kennedy Onassis, Julia Child, and Anne Frank, you would expect that educators would study this district thoroughly. However, Montessori, despite its widespread success, garners relatively little attention in the United States. Many influential researchers in psychology had Montessori connections: Jean Piaget was the head of the Swiss Montessori Society, Erik Erikson held a Montessori certificate, and Bruno Bettelheim married a Montessori teacher. Even Mister Rogers was a strong supporter of Montessori education. When Barbara Walters asked Larry Page and Sergey Brin (the cofounders of Google) if they attributed their success to support from their parents, who were college professors, they said no. It was *Montessori* that taught them to be self-directed.

Indeed, the Montessori system provides a model of what a game-based learning system should look like. Not that Montessori is perfect (no system is). However, Montessori is based on similar principles and has many connections to video games, making it a great test case for arguing for the viability of a video-game-based curriculum.

My firsthand experience with Montessori began in 1995. After teaching at McGuffey School, I was hired as a teacher's assistant (and later teacher) at the Knoxville Montessori School and trained there as a Montessorian. Montessori is a system devised by Maria Montessori, who was the first female Italian medical doctor and who practiced education in the early 1900s. I'd highly recommend that anyone interested in education read Montessori's original work, starting with *The Secret of Childhood* (1936). Working with poor kids who were said to be unable to learn, Montessori developed a theory that all children *could* learn if put in the proper environment. She developed an intricate, thorough system that goes from birth through adulthood. Today, Montessori is often dismissed as an elitist due to the high cost of enrollment in private Montessori academies, but the Montessori system was originally designed to work for the poor and did very well in that context. Sure, elites are choosing this system for their children, but shouldn't *all* children have access to this quality educational experience?

The typical Montessori day begins as students (as young as 2) arrive, independently put away their clothing, and select a lesson from the shelves (see Figure 3.1). The group often convenes for a brief "line activity," at which time the class will sit on a line together and share housekeeping notes. Here, they deal with issues such as impending birthdays or someone not picking up after themselves—a little like the meetings my wife calls at our house.

The next 3 hours (the morning work period) is the cornerstone of the day. Children select material to work on individually or with other children. The rules are simple: Children may use materials that have been demonstrated by a teacher (or a child skilled with that material). They are to use the materials properly and return them to their spot when they are finished. They also may choose to read silently, have a snack, or in some cases "do nothing." You'd be surprised how difficult it is to "do nothing" for 3 hours straight (ask anyone who meditates), so it happens less than people fear.

This unique morning work period embodies foundational principles of Montessori education. Children are *naturally* motivated to learn as a *normal* part of development. Learning cannot occur if children are forced to sit with their attention on their teacher; learning requires the ability to follow one's interests, engage

**Figure 3.1.
Montessori Shelves**

Photo courtesy of Amru Zainal Abidin. Used under Creative Commons.

the senses (and Montessori famously includes all of them—sight, hearing, touch, smell, and taste), and test ideas. Learning also requires *concentration*, which is why children have a 3-hour block of time. The Montessori system assumes that *all* children are capable of this kind of concentration and *need* opportunities to cultivate this concentration in order to become healthy adults.

No one tells children what materials to work with, when to take a break, or when to use the bathroom. It is expected that these are all choices that children are fully capable of making for themselves by the age of 3 (apparently, unlike most American high schoolers). In some Montessori schools, children set weekly target goals, which are done in consultation with teachers and parents. Snack, one of my favorite times, is taken by children on their own, and they are responsible for getting out the snack, setting the table, clearing the table, and doing the dishes. Indeed, in Montessori schools the children *themselves* are responsible for classroom cleaning and upkeep; being responsible for one's immediate environment is an important value. In contrast, many American public schools (again in the name of efficiency) reinforce not taking care of space, something Montessori would have considered unethical, as it prevents students from gaining the natural feedback (a messy room) from their actions (working sloppily).

In the afternoon, there is more variation in how schools implement the Montessori philosophy. The school I worked in dedicated the afternoon to free reading, special projects, and group work, including playing *SimCity* and making hypercard stacks (which the 6-year-olds loved). Most schools use the afternoon to pursue individual interests in greater depth (one 9-year-old mastered every world map, with capitals); others worked on art or music projects or wrote and published their own books. Many schools have enrichment activities at this time. My coteacher, Dawn Bullen, once led a multiweek optional science activity that culminated in students as young as 6-years-old dissecting fetal pigs. We discussed the ethics of dissecting animals at length. Because the fetal picgs were harvested from a slaughterhouse (and thus were already dead), most students opted to do the activity. We didn't, however, discuss the ethics of factory farming or the potential for animal-free economies.

Today, it is widely acknowledged that toddlers have an inherent desire to learn as they acquire language. However, later learning is often "laborious," and education generally becomes something done to you rather than something you undertake for fulfillment, or even as a sociobiological necessity. The trick for the teacher is to become a keen observer of children and to prepare a stimulating environment. So the Montessori environment is *anything* but a free-for-all. Kids *need* an environment *designed* to pique their interests, instill a sense of order and pattern to the world, and push them toward developing deep understanding. They need freedom, but within boundaries.

Children by and large do concentrate for extended periods of time without coercion. Some (mostly liberal) educators fear that Montessori is rigid or "not creative," especially with younger children, perhaps because of the lack of fantasy toys (see Kilpatrick, 1914). The guidebooks themselves are quite structured and include detailed instructions on how to use materials, including with what hand the tray should be lifted and so on. In my experience, this is interpreted differently according to the personality and approach of each instructor. Many (maybe even most) creative people are particular in the details of their craft (such as how to hold a harmonica properly or prepare one's creative work space). However, you can find enough variance among instructors to remember that it's never just the system but the *enactment* of a system by teachers, students, and parents that matters. If students, parents, and teachers want more dramatic play in a Montessori classroom, there are ways to do it.

Other critics may say, "Well, those kids must be different, because I know my teenager, and that wouldn't work for her." They are correct. If you let an average 12-year-old "study whatever he or she wanted," maybe many would goof off or get into bigger trouble. Most of us were raised in a system that squelched our natural desire to learn and engrained a deep sense of passivity. "I don't want to figure these things out . . . Tell me what I need to know!" That mentality is the *enemy* of the Montessori approach. According to Montessori, the problem with most of us is that we weren't "normalized." Normalization is at the heart of what the Montessori system has to teach us (especially educational game designers) about children, learning, and school design.

Normalization

Normalization is a simple, but powerful, idea: Children who are allowed to develop "normally" have a deep psychological and social need to learn as self-directed, productive members of society. This normalization develops "through 'concentration' on a piece of work." Again, adults are not absent but "must provide motives for activity so well-adapted to the child's interests that they provoke his deep attention." This is like a game designer who creates levels that pique players' interests, require creative problem solving, and reward a job well done. Montessori writes:

> "Normalized" children, aided by their environment, show in their subsequent development those wonderful powers that we describe: spontaneous discipline, continuous and happy work, social sentiments of help and sympathy for others. . . . An interesting piece of work, freely chosen, which has the virtue of inducing concentration rather than fatigue, adds to the child's energies and mental capacities, and leads him to self-mastery. . . . One is tempted to say that the children are performing spiritual exercises, having found the path of self-perfectionment and of ascent to the inner heights of the soul. (1967, p. 206)

Montessori thought this discovery of normalization (something observed across time and cultures) so important that she described it as "the single most important result of our whole work" (p. 204). Montessori chose to label the process *normalization*, in order to emphasize that it's a completely *normal*, natural part of development and *socialization*. Montessori is careful to describe normalization not as simply a "flowering" of a child but as a natural process "aided by the environment." Because Montessori refers to an environment prepared by an adult, this must be understood as a process guided by adults.

For example, as I write this, my 2-year-old is obsessed with playing with our dog's food, which he knows he should not do. As I stop him, I also observe what he's doing and ponder what this is really *about*. It might be his interest in sorting small objects, playing with the dog, pushing rules, or getting my attention (or all of the above). My short-term response is to reorganize the environment by putting up the dog bowls, but the longer-term response for me is to figure out what is driving that impulse and to channel it toward concentrated work. My wife later developed a Montessori-like activity involving sorting coffee beans into different cups and piles, which has satisfied his desire for fine-motor-skill development.

Preparing the learning environment (similar to designing games) is a key task for educators. Montessori explains, "The essential thing is for the task to arouse such an interest that it engages the whole child's personality." Montessorians identify the characteristics of normalization as a love of one's work and a love of order, concentration, self-discipline, independence, helping others, generosity, and joy. Almost anyone who observes a classroom of elementary children working autonomously recognizes it as inherently good and peaceful. *This*, rather than standardized test scores, sounds like a good educational outcome.

Thus, a related concept of normalization describes how groups settle. There is a "you know it when you see it" quality to a normalized class. Children are working intensely with materials alone or in groups. No teacher is telling them to get out their pencils and workbooks, no teacher is telling them what lesson to choose, and no administrator is concerned about who is on what page of the standardized curriculum because it is 2:00 p.m. on a Tuesday. That would be contrary to the very *purpose* of education.

Traditional public schools in fact "block" the normalization process. I would describe typical school experiences as training *docility* and preparing students for more schooling (something Ted Sizer describes eloquently in *Horace's Compromise*). Indeed, if concentrated, self-directed engagement is central to development, then our schooling system is not just ineffective but also ethically irresponsible.

Montessori argues that blocking children's developmental impulse to master their worlds and function independently in society is actually *deviant* (something I find amusing when applied to educational policy makers). However, it's not that adults are deviant if they say no every time a child wants cookies. Deviance can come from the child, the environment, or adults' imposing their will upon children. Adults must prepare the environment for healthy development. When such deviations are observed, the adult's job is to restructure the environment, much as my wife did with the coffee beans.

In Montessori, this normalization is what children engage in from the age of 2 or 3. This should be the core "game mechanic cycle" of education. Outside schools, children (particularly those with supportive home environments) do this regularly, and such experiences can even be found in popular culture, such as in video games.

Materials and Systems

The materials used in Montessori environments are ingenious and widely recognized for their elegant design (see Zuckerman, Arida, & Resnick, 2005; see Figure 3.1). In fact, they share many qualities with well-structured games. Each material is self-contained and self-correcting and is designed to teach particular concepts while reinforcing several others and "previewing" concepts that are much more advanced.

The pink tower in Figure 3.2, for example, is a set of 10 cubes, with the smallest cube being 1 cm^3 and the largest cube being 10 cm^3. Teachers use them to introduce the concept of three-dimensional size, to teach children how to stack (a motor skill), to illustrate properties of weight, and to reinforce measurement principles. The pink cubes implicitly introduce children to the "base 10 system" and cubic roots. The cubes themselves are *self-correcting* in that you can visually see whether they are in the correct position (it is difficult to stack them incorrectly). In addition, the teacher can introduce language for colors (*pink*), mathematical units (*cube*), early geometric terms (*edge, corner, center, vertical, horizontal*), and comparisons (*small* and *large, smaller* and *larger*). The key design principle is that good learning grows from robust intuitions about systems. In physics, educators have tried to design educational video games (such as *Surge* or *Supercharged!*) based on this same principle.

Subsequent materials extend these understandings. Students can also use control cards (which most lessons have) to check their work. These control cards present the same information, but on a 2-D plane, which introduces abstracted representations at an early age. Control cards function for learning much as walk-throughs do in video games. They enable skilled players to see complex problems solved correctly and to test their own understandings and performance in relation to them. Observe how much control is in the hands of the *learners*: They select the problems, they master the material, and they assess if they are doing the problem

Figure 3.2.
Montessori Pink Tower

correctly. In addition to the students' self-assessments (which occur in multiple forms throughout the curriculum), teachers also assess students' learning as they probe understandings during lessons. In this scenario, teachers function much as game communities do, as a social pushback on understandings. Students must convince outside communities (i.e., the teacher), not just themselves, that they have mastered the content before they can move on.

An epic Montessori material that embodies these ideas (and makes geeks swoon) is the trinomial cube. The trinomial cube is a puzzle designed to develop children's visual perception of patterns and indirectly prepare children for algebra. The cube is a visual representation of the algebraic formula $(a+b+c)(a+b+c)(a+b+c) = aaa + 3aab + 3aac + 3abb + 3bbc + 3acc + 3bcc + 6abc + bbb + ccc$. Each variable corresponds to a particular length, so there is one cube of size a^3, 3 solids of dimension aab, and so forth. If you ever wanted to *see* algebra, get one of these cubes.

The Curriculum

To see the Montessori curricular progression, just look at the shelves. The curriculum is divided into six categories: mathematics, language, science, culture, practical life, and sensorial experience, each of which is located in a particular region of the room. Famously, the Montessori curriculum goes from concrete to abstract in each area, arranged from the bottom of the shelf (most concrete) to the top (most abstract). Children begin learning mathematics through activities such as the pink tower (described earlier) and then move on to the stair. The stair leads to a variety of number lines, which are used to teach basic number theory. Next, they use mathematics manipulatives such as gold beads, which introduce the decimal system. The manipulatives get most of the attention, but the abstract materials, like the Pythagoras Board, are also important for developing mathematically literate students[2].

The curriculum has a *transparent* quality, in that modes for progression from the initial concrete levels (at the bottom of the shelves) to the more advanced abstract levels (at the top of the shelves) are clearly visible. Students progress along this trajectory at their own rate and go as far as they like. As such, the curriculum is also *meritocratic,* in that you can and should go as far as you can. A mature game-based pedagogy would also require letting go of lockstep group instruction.

---

2. The Pythagoras Board is a wooden puzzle of the multiplication table that encourages students to master multiples in their most abstracted forms and see patterns across them.

A last feature to explore is the social nature of the curriculum. Although Montessori has been criticized for being insufficiently social (see Kilpatrick, 1914), my experience is the opposite. Montessori classrooms are multiage, meaning that younger students observe older, more advanced students working (a form of modeling). In my brief stint at Montessori and McGuffey, teachers grouped students in a variety of ways for many different purposes (indeed elementary teachers often do this). Sometimes it was to help a socially awkward child develop self-confidence by working with a friend. Other times, in order to slow down a fast learner who wasn't understanding deeply enough, the fast student would be asked to teach a slower student, forcing the fast learner to reflect on his or her learning. Thus, although the curriculum is personalized, it's much more social than standard group-based instruction.

Measuring Success

Many critics may ask, "Can we prove the positive effects of Montessori while using other systems?" In the Coda to this book, I address issues of experimental design in educational research. However, a big challenge is showing which effects are caused by the Montessori system and which were influenced by factors like self-selection or parenting. Did Larry Page and Sergey Brin (the cofounders of Google) become such successes because of the Montessori system (as they believe) or did their parents also help? The answer is "Probably both."

Yet with the new wave of public Montessori schools and charter schools, we are beginning to see more research. Mihaly Csikszentmihalyi, *inventor of flow theory (a theory that is central to video games; see Chapter 10), and Kevin Rathunde (2005) studied middle school students and found that "Montessori students showed more intrinsic motivation; were more on task; and reported greater affect, potency* (i.e., feeling energetic), intrinsic motivation, flow experience, and undivided interest (i.e., the combination of high intrinsic motivation and high salience or importance) while engaged in academic activities at school." (p. 341). Ideally, we'd want to see measures of academic achievement, but the importance of studying motivation shouldn't be overlooked. In fact, in a digital age in which information is freely available and people are expected to be lifelong learners, these positive learning associations are far more important than test scores.

Montessori also complicates the research literature on learning. For example, a large body of literature shows that learners are not capable of exercising control over their own learning (see Kirschner, Sweller, & Clark, 2006). Some researchers will claim that this is evidence for why constructivist-inspired approaches cannot work. This view is partially correct; novices are generally not capable of learning without a well-prepared environment. The prepared environment gives the novice freedom in doses that he or she can handle. The materials themselves structure and guide the exploration on a certain path. Indeed, the Montessori curriculum is *incredibly* structured; recall that the pink tower is carefully constructed, not just to teach motor skills and rudimentary measurement and vocabulary, but also to preview concepts such as the base-10 number system.

However, control isn't so much a *tool* for learning as a *goal* of education. We want students to identify problems, muster the resources to solve them, moderate their learning, and then check for understanding. That is the *point* of education. If students are not able to work with minimal guidance, then that's all the more reason to reform education.

There is a dangerous assumption prevailing in current education policy that education is really a problem of finding the "right" program (such as Success for All) that will work for *all* children and teachers across *all* situations. As opposed to treating education as a human endeavor that is driven by kids, teachers, and parents in complex social situations, this "magic bullet" approach makes educational *programs* the source of agency. It assumes that if you find the right program, you will "fix" education, end poverty, and save the world.

I want to be clear that I'm not claiming Montessori is "the answer." No one system is right for all children all the time. Perhaps it's the *teacher's* job to make such decisions at the classroom level (with input from students, parents, communities, and the nation at large). Of course, this leaves classroom instruction up to local control, and there's no simple way out of this conundrum. In our work with teachers (see Chapter 9), we present curricular models that we expect to be *adapted*, not *adopted,* and we try to engage in a deeper conversation about the goals and methods of education.

TOWARD GAME-BASED PEDAGOGIES

Approaches such as the Montessori system provide models for educational game design. Indeed, the connections between Montessori materials and games runs deep. Designer Will Wright often compares his games, such as *The Sims* and *Spore,* to Montessori toys (see Crecente, 2009). Like Montessori materials, they guide students through cycles of discovery. Both involve perceiving patterns and relationships through cycles of action, observation, and feedback (see Chapter 2). And both push back on understandings in *a self-correcting* way as learners strategize, fail, and revise.

Like Montessori, *SimCity* at its best engenders intuitions about systems. On the surface, players may be learning about laying roads or zoning areas, but they are also developing intuitions about supply and demand, growth cycles, delayed feedback loops, and traffic patterns. At its core, *SimCity* (as Wright confesses) is more about nonlinear complex systems than about how cities operate.

Critics of *SimCity* argue that it lacks realism. In *SimCity*, you're not a mayor, a city council member, or anyone with a historical analog. You are this weird, God-like presence with the ability to tinker with abstract variables. It's precisely its implausability that makes the game compelling. Games enable the direct manipulation of variables, similar to how a novel provides access to internal dialogue. Of course, games built on the real-world practices of being a mayor might also have value; in fact, role-playing games often do this. However, bringing in fantastical elements (like speeding and compressing time) or the direct manipulation of variables opens the possible worlds and learning experiences unique to games, as discussed in Chapter 1.

I experimented with using games in my Montessori school. Although there is debate about computers in Montessori classrooms, every student had a computer at home, and parents actively encouraged their use. In fact, as I observed them interacting with the Montessori materials and computers, my students gravitated toward the computer in the same ways Maria Montessori's students engaged with her materials in the early 1900s. They were enraptured, trying to understand how it works, repeatedly puzzling through problems until they accomplished mastery.

With this in mind, I used *SimCity* with my 6- and 7-year-old students to introduce them to elementary social studies concepts (such as electrical, water, industrial, commercial, and residential systems). Within the Montessori system, teaching with *SimCity* was easy: Simply set up a computer in the back of the room and devise a series of lessons on how to play. There were none of the big "concerns" of fitting games into traditional classrooms and curricula. Short time periods, setup, differential learning outcomes, individualized pacing and progress were issues. As the children became comfortable with the game, they all wanted to tell me about their cities (much as a typical 6-year-old would be dying to tell you about *Pokémon*).

To build on this natural inclination for reflection, I borrowed an idea from my educational technology professor, Chris Wolfe, and introduced HyperCard. With HyperCard, students could take screenshots from their games and explain key accomplishments (such as showing off their bridges or public transportation systems). Not surprisingly, they loved it.

THEORY AND PRACTICE

We opened with the question "Can we put cutting-edge games into classrooms?" My experience suggests that the answer is yes. However, to do so requires changing the status quo of schooling and making a new commitment to interest-driven learning, differentiated learning trajectories, multiple levels of expertise, collaboration and competition, and learning through design rather than administrative efficiency.

Thus, we should not ask, "Can we adjust schools to accommodate games?" any more than we should have asked 500 years ago, "Can we adjust universities to accommodate books?" The real question we should be asking is, "What are the key features of a powerful learning environment that need to be leveraged to implement a mature vision of game-based learning?"

- *Game-based learning environments require a deep commitment to interest-driven learning.* The teachers at McGuffey valued understanding and unpacking students' interests and extending them into new academic domains. Some systems such as Montessori (but also Waldorf and Reggio) are set up to naturally promote such interest-driven learning and production-oriented designs. Without a deep commitment to such interest-driven learning, it's easy to imagine game-based learning failing, because opportunities to extend expertise in unique directions are squashed by standardization pressures.
- *Game-based learning environments might empower teachers to act as coaches, advisors, and producers rather than as content dispensers and police officers.* Once kids are interested in learning and engaged in focused work, teachers' work becomes much easier and they become resources, rather than obstacles, for students enacting their goals. Games allow this independence. But the brilliance of principal Janet Kretschmer's move to join her kids in gaming stems from a sophisticated conception of adulthood that sees teaching as providing progressive freedom.
- *Game-based learning pedagogies require dedication to* design *as a worthy goal of education.* The most advanced, sophisticated forms of participation in games culture—designing levels, mods, fictions, or guilds—are largely unacknowledged, if not derided, by mainstream educational institutions. We might recognize the genius in Nate and Eric's creation of the McGuffey Foundation School as a game level, but we realize it would be *banned* by many schools rather than encouraged. Further, the original creation of complex media, while being self-evidently a goal of education, simply isn't valued by today's mainstream education assessment mechanisms.

In 1995, when McGuffey kids explored the dark corners of the Internet and found MUDs, it was an esoteric phenomenon. Subsequently, such participatory cultures have become mainstream. The next chapter probes the nature of these communities and suggests how they might be powerful metaphors for the future of education.

CHAPTER 4

Community Organizing for Participatory Learning

Montessori provides a model for integrating games into classrooms, but how might games and participatory culture also change schooling?

In 1999 or 2000, this idea that video games and gaming culture could have *anything* to say about schools was controversial. When educators thought about video games at all, they thought of *Mortal Kombat*, *Lara Croft*, and *Doom*. Yet games were changing. MUDs highlighted the educational potential of games (see Bartle, 1996; Bruckman, 1993). Role-playing and "God" games, such as *Ultima*, *Deus Ex*, and *Black and White,* showed that games could ask complex moral questions (discussed later in this chapter). And games such as *The Sims* and *Civ* were complex simulations that enabled users to *create* media.

The educational potential of video games is not just about the *software*, but also about the participatory communities that games often inspire. This chapter uses the example of Joystick101.org, a web community for the study of games that I cofounded with Jon Goodwin in 1999, to argue for the importance of participatory media spaces—spaces that function outside formal schooling—as important sites of learning. They provide opportunities to forge new identities, follow one's passions, develop unique expertise, make new social connections, and ultimately participate in real practices. When you can access better information, attain deeper understanding, and get better feedback through informal participatory networks than you can through formal ones such as school, the basic model of schooling (even progressive schooling) can be called into question.

This chapter argues that learners need opportunities to participate in—and even *create*—their own self-organizing learning communities. Education, in this view, should help people identify and pursue their own passions. This chapter uses my own academic career as a case in point, but the reader can consider his or her own aspirations (or his or her students' passions) and ask how we as educators might create similar opportunities for *everyone*. Prior to 1999, I was another struggling graduate student trying to study video game cultures and the field of digital media and learning didn't yet exist. A little luck intervened so that I could pursue the ideas I loved. For today's students to succeed in a world of tomorrow that hasn't yet been created, we need more than luck; we need mechanisms for students to identify their skills and passions, refine them, and channel them into productive future selves.

CREATING A COMMUNITY TO LEARN WITH

"You, me, and a team of trained monkeys could do better than this crap," Jon Goodwin said as he threw a *Daily Radar* article on the table. I don't remember which article it was. Maybe it was "The Top 10 Hot Mom Pickup Lines"; it could have been list of torture devices. Regardless, it was typical of games journalism in 1999. Few people outside the industry took video games seriously, and few people within it did either. This was before exhibits such as Game On, which played at the Barbican in London, or the formation of the Digital Games Research Association (DiGRA), the international community of video games scholars. As a video game scholar, your resources were J. C. Herz's (1997) *Joystick Nation* and Justine Cassell and Henry Jenkins (1998) at MIT, who edited *From Barbie to Mortal Kombat*. That, and our little Simulations and Gaming class at Indiana University (see Video Game Studies sidebar).

As we read through the *Daily Radar* feature, I told Jon, "You know, you may not even have to train those monkeys. This is bad." We hatched a plan: We would skip the monkeys and instead recruit students to build a collaborative website (back before *blog* was even a word) for the in-depth study of games. We envisioned running a Slashdot.org clone (see Slashdot.org sidebar). I was interested in how blogs might be a new model for professional development. (Imagine requiring students to participate in a blogging community instead of a traditional seminar. I'd still like to try that, actually.)

We chose to use the SCOOP code (which the progressive blog *Daily Kos* is also based on) because it enabled more transparent ways for ordinary users to become involved. Any person could register, write a story, and post a story to the moderation queue. There, readers rate the story, give qualitative feedback, and make a *yes* or *no* decision. With enough yes votes (5% of registered users), the story automatically appeared on the front page. In a very direct way the content was user generated and user moderated. However, Jon and I maintained the power to edit and revise any text. We extended this editorial privilege to several others (most of whom we only met online).

Video Game Studies

How quickly perceptions of video games have changed! There are now conferences, books, and journals dedicated to game studies, and many institutions offer majors in video games. But only a few years ago, in 2000, when Robert Nideffer proposed a video game minor at the University of California, Irvine, the dean of the college said, "An academic program of study officially listed as focusing on gaming studies runs, I think, the strong risk of attracting people on the basis of prurient interest" (see Dean, 2001). To him, Nideffer might as well have been talking about studying porn.

I was fortunate to have access to a venue for discussing video games as a cultural form through teaching probably the only class on video games and learning that existed at the time. In the 1990s, two entrepreneurial Indiana University graduate students, Tony Betrus and Edd Schneider (both now faculty at the State University of New York, Binghamton), redesigned an upper-level education course on games and simulations to incorporate video games. They exploited a loophole in which no faculty actually knew what they were teaching in the class, so they used the class to discuss MUDs, competitive games such as *Quake* and unique games such as *Dance, Dance, Revolution.*

I got to teach the class largely by luck. Edd was graduating, and he didn't want to see the class die. One day he pulled me into the classroom, which had giant monitors showing gory games such as *Quake*. I was petrified, but did it anyway. I learned that if you remain open to learning from your students, you can teach games.

Slashdot.org

Slashdot.org is a technology news site that aggregates and links to stories on other Internet sites. Users submit stories to Slashdot.org and discuss and debate those stories, earning "karma" for posting good insights. With hundreds of thousands of readers, Slashdot.org has a reputation for crashing the servers hosting the stories it links to.

In the late 1990s, tech websites such as Joystick101.org were springing up all over the Internet, as anyone with a Linux machine and Internet connection could use these free code bases to launch a website. We all lived in a weird symbiosis with the Slashdot community as we used their code, provided them content through our published stories, and then relied on them to push users to our site (see Chan, 2002).

If we are going to support students in identifying, leveraging, and even creating such communities for learning, it's critical for us to understand, not only how they work, but how social values are embedded in code.

Understanding Affinity Spaces for Learning

For those unfamiliar with online affinity spaces, they are groups that voluntarily gather to learn (see Wiley and Edward's [2002] work on self-organizing learning communities). James Paul Gee (2005), who coined the term "affinity spaces," noted how they form through voluntary associations (i.e., we all are there by choice) and the sharing of knowledge and expertise. Some, but not all, of these affinity spaces can be described as *communities*. Communities typically have a longer history, deeper culture, closer social ties, stronger commitment to the group, and mechanisms for enculturation.

Whether or not one thinks online affinity spaces are models for education (I think they are), they are an important way that people learn and interact in the modern world (see Gee, 2007). They are relatively *open*: Anyone with an email address can join and post content. Your age, educational degree, or geographical location doesn't matter. Affinity spaces *do* police members in subtle and not so subtle ways. They can be hostile toward outsiders who violate the group's norms (one of their downsides, but this is also true of schools).

Most affinity spaces include mechanisms for "ordinary users" to contribute and moderate content. Many affinity spaces strike a balance between "official," editorially approved content and the purely user-generated stuff. Critical digital literacy requires knowing the difference between a diary and front-page story (just like distinguishing between a news story and an editorial). Usually, editors write the front page, but sometimes, as with Joystick101.org, anyone's content can become the headline. Thus, every site is a unique mix of information with varying degrees of formality, credibility, and sanction. Being literate means understanding what content belongs where as well as the relative credence of information in each context.

This interplay between "official" and "unofficial" content makes participating in affinity spaces engaging, but it also can create confusion. For example, Wisconsin Public Radio (WPR) recently botched an interview with Markos Moulitsas, founder of *Daily Kos* and author of *Taking On the System: Rules for Radical Change in a Digital Era* (2008), due to such a mix-up. The WPR host pulled a few racy quotes off someone's unofficial post on *Daily Kos* and then acted as if *Daily Kos* was directly accountable for the statements (Bill O'Reilly also does this, something that Steven Colbert famously mocks). *Daily Kos* was no more responsible for that person's comment than a mayor is responsible for someone ranting at a town hall meeting. In most cases, community members moderate offensive commentary. But blogs are venues for people to test ideas, which makes them very different from broadcast media.

This type of social organization—which has multiple interest-driven trajectories, opportunities to learn with experts, paths toward becoming an authentic participant, and ways to lead the group itself—is a good model for schools struggling with how to provide expertise to a classroom of kids who have unique interests. Whether schools embrace affinity spaces remains to be seen, but if history is a guide, media-savvy parents will use affinity spaces with their children to further the children's interests in dinosaurs, robots, or games through podcasts, websites, and gaming communities. Parents value the 21st-century skills gained by participating in affinity spaces, similar to those exemplified in the "gamer disposition" (see The Gamer Mindset: Xzins sidebar). To explain, let's return to Joystick101.org.

The Gamer Mindset: "Xzins"

As Will Wright (2006) says, there's something scientific in how video game players experiment (i.e., develop and test hypotheses in games).

Google "Xzin" and find his videos playing five *World of Warcraft* characters simultaneously—he's really good. Xzin's goal was to build a pvp, or player vs. player (competitive gaming) machine, and he succeeded, taking five of the seven top rankings on his server. It isn't unusual for Xzin to single-handedly change the course of 80-player battlegrounds.

You might think, "This must be cheating." No, he's not cheating, said Blizzard officially, because he is in control of all five characters. He's running an experiment: Can one person, using custom-configured hardware, be as good as five humans? After playing MMOs, the thought of grinding up a character sounded . . . boring. Why not try five at once?

The key to this setup is the keyboard multiplexer, a device that allows one keyboard to send commands to more than one machine. Multiplexers strung together, hardware tweaks, and creative keybinding and macros allows Xzin to control all five characters in real time.

Xzin is a dramatic example of how modders create new game interfaces and how guild leaders create rules, structures, and groups. Our single greatest challenge in education is that our schools are not teaching kids to innovate. Entrepreneurial thinking is every bit as important as mastering preexisting objectives. Yet, traditional schools are designed for uniformity and conformity, and not for producing (or even handling) the "Xzins" of the world. Games show us the future of education.

Designing an Affinity Space for Learning

Here's what we hoped for our site: A reader learns of Joystick101.org from Slashdot.org. She adds Joystick101.org to her bookmarks and checks it regularly. Eventually, she develops an interest in an issue in a game—say, representations of race in *Grand Theft Auto*. At the time, there was no venue for serious and critical discussions of games, and we hoped to draw students, professors, game designers, fans, and ordinary game players who had something to say. Let's say our participant writes an article and submits it to the moderation queue, where it receives feedback, editing, and proofreading by the community. When enough readers or editors deem it worthy of publication, it is posted to the main page. She enjoys being an expert in this area and Joystick101.org extends her hobbies into quasi-professional identity.

After publishing a few articles, our author might develop a reputation for a particular area of expertise, like gender and games. She might become a feature writer and obtain organizational affiliation. She could make business cards, conduct interviews leveraging the Joystick101.org affiliation, request review copies of games and books, and attend events such as the Game Developers Conference on a press pass (saving thousands of dollars). The most committed members would be promoted to "moderator" status, giving them all the same abilities we founders have (including deleting content).

This may sound like an obscene amount of trust to give a stranger, but it happens all the time in online groups such as guilds in *World of Warcraft*. One reason, as Steinkuehler (2006) points out, is that people in such communities are engaged in joint activity. They are working together on a shared project in which everyone is emotionally invested. People in such communities aren't naive; they have *built* trust. Trust-building mechanics are the basis of most team-building seminars. In self-organizing affinity spaces, these principles are inherent.

Here's what actually happened. Slowly, the Joystick101.org readership—and authorship—grew to a few hundred people. As we posted stories that were picked up by video game fan sites and niche gaming sites, we would attract about 2,500 new readers, which tapered off to a small, but growing group of committed participants, and even a few volunteer moderators. Not astounding, but more than the readership of the average academic article. Now how to build a real community?

Community Organizing with Participatory Media

There is an ecology created among the readers, authors, and websites in affinity spaces. It's not a case of "established versus participatory" media, where one wins and the other loses. Instead, they feed off each other for content, publicity, ideas, and legitimization. Savvy producers understand this ecology and craft messages so that they flow back and forth across channels, as described in Al Giordano's brilliant essay, "Global Tanning: Anatomy of a Media Virus" (2008). Understanding these ecologies *should* be a cornerstone of media literacy education, but the discourse surrounding popular culture and education is hopelessly caught up in the debate over whether to trust established corporate media (i.e., the *New York Times*) or laud the emancipatory potential of participatory media. True media literacy would involve learning to leverage these channels for communication.

The key to scaling became apparent in the fall of 2000 with the release of PlayStation2 (PS2). Its success or failure would shape the industry and be worth billions to its parent companies. For Joystick101.org, a feature on the PlayStation2 release could be our grand entrée into the field. Over beers we hatched a plan. I would chronicle the travails of those brave souls camping at electronics stores with the hopes of obtaining a PS2 as soon as it was released and write the story overnight. Jon would post it to Slashdot.org and ensure that our server withstood the onslaught of readers.

This strategy worked even better than we had planned. The story, "PS2 Launches! Word from the Street," (available on kurtsquire.info) was picked up by Slashdot.org and other sites shortly thereafter. Next came Wired.com, and soon we had 250,000 unique visitors in 48 hours. Literally overnight, we had a regular readership with 2,000 to 10,000 daily readers. As a graduate student, it felt weird to have 250,000 people read my work. I wasn't ever sure my professors actually read my papers. Even academic articles reach four or five people, at best. Here was a chance to reach a lot more people while also learning to write and edit in public.

What to do with this platform? Immediately, we used it to expand our social network, reminding us of how infrequently students can do this in schools. We interviewed game designers such as Raph Koster and Eric Zimmerman and academics such as Henry Jenkins. We were unique in featuring analyses of games culture, too. A favorite was a story on homemade hardware hacker Benjamin Heckendorn (benheck.com), who made his handheld Atari 2600 by hacking up a used Atari 2600, and adding a pocket tv screen and batteries. He later wrote a book, *Hacking Video Game Consoles* (2005), which describes how to make an Xbox 360 laptop and homemade pinball machines (such as his table, based on HBO's *Big Love*). And, yes, we earned passes to the Game Developers Conference (see Game Developers Conference sidebar).

Game Developers Conference

The Game Developers Conference, or GDC (gdconf.org), is an annual event where tens of thousands of game developers, including luminaries like Will Wright, Shigeru Miyamoto, Doug Church, and Sid Meier, gather to share ideas about their craft. Attending GDC is exciting, at least for those of us used to academic conferences. The presentations themselves are full of humor, self-deprecation, and, most important, passion. They also acknowledge failures—and even celebrate them—as a key part of learning. Attending GDC changed how I thought about my professional speaking, and I've heard many academics (such as Henry Jenkins, James Paul Gee, and Jane McGonigal) say similar things.

Joystick101.org tried to embody the ideas of participatory culture by helping readers to become writers. We wanted them to use the site as a platform to express *their* voices and further *their* careers. Around 50 different people wrote original, feature-length articles, though I met only one of them personally. Contributors ranged from graduate students in anthropology to high school students hoping to enter video game journalism, to "professionals" such as Steven Poole from the *Guardian*. RevRaven (who I think was a high school student, but who knows) became a popular poster through his provocative prognostications, such as in "The Great Video Game Crash of 2000." (I searched for a link to this post on the web and on archive.org, but to no avail.)

For a great example of how people used the site, take Kyle Orland, a high schooler who ran a website called Super Mario Brothers Headquarters. I emailed him and learned that Kyle wanted to become a games journalist when he graduated school. Kyle started posting stories to Joystick101.org and other sites, and pretty soon he developed a following. I fell out of touch with Kyle for a few years, but I recently heard he was the host of National Public Radio's gaming podcast *Press Start*.

Joystick101.org didn't "cause" Kyle to become a games journalist. However, sites such as Joystick101.org and Gamecritics.com provided Kyle with opportunities to develop and hone his craft and his identity as a professional writer. The same was true for me, really. Kyle, RevRaven, Jon, and I all had doors opened to us. Our age, origins, or academic credentials weren't as important as what we had to say. (Of course, those things probably affected what we said and how we said it).

Affinity spaces can be profoundly democratic. However, this does not mean that they are equal opportunity. There are equity issues regarding who has access to such communities and whose voices are heard within them. (Many sites in games and technology are marked by a strikingly male discourse). Starting Joystick101. org required a passion for learning about games, a knowledge of how to leverage Slashdot.org, access to a server and bandwidth (an expensive investment), decent writing skills, and colleagues ready to hatch this plan. (For a similar deconstruction of successful dot-com era inventors, see Gladwell, 2008) This last element—access to a peer group to help inspire and implement ideas—seems endemic to most similar successful ventures.

INSIDE ONLINE AFFINITY SPACES

As the world becomes increasingly networked, knowing how to identify, navigate, and even *start* affinity spaces such as Joystick101.org is an essential skill for furthering one's professional development. A new kind of entrepreneurship is emerging, fueled by an intersection of freely available code bases and an ecology of media outlets that enables new voices to proliferate. Online systems make it possible to extend one's social and professional ties beyond immediate geography and reach a broad audience.

Affinity spaces are equally influential outside video games in areas from sports to politics. My first initiation to affinity spaces was following Indiana basketball via Peegs.com, a message board run by Mike Pegram, an accountant. Pegram eventually quit his day job to run what would become the premier source for information on Indiana basketball. At Peegs.com, teenagers, high school coaches, and professional reporters all shared analysis of recruiting, players, games, and gossip. If a recruit hurt his thumb in a pickup game in Fort Wayne, it came up on Peegs.com first. There was no way a sports page could keep up with thousands of basketball fans spread across the state. Stories broke on Peegs.com and then were picked up by reporters. Media scholars such as Henry Jenkins (2006) have described such places as sites of "collective intelligence" because together they know more than any one person could. Mike Pegram was soon doing interviews on CNN and other major networks.

Bill Simmons, now an influential ESPN columnist, got a similar start by publishing his writing online. He covered topics such as fantasy baseball, which most newspapers *still* won't touch (no wonder they are going out of business!). He now has a podcast with hundreds of thousands of listeners and a Twitter feed with over 1 million followers, and his book, *The Book of Basketball* (2009), topped the *New York Times* best-sellers list. Simmons built his career in establishment media by navigating the same digital media landscape that our friendly WPR personality treated with derision (see Institutions in a Participatory Age sidebar).

Institutions in a Participatory Age

If educators are going to embrace participatory media for education, we need methods for addressing the diversity of opinions online. Witnessing the sort of ludicrous claims that flourish online (for example, that Barack Obama isn't an American citizen), it's easy to write off participatory media as anathema to education. Before one criticizes participatory media too harshly (see Bauerlein, 2009), it's important to recall the poor quality of information in many establishment institutions, particularly profit-driven entertainment news media, which is beholden to shareholders and not the public good. There are also schools that teach intelligent design in science and use heavily biased social studies textbooks (see Loewen, 1995).

Indeed, educators should take solace. As troubled as schools can be, media institutions may be worse. We all know their recent failures, including not challenging questionable claims by the Bush administration prior to the Iraq War or informing the public of the differences between Osama bin Laden and Saddam Hussein. It's still shocking how few Americans know that the architects of the war in Iraq had openly been advocating attacking Iraq since January 1998, something many blog readers know. So we must interrogate the quality of information in establishment institutions as well as participatory ones. Recent uprisings in Egypt, the cholera outbreak, or even the historic civic uprisings in my own Madison, Wisconsin, are all good examples of mainstream media's failure to cover stories important to citizens.

For how not to deal with participatory affinity spaces, consider how establishment media handled the 2008 election. During debates, mainstream reporters such as George Stephanopoulos and Brian Williams repeatedly asked Barack Obama questions based on falsehoods, with Williams reading from an email alleging that Obama hid the fact that he was Muslim, gave the oath of office on the Koran, and would "not pledge allegiance to the flag or respect it." Rather than debunking such falsehoods or asking why the media had failed to inform the public of these matters (which professional journalists should be obligated to do), the newscasters simply revoiced these ideas, acting as if giving credence to a rumor is democratic.

Established institutions such as *The New York Times* or our public schools must interact with affinity spaces to stay relevant. As institutions such as newspapers struggle to prove their viability in a digital age, it is a reminder that traditional schools are the product of particular historical patterns and that deeper cultural and economic changes need to be leveraged to make schools more equitable, democratic, and humane.

EDUCATION IN A DIGITAL AGE: PARTICIPATORY EDUCATION

More than just educating learners to evaluate information, schools need to teach learners to evaluate *communities* in order to understand their strengths, weaknesses, and biases. We have to teach students to have a critical literacy of participatory culture.

In fact, entertainment game designers, you might be surprised to learn, rarely start with games as the solution to the pitfalls of our education system. Most often, game designers focus on the values of *participatory* culture. I once had the pleasure of hearing Bing Gordon, the former chief creative officer of Electronic Arts, address a group of prominent educational game designers. Gordon explained that instead of building a game, he'd simply start by requiring that kids do something "real" in the world. If designing a game, he'd emphasize physicality in games for tween-age boys (fighters, platform jumpers), identity development in games aimed at young adolescents (role-playing games), and social networks in games aimed at older adolescents and adults (cooperative games). But more important, he'd use those values to rethink education. When teaching at the University of Southern California, he said that to get an A in his class, you had to do more than fulfill his expectations. You had to make something that people would actually use—just like how we started Joystick101.org to learn about video games.

Gordon articulates a *participatory* approach to education. Given today's tools, from a development and a production/distribution standpoint, there's no good reason for students to wait 20 years to do something consequential. Use the Internet (or your cell phone) to get involved in a community that is doing the thing that you want to learn. Since that lecture, Gordon (2009) has become a proponent of video games in education and argues that games will one day replace textbooks. Again, it may be less games as a technology and more games as a cultural practice that encourages experimentation, systemic thinking, and authentic participation.

LEARNING THROUGH PARTICIPATION

The primary challenge of participatory media, however, is to open new horizons for participation. Let's finish with the story of how Joystick101.org brought me to MIT. It was the spring of 2001. Jon Goodwin and I were scrambling about in the Game Developers Conference pressroom posting an analysis of Bill Gates's keynote address launching the Xbox.

Up strolled Jordan Raphael. Jordan wrote for *Inside* magazine and was higher up the media food chain. You could tell this because he was leisurely enjoying his coffee rather than fumbling over his laptop. Jordan looked over and saw what must have looked like two characters in a Will Ferrell movie.

"Hey! I know you two," Jordan interjected. I looked around. He *was* talking to us. Why did he need to harass two guys running a website for no pay?

"No, seriously. I read you guys every day. Henry Jenkins told me about your site." I paused. This was plausible.

"Henry is throwing a party tonight. You two should come." Jon and I did a double take. Henry was an academic rock star.

Jordan just needed to email his contact, and we'd be in. A few minutes later, his contact Alex emailed saying, "Yes you can come. Henry likes you. But please, if you see Jordan, kindly ask him to stop inviting people." Alex's message was clear: We could come, but be on our best behavior.

We were invited to our first "insider" party. Later that night, as Jon and I scanned the crowd at Dr. Jenkins's suite, every face was recognizable. That is, every-one but us. On one side of the room, Warren Spector and Will Wright were drink-ing Sierra Nevadas. We could see J. C. Herz, Eric Zimmerman, Brenda Laurel, and the beat reporter from the *San Jose Mercury News* behind them. Henry was enter-taining Microsoft bigwigs. So Jon and I did what anyone in our situation would do; we grabbed a couple of free beers and parked ourselves next to Will and Warren.

"So Warren, if you don't mind me asking," Jon started, before realizing he was sounding fan-boyish. I knew what he wanted to ask: In *Deus Ex*, why did Warren include a scene with the bartender in which you can unlock a conversation about political philosophy from the perspective of a Chinese businessman critiquing U.S. capitalism (see *Deus Ex* sidebar)?

Warren pleaded the fifth, but gave a great producer line, "I don't know for sure, but I told my team that if each of you doesn't put something in there that will get you fired, then you're not doing your job." Eventually the conversation turned to our colleague from Microsoft, the party sponsor.

"We're going to revolutionize education through games," the Microsoft guy said. I nearly choked on my appetizer.

Warren saw my surprise. "What's up with you?" he followed.

"Nothing." What to say? I had felt out of place until now. This party was all for games in education? Although I hope games *could* revolutionize education, I know there are no silver bullets.

I explained that in my "other life" I studied games and education and that I felt marrying academic content and game play was tricky.

The guy from Microsoft went on about *Reader Rabbit*, a flashcard-style game, and how if games worked for 3-year-olds, they could work for high schoolers. He wanted to create the next generation of science education based on *Reader Rabbit*.

I looked around at Warren, Will, and Jon. Warren could see the wheels turning in my head. "C'mon, say it! You are getting a PhD in this stuff, right?"

Deus Ex

I can't think of a more prescient piece of media in 2000 than *Deus Ex*. In *Deus Ex*, a group of former government-sponsored "freedom fighters" have been mobilized by the government. They lock themselves in the Statue of Liberty, taking hostages. The game asks the player to decide where his or her allegiance lies; is it with family, religion, or government?

In one scene, two characters get into a political discussion where they debate the merits of American capitalism versus Chinese socialism. The conversation goes as follows:

J. C. Denton: What does China fear?

Isaac: China is the last sovereign country in the world. Authoritarian but willing—unlike U.N.-governed countries—to give its people the freedom to do what they want.

J. C. Denton: As long as they don't break the law.

Isaac: Listen to me. This is real freedom, freedom to own property, make a profit, make your life. The West, so afraid of strong government, now has no government. Only financial power.

J. C. Denton: Our governments have limited power by design.

Isaac: Rhetoric—and you believe it! Don't you know where those slogans come from?

J. C. Denton: I give up.

Isaac: Well-paid researchers—how do you say it?—"think tanks," funded by big businesses. What is that? A "think tank"?

J. C. Denton: Hardly as sinister as a dictator, like China's premier.

Isaac: It's privately funded propaganda. The Trilateral Commission in the United States, for instance.

J. C. Denton: The separation of powers acknowledges the petty ambitions of individuals; that's its strength.

Isaac: A system organized around the weakest qualities of individuals will produce these same qualities in its leaders.

Fun stuff. And who said games don't express ideas?

I mumbled something about being nice to my hosts (remembering Alex's admonishments), underlying epistemological issues, and some other blather, but Warren wouldn't have it. "Look, I spend all day surrounded by people talking about things that they don't know. If you know something about this, then say it. I'm an old academic who quit his PhD in film to make games."

I looked at Jon and thought, Why not? The worst they can do is kick me out, but if I could entertain Warren for 5 minutes it was a good night.

I launched into a mini-rant about games and learning and how *Reader Rabbit*, a flashcard-style game, doesn't tap into the deep educational potential of games (as covered in chapters 1–3). I explained how games worked under a different epistemology, or way of knowing things. Flashcard-type games assume that the learner will buy into whatever the designer tells him or her. It's essentially memorizing words. Yet, games have the potential for people to *test* ideas because they work in the world for them. Recall how players learn geography in *Pirates!* because it's useful to them. You know something is true in games because you've used it in many different situations. Games embody Dewey's pragmatic philosophy, "That which is true is that which works in the world." Combine this knowing-through-doing with the authorial opportunities within games in participatory media circles, and you have a pedagogical model far beyond *Reader Rabbit*. The trick was that no one had done it yet, so it was just a theoretical possibility.

Microsoft Guy scuffled off and Warren looked mildly entertained. Soon, Microsoft Guy returned with his boss Randy Hinrichs, who said, "So I hear you're pestering my guy." I backpedaled, but Randy laughed. "Come, I want you to meet some people." Randy dumped me off with Alex Chisholm, our contact.

"What did you do?" Alex asked. Jon explained how Warren requested that I unleash my academic tirade on Microsoft Guy.

"Well, it seems like Henry likes you. Would you visit MIT to help us think through these issues?"

"Do people ever say no to that?" I asked?

When I returned to Indiana, my advisor was skeptical. I was the crazy guy speaking about a "mystical partnership forming between MIT and Microsoft to build educational video games." More than once I was asked, "How many Sierra Nevadas did you have?"

Yet, within a month, I was driving to Cambridge, Massachusetts, to not just study games culture seriously, but to actually start *making* games based on those ideas. It was all quite shocking. We would challenge the preconceived notion that games are misogynistic, violent, and overly competitive by building interesting ones that buck those stereotypes. Not only would I be allowed to play—and study—games in the open, but I would be encouraged to collaborate with designers like Wright or Spector.

THEORY AND PRACTICE

In this chapter, we've established that people learn things through video games, and that some of this learning is socially valued. Games are capable of expressing complex ideas, but do so in ways different from books or film. There are even models for how we might incorporate them into schools through systems such as Montessori as well as precedents for thinking about how students might become designers of products (e.g., MUDs or blog articles) and social systems (e.g., communities like Joystick101.org).

- *Participatory culture might change schooling*, and while our story of Joystick101.org doesn't tell us *how* to do this, it demonstrates the potential for learners to self-organize and use learning communities to further their interests and passions and to make a demonstrable impact on the world. People do this every day in everything from sports to politics, and given the dramatic educational potential of these spaces, educators (particularly those interested in games) need to consider how to incorporate these spaces in educational game design.

- *Learners should be empowered to seek out, leverage, and even create communities to further their interests.* These spaces might take many shapes and sizes, but they are organized around this participatory ideal. A 15-year-old girl in Detroit interested in women in hip hop could benefit from being taught how to find—and, if none exists, to create—a community within which she can pursue her interests.

- *The digital age is profoundly participatory* (for *some*), *and there are avenues for developing expertise and for using it to participate in broader systems.* Internet technologies make it possible to participate in legitimate activities that have an impact on the world, and learners are doing so everywhere all the time (except perhaps in schools). My own career (and those of thousands of others like me) is a testimony to this, as it was launched largely through my work at Joystick101.org, where I could reach tens of thousands more readers than I could as a student writing for a professor. The key is to bring such experiences to people equitably.

- *There is a deep affinity between games—a participatory medium that players co-create—and the logic of participatory cultures in which participants co-create the organizations themselves.* MUDs, gaming guilds, clans, and even gaming communities such as Apolyton (see Chapter 7) all function by a similar logic, one that values a sort of meritocracy, rather than credentials. Later chapters explore how this affinity has pushed our team to create game-based pedagogies that help kids participate in the world in meaningful ways. As fields of knowledge continue to coalesce, specialize, and dissipate, we might expect that knowledge of creating, participating, and leveraging for one's own ends will become *essential* for successful participation in social, economic, and civic life.

CHAPTER 5

Games-to-Teach: Designing Games for Learning

Having discussed what properties cutting-edge games should include and why we need to design social interactions around them to make them participatory, we turn our attention to designing games for learning. Specifically, this chapter asks:

- Can we design games for learning that reflect the best contemporary gaming and learning theory?
- What would next-generation educational games look like?
- What kinds of design teams and processes do we need?

Let's start with my first day on the job at MIT.

BROADENING THE DISCUSSION OF EDUCATION AND GAMES

"Kurt, why don't you tell them the story of *Pirates!*" Henry Jenkins suggested. I scanned the room of 25 MIT scientists. Many were skeptical that you could learn science from a video game. Heck, *I* was skeptical. But this was exciting. Microsoft Research had funded iCampus, a collaboration with MIT to develop educational technology. They wanted to combine MIT's tradition of inventing new technologies with Microsoft's publishing power.

The Games-to-Teach project, led by Henry Jenkins from MIT's Comparative Media Studies department and Randy Hinrichs at Microsoft, strove to ignite a global conversation about educational games. This was back in 2001 and video games were mostly considered violent or misogynistic at best. Henry wanted to change that.[1] At about the same time, the serious games movement, led by Ben Sawyer with support from David Rejeski (2002) at the Woodrow Wilson Foundation, made similar observations. The serious games movement asks, How we can promote the nonentertainment use of gaming tools, knowledge, and teams?

So I related to the scientists my anecdote about swashbuckling in high school. In response, Matt Ford, a game designer working on *Asheron's Call*, shared how, after playing *Starcraft*, he surveyed the blighted battlefield and couldn't help but see the futility of war. Could kids *play* games in academic domains and *reflect* on them?

Henry shared how his son, Henry IV, tried to bring Doonesbury's Election Game (1996) to school. Playing at home, Henry IV noticed that the 1996 election would come down to California, because it was the only remaining large swing state. He showed the game to his teacher, but she sent it home because video games were banned. Henry was appalled. How could you ban an entire medium, regardless of content? If game designers didn't do something quickly, video games would go the way of the comic book. Comic books were a mainstream medium in the mid-20th century, but because of concerns about their effects on children, a "comic code" was enacted limiting what content could be displayed in comic books. Now most people think of them as media for children, although Spiegelman's *Maus* (1986), the story of a Holocaust survivor, is but one example of how graphic novels can convey mature content. (For more on this topic, see Michael Bitz's [2010] *When Commas Meet Kryptonite,* one of several recent texts on how literacy skills can be developed through comics.)

Over cocktails at the Electronic Entertainment Exposition (E3), Henry and Alex (with me along for the ride) outlined a plan to produce 10 prototypes that would demonstrate the potential of educational games. Our goal was to create a suite of games with a wide variety of features, rather than a one-off game that could be critiqued for its specific features (such as for being multiplayer or not being multiplayer and for being too open ended or being not open ended enough).

I returned to Bloomington to explain that I was taking off to MIT to work with Henry Jenkins, a guy who researches video games, pro wrestling, and *Quentin Tarantino's Star Wars*. My colleagues expected me back within a few days, and frankly I wasn't sure what to expect.

---

1. Ironically, Henry has written extensively about both, as they are unavoidable topics. For two excellent examples, see "Professor Jenkins Goes to Washington," the story of his testifying after the Columbine massacre, or Henry's work on video games as gendered spaces. As I raise my own boys, I appreciate Henry's argument that many games are based on traditional boys' play and that parents' discomfort with games is in part due to mothers' unease with boys' culture in their living rooms.

But back at E3, Blizzard was introducing a little game called *World of Warcraft*. The Blizzard fan boys were fawning. I got a walk-through and saw nothing remarkable. I said, "We already had three fantasy-themed games about elves and orcs, and they all compete for the same 500,000 people. Why will you succeed when they can't?"

As everyone knows, I was wrong. *World of Warcraft* has sold upwards of 12 million copies and is one of the largest media franchises ever. Why? Lots of reasons (see Wallace, 2006), but a big one is that *WoW* was *incredibly* polished. Blizzard spent more money developing *WoW* than had ever been spent on a game, including a several-month beta period.[6] Educational game designers—and funding agencies—could learn from their policy of never shipping a game until it's ready.

Yet the game itself offered almost *nothing* new.[7] On the surface, the core features of *World of Warcraft* were a simplified version of what already existed—in a market in which *more features* are considered good! The character progression system was taken from MUDs. The quests were from *EverQuest*. Famously, the death mechanic was lifted directly from *Ultima Online*, causing Rich Vogel to comment that Blizzard used good mechanics that other developers *forgot* about. What worked was not the idea as much as Blizzard's *execution*.

Games Literacy

In education, we don't test *ideas*; we test their *execution*. This is why educational game designers need to be literate with the medium. Just as educational film directors know about composition, sound, lighting, cuts, and so on, educational software designers need to understand avatar creation and customization, overlapping roles, reputation systems, embedded narratives, and other elements (see Prejudice in Educational Media Design sidebar). Indeed, the idea that researchers or designers should even *play* games is controversial. Some educational game designers haven't even tried *WoW*. If asked why, usually they claim they are too busy (imagine an author being too busy to read best-selling books). I would love it if they said, "Well, I don't play *WoW* because it's a rehash of 1990s MUDs, and I'm more

---

6. Outside forces intervened, as well, including the maturation of the games market, a lack of good PC games at the time, cross-platform availability (it was one of the only AAA titles to launch on the Mac), the penetration of broadband, and the growth of the global games market. Blizzard has a huge reputation in East Asia thanks to *Starcraft*, and it had the infrastructure to pull off a strong Asian release. *WoW* sells as well in China as it does the United States.

7. The implementation of the rogue and warrior classes were new, as was the concept of warlocks and druids. I still get misty-eyed when I think of my warlock.

interested in indie games such as *Flower*, *Braid*, or *Parallel Kingdoms* (see Chapter 10), but that generally doesn't happen. Others don't want to become game "advocates," lest we lose neutrality. Imagine proudly proclaiming that you don't read books because you don't want to become biased toward reading. It's thinly veiled cultural fear.

Prejudice in Educational Media Design

Imagine wanting to publish educational books, but only by people who don't read. Could I have used that as an excuse for my poor term papers in English class? I could have justified my lack of theme, narrative structure, or spelling by arguing that I don't want to waste my time reading and don't trust the teacher and his culture of books. (In fact, many struggling readers react to school just this way.)

Many of the designers of educational games aren't players. Imagine a social science researcher damning book culture because he or she watched a few people reading books at a coffee shop, ran a few studies, and found that if people were forced to read violent books (e.g., *Beowulf*, Shakespeare, or the Bible), they reacted with aggression to fictional literary characters, thus proving that reading violent books causes aggression.

As a result of educational media specialists' negative bias toward video games, some of the materials being tested as "game-based learning" don't contain the core features of games as we defined them in the opening chapters. Many educational games lack transgressive play, character progression, competition, interesting choices and consequences, the chance to try on different social identities, or interesting artwork. It's as if someone strung a bunch of words together on paper and then dismissed the educational potential of books because no one could understand the text.

We need to treat the first wave of game-based learning research with caution. By way of another analogy, it's as if we're in 1925, we've given educators films and cameras, and we want to make judgments about the medium. We would never expect to definitively evaluate the educational potential of motion pictures for all subject matters, across all time and space. Indeed, the enterprise of "judging" a medium assumes that execution is more or less trivial.

This execution is why Robert Kozma (2000) described educational technologists' task as *making* links between media and learning, rather than *discovering* them. We don't just discover media in the wild; media are designed, developed, executed, and implemented within particular contexts. There is no "one" television, but there are *Sesame Street*, *Super Why*, and *Bill Nye the Science Guy*. And, there's no one way to watch these shows. Cook and Conner (1976) showed that many learning effects of *Sesame Street* came from parents' and peers' encouraging children and friends to watch and participate in media. Some social scientists sought to isolate the effects of watching *Sesame Street* from this context, as if watching alone in a controlled setting was somehow natural. If our goal is make connections between media, learning, and context, then we need to *identify* issues such as encouragement to view and build better mechanisms to support learning. Basic and design research need to reinforce one another so that we understand how mechanisms like in-jokes work and how parents' participation in viewing reinforces good viewing habits.

We cannot study the educational benefits of media until after they are designed, so that our findings are linked to those designs. Similarly, we can never draw summative conclusions about a medium from one example; indeed, we probably can't draw summative conclusions about that medium in any circumstance, given the nearly infinite ways that ideas can be expressed. Thankfully, most teachers understand that some media work with some kids some of the time but, other times, might be less effective.[8]

These same design techniques flow seamlessly across *non*game websites such as Facebook and eBay. Designers who can employ these features toward learning software have a huge, untapped market waiting for them. Those designers who act like it's still 1996 will struggle.

DESIGNING GAMES FOR LEARNING

The remainder of this chapter shares experiences from the Games-to-Teach project, in particular the games, genres, and research on learning from game play. However, the biggest successes are actually the dozens of people who, like myself, are out leading research groups, working in games companies, and exploring these ideas

---

8. Janet Kretschmer, from the McGuffey School, once said that the "way" her school worked was to not have one way. The trick was getting different teachers, methods, materials, and programs to work in concert toward meeting kids' needs. Some kids at certain times need certain methods (including certain teacher personalities), and other kids at other times need other ones. Teachers (as professionals) understand the dynamics of implementing different instructional techniques and do so creatively as the situation requires. Games like *Model UN* played a role in the McGuffey curriculum, but McGuffey would never propose that students play games all the time.

in different ways. Altogether, we created 17 game prototypes (ideas demonstrated via a variety of media that are available on the archived Games-to-Teach website), and four were developed into playable, testable games.[9] The two that we produced internally (*Environmental Detectives* and *Supercharged!*) are described in this chapter. Here's what we learned.

Art Direction

Visual artists approach game design differently from the way most educational researchers do, and it is critical to have visual artists involved early in the design process. Whereas I might think about themes, concepts, and relationships, visual designers might think about settings, characters, colors, and worlds. Coming up with "fantasy" ideas (such as those leafy shoulders on my druid) is second nature to most visual artists. Educational researchers pay virtually *no* attention to aesthetics. Our educational system seems to weed out skilled visual communicators through year after year of text-heavy assignments. In many educational games, graphics, inasmuch as they exist, are merely functional. *Good* graphics are derided as "eye candy," suggesting that a pleasurable visual experience detracts from learning.

Cuckoo Time! is a great example of how good games require creative visual thinking. Our team was discussing games about elementary physics that included gears, pulleys, levers, and pendulums. David Moisl, an animator, took that idea and designed an entire world of fat little gnomes set inside a cuckoo clock (see Figure 5.1). Their iconography became power-ups so that Birkenstocks boot other gnomes, while accordions move the cuckoo bird. Knockwurst added mass, while lederhosen reduced mass. By using visual humor, David took an *academic* idea and made it a *game*.

Lessons from *Biohazard* (a game developed by partners at Carnegie Mellon's Entertainment Technology Program; see Figure 5.2) reinforced the same thing. *Biohazard* was designed to teach AP-level biology through investigating diseases, an idea that has spread into subsequent games, some of which I describe in Chapter 9. We wanted the student who was playing the role of the doctor to feel emotionally compelled to help people. Players become specialized forensic scientists by investigating anthrax scares, flu viruses, and so on, drawing on the appeal of shows like *CSI*. Carnegie Mellon University's team adapted our design to use *Biohazard* with emergency responders who were preparing for terrorist attacks.[10]

---

9. When it goes down, put http://educationarcade.org/gtt/index.html into the wayback machine at archive.org.

10. Pursuing homeland security grants was common after September 11, 2001. The

Figure 5.1
Cuckoo Time!

I studied firefighters, high schoolers, and children as young as age 3 playing Carnegie Mellon's version of *Biohazard*. The most critical part of the game was its artwork. The moment players put on those suits, no matter who they were in real life—firefighters, paramedics, college students, 3-year-olds—they became heroic saviors. The appeal of this fantasy is nearly universal; everyone enjoys braving danger to help people.

The firefighters loved using *Biohazard* as a training tool. Rural firefighters wanted to play authentic scenarios, such as an urban anthrax outbreak or rural water contamination, and compare their performance with that of urban units. "Let's see how the New York Fire Department deals with a Brown County brush fire!" one challenged. They believed that if an online training game that included tournaments, high scores, and bonus levels for advanced techniques was in breakrooms, it would be so popular they'd have to tear it away.

Skeptics often argue that educational games are inherently not fun, but I think the opposite is true. If done well, there are *few* fantasies better than having a positive impact on the world. If a player can put down the game and know that he or she is better at something useful, all the better. This allure of self-improvement is part of the success of games such as *Brain Age*. The trick is that educational game designers have to use art, aesthetics, and design in the same ways that entertainment designers do.

Bush administration gutted educational technology research programs such as the Fund for the Improvement of Postsecondary Education to give out earmarks for programs such as the Strom Thurmond Wellness and Fitness Center at the University of South Carolina. In fact, we spend much more on educational technology in the military than we do on such technology in all public K–16 schools combined. See National Academy of Sciences (2003).

Figure 5.2.
Biohazard

From Content to Experience

Once the design is set and artists are involved, designers focus the game *experience* so that it requires thinking with content rather than just memorization. How do you design this sort of game play? We developed *user scenarios*—game play descriptions written from the player's perspective. Here's an excerpt from *Hephaestus*, a game prototyped in Mathematica (a high-end mathematical visualization software—seriously).

> Ana's father purchased *Hephaestus* to encourage her interest in engineering. Ana gives Strider, her robot, a three-speed gearbox, allowing her to switch between 1:1, 1:4, and 1:10 gear ratios so that she can have fast movement or raw power. Strider will need to traverse diverse locations from marshes to mountains, so she purchases an engine with power to spare. Her friend's robot has a recharging station.
>
> In an after-school robotics club, Ana plans to build a "real" version of Strider, using *Hephaestus* as a design tool.

This design exercise requires entering the player's head, speculating what he or she might be thinking, and then using that knowledge to enable academically valuable interactions. *Hephaestus* featured a *design-then-play* rhythm. This combines visceral game play (scouting the terrain, mining resources) with reflection through design. It also explored how to connect home and school and how to relate educational gaming with hobbyist pursuits such as robotics.

Connecting to Learning Theory

We tried to engineer "memorable moments," a phrase that describes how players' intentions, game systems, and representations on screen converge to produce transcendent emotions.[11] Can we trigger game play that challenges our current models of the world and creates flashes of insight? As we fleshed out the design, we began scouring the research literature for design ideas. Hopefully, that sentence caused pause. How could educational research be useful in such a nuts-and-bolts endeavor? When viewed from the prism of a game designer looking for puzzles and problems, research is actually full of potential.[12] We asked several questions: (1) What are the *purposes* for learning that content? (2) What is known about *how* people learn in that domain? and (3) What *strategies* have worked in the past?

To explain, consider *Cuckoo Time!* We had a relatively creative idea (learn Newtonian physics by jumping around the inside of a cuckoo clock). David's sketches proved to us that it could be a game and that it could be fun (or better, or interesting) to use power-ups to change velocity, acceleration, mass, or gravity. But how would players *learn*?

The research literature shows that most people have really bad understandings of classical mechanics. For example, what's the effect of changing the mass of the bob of a pendulum on its period? How do mass, length, or gravity affect angular acceleration? Knowledge areas in which people have naive misconceptions make *great* starting puzzles. For example, people often think that the heavier a pendulum bob, the shorter its period. You could imagine someone swinging on a pendulum, hoping to fly up to a new platform. They miss. So they use a power-up to reduce their mass and swing higher. It doesn't work.

Integrating content and game play can produce *puzzlement*, as constructivists like John Savery and Tom Duffy (1995) would call it. The idea of puzzlement is that we're naturally motivated to learn when the world does not conform to our expectations. As this puzzled player tries different power-ups, he or she might check the "hint" section, which offers a textbook-style physics explanation. This puzzlement would drive the intellectual life of the game (beer 'n' brats drove the fun). Because

---

11. I won't bore you with more of my memorable moments, which range from epic space races in *Civ* to my first confrontation with marines in *Half Life*. Drew Davidson's ongoing Well Played book series does a good job of relating such experiences and tying them to theory.

12. Entertainment game designers do this, too. Tower of Hanoi, the classic mathematical puzzle used in cognitive science research, has been used in many games, most famously *Star Wars: Knights of the Old Republic*.

Cuckoo Time! is *collaborative*, players could also teach one another or debate ideas while playing, just as *WoW* players can argue about strategies.

Across all 10 prototypes, we proposed how intrinsically interesting aspects of science could be turned into games. The upshot of this work was a general process for finding the game in the content (Rieber's notion of endogenous games), published by the Games-to-Teach team (2003). Before the project, people mostly laughed at the suggestion, but now we had a process for thinking through design and development. Next we needed to build a game and try it out.

BUILDING AN EDUCATIONAL GAME FROM SCRATCH

"Have you seen the real-time physics in *Halo*? They're incredible!" said Dr. John Belcher, a winner of NASA's Exceptional Scientific Achievement Medal. Belcher had played *Halo* with his grandson and was now lecturing me on its real-time physics engine. For years, Belcher had been building electrostatics visualizations to help explain ideas to funders and to physics students. The problem was that these visualizations weren't *interactive*. You watched them, but you couldn't *test* your understanding. Belcher thought that video games were the next logical step. It was insanely cool to hear this from someone who led experiments on the Voyager spaceship.

Finding the Game in the Academic Domains

Over the next few months, John explained to us the big ideas students needed to learn, what they struggled with, and what he thought were good game ideas. Our first idea involved manipulating electrostatic forces in a simulated world game like *Deus Ex*. Players could send electricity through wires to create magnetic fields, or somehow change the Earth's magnetic field. I knew nothing about electromagnetism, so John invited me to audit his technology-enhanced physics course. I was blown away. John used simulations, probe wear, clickers, circuit boards, and lectures in one integrated course. And he did it with an *entire class* of *144* students.

However, we struggled to design a simulated world electrostatics game. Simulated world games rely on what Doug Church (2005) calls *problems*, not puzzles. *Problems* are challenges facing the player that can be solved any number of ways. Consider *Thief* (a game he designed), in which the player must break into a house. He can march in the front door and knock out a guard, he can distract the guard with a noise and then sneak in behind him, or he can break in through a window and dodge the guards altogether. There are *many* ways to succeed, and the "fun" is thinking creatively to solve the problems. The educational content in such games comes from learning the underlying properties of the system. *Thief* players learn the layout of the house and the rules governing how guards react; we wanted players to learn the rules of electromagnetism. This basic model is at the core of how I think about educational games, but our game just wasn't gelling.

Our best game ideas all involved *puzzles*. *Puzzles* have single solutions. Adventure games are full of them. The classic format is "find the key that unlocks a door." To solve an electromagnetic puzzle, players might set an electric wire next to a compass in order to alter the magnetic field immediately surrounding it and unlock a new level. Sadly, we couldn't identify "problems" that could be solved a variety of ways. Puzzle games are certainly OK. Puzzles are especially good at serving as *choke points* to test understandings. But for a physics game—a content domain that is capable of being simulated—to be built entirely around puzzles and not simulated problems seemed ironic (and not in a good way). Adding to our distaste for this approach was our play-testing of *Physicus*, an adventure game featuring physics puzzles with minimal simulation. *Physicus* made sense as a game, but playing *Physicus* confirmed our fears that a physics game *not* based on simulation felt flat.

We were finally rescued by a visit from Alex Rigopoulos and Eran Egozy, two Harmonix game developers (fittingly suggested to us by Doug Church). As Alex and Eran riffed back and forth with one of our team members, Walter Holland, they proposed that the way to do an electrostatics simulated world game was to build an abstract world around Maxwell's four equations. Maxwell's equations can be used to determine electric force, and force can be described through movement. This could translate readily into game mechanics. They argued for keeping it simple, so that anyone playing the game developed an intuition of these ideas, which are the foundation of electrodynamic physics.

Thus *Supercharged!* was born. *Supercharged!* was a 3-D simulation game designed to help introductory physics students develop intuitive understandings of electrostatics. (See Figure 5.3.)

Players control a spaceship that places charged particles. They spin and fly about the world, bouncing off walls and soaring through abstract spaces. It is possible to use the game as a *predictive simulation* by taking note of your position and conducting measurements to mathematically infer Coulomb's law or Maxwell's equations, but we didn't think any normal person would do so. We did think, however, that students might develop a better grasp of these underlying concepts, working back and forth between homework problems, lecture notes, and the game to think through the content. To encourage this sort of thinking, levels were designed to correspond with classic textbook problems and thought experiments.

We knocked out a narrative: After a physics experiment goes awry, the player is sucked into an abstract world of electrostatic forces. The art direction followed the bright, abstract style used in *Rez* and *FreQuency*, which was in vogue as a reaction against many developers' obsession with photorealism. This approach enabled us to make a fully 3-D game while avoiding costly character modeling and animation, which we didn't have the resources to do well.

We ran the idea by John Belcher, who signed off. Belcher confirmed that most students lack an intuitive grasp of Maxwell's equations. I delved into the research literature and found plenty of confirming evidence. Andrea DiSessa's (2000) and Kenneth Forbus's (1996) work showed that intuitive, qualitative understanding in physics is desirable *before* learning physics equations.

I started designing levels to walk the player through a series of classic physics problems after closely studying John Belcher's teaching in his classroom. John frequently used thought experiments such as, "Imagine that you are a charged particle flying through a magnetic field that is perpendicular to your velocity. What direction would you go?" There were even more basic ideas that we could translate for younger audiences, such as Coulomb's law, or the inverse square law, which states that some physical quantity or strength is inversely proportional to the square of the distance from the source of that physical quantity. Through games, players could inhabit these fundamental laws and test them interactively.

Design Research: Developing Supercharged!

We hired a team of four undergraduate programmers, managed by Philip Tan (now an executive director for the Singapore-MIT GAMBIT Game Lab) to make *Supercharged!* Immediately, we had questions: How does the world look when viewed from the perspective of a charged particle? Should players be able to move their ship however they wish, or should they be forced to move according to electromagnetic forces, like a ping-pong ball getting bounced back and forth? We argued about this for a few days, and finally one of the undergraduate students, Rob Figueroa, coded a demo in Direct X over the weekend. The demo revealed that it was kind of viscerally enjoyable, but discombobulating, to be spun around by these forces. Having no direct control was frustrating, and placing charged particles in real time while flying was not going to happen—at least not in 3-D. Prototyping saved us countless hours of arguing, and to this day I'm a fan of prototyping early and often rather than writing design documents (for a thorough case study, see Jenkins, Squire, & Tan, 2003).

Figure 5.3.
Supercharged!

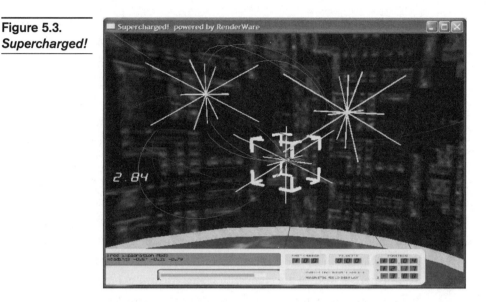

This still didn't resolve the artwork concerns. Because 3-D artists were in short supply at MIT, we hired an award-winning artist, Patricia Beckmann of Bunsella Films, to create art assets and manage a team of students. We soon learned that when you want game-ready art that works in-engine, it's best to have a professional. Novice artists are great for conceptual art, but for final art, find a "pro" or be ready for students to learn on the job.

One mistake we made (lo and behold) was to get too far in game play design without active art direction. Ideas coming from the art team were inevitably bumped down the priority list because programmers thought the "fuzzy little creatures" or "eye candy" were silly. Yet game art must *communicate* concepts such as providing feedback on players' actions or guiding players in ways that other media don't. This was an incredibly useful insight for me as a games theorist. I appreciated the *functional* role of art in games, but I didn't understand just how critical art was for communicating concepts to the player. For example, our initial walls were translucent, which meant novice users had no idea what they were. As one asked, "What is that thing? A warp shield?" Through play testing, we learned that walls must communicate their "wallness" as well as the player's position and velocity. Similarly, the goals in the game needed to call out to the player, "Hey! I'm where you want to go," so that the player intuitively understood the point of the game without having to think about it. In games, as in life, we use objects in the environment to understand where we are, how fast we're going, and so on, and some objects are better at this than others. Interestingly, this finding comes from Gibson's (1979) work on visual perception, which is foundational to situated learning theory.

Everything in a game has to show players how to play. A well-designed game builds loads of information into the environment (e.g., high-up ledges suggest jumping). Good art makes important clues "pop" off the screen. Good games use more-subtle techniques, such as color saturation to communicate the boundaries of walls or enemies. Otherwise, the game becomes about navigation rather than more-interesting concepts. When it works in harmony, the art is pleasing while underscoring what the gamer needs to be doing. It's truly an art form.

More broadly, designers must communicate the goal of the experience itself. Our first user tests included various types of levels (flying levels, 2-D mazes, and rail-tunnel levels), but players didn't understand anything *except* the maze levels. Once you give someone a maze, he or she immediately has a frame for the activity. The person knows the goal; anticipates constraints (such as time pressure or an enemy); and—hopefully—develops a desire to get out.

Helping players develop goals may be elementary for veteran game designers, but this was new to me. Given how incredibly *simple* this example is, imagine what we could learn by studying larger projects. For example, I recall a conversation about *Metroid* with Nathan McKenzie (a game designer who used to work at Raven and Rainbow Studios). I was impressed by how the levels alternated closed and open spaces, providing a rhythmic feel. Nathan agreed, and he pointed out that this alternating structure enabled the levels to load while playing. I had never bothered to think about how such loading concerns manifest themselves in design, but as a practicing developer he couldn't miss it. This anecdote isn't to suggest that all game theorists need to become designers (although it might be useful to do so) but, rather, that substantive conversation across areas of expertise can generate new insights. If only more game developers allowed researchers to study their practice For notable exceptions, see Malaby's, 2009, study of Linden Lab and Daer's, 2010, study of GameLab).

Implementing Games-Based Research in Classes

By the spring, the game was ready to test in classrooms. This was a fast development cycle (from concept to classroom in under 1 year), but we wanted to test in early stages. Our plan to work with John Belcher's Technology Enabled Active Learning (TEAL) course met some snags. The course was expanding so that in the following term, *all* sections of Introduction to Electricity and Magnetism (about 1,000 students) would learn through TEAL's innovative, hands-on approach. The conversion wasn't going well. Many students feared that they were receiving "easier" assignments than previous courses. (Only at MIT could students be personally affronted by the lack of difficulty in problem sets). In reality the problem sets were the same. Students also feared that they missed the "real" information from traditional classes, a common fear in any non-survey-style course. By March 2003, a group of students threatened to walk out of class (LeBon, 2003).

Yet when they studied learning through TEAL, Dori and Belcher (2005) found that students *did* in fact show higher learning gains via TEAL than through traditional methods—almost twice as much. It's hard to communicate how impressive this was; the majority of such studies rarely finds *any* statistically significant differences. Belcher and colleagues have since smoothed over the transitional difficulties, and the course is integrated into MIT life. This goes to show you how things change if you have patience, and how different a story looks depending on when you tell it. The story of TEAL in spring of 2003 looked like a failure. Now it's a crown jewel in MIT's undergraduate curriculum.

Regardless, John didn't want to make things even more difficult by introducing a video game. He allowed us to recruit 20 students who would use the game and do interviews with us about the experience. If the project continued, he would use the game at the beginning of the course to build students' conceptual understandings and then refer back to it throughout the term.

Working in Schools

We set out looking for another site to test *Supercharged!* We did demonstration projects in a few secondary schools, including a technology charter school. Massachusetts (like many states) was moving toward a physics-first curriculum, where physics would be the first science course in the high school curriculum. Teachers, of course, had no idea how to teach physics to 9th graders. *Supercharged!*, which built on Forbus's idea of qualitative physics understandings, seemed like a good place to start. We hoped to show how games for higher education *could* migrate across markets, such as K–12 schools or homes. Mike Barnett, a colleague at Boston College, had a master's in physics and was willing to teach the unit to middle school students. We taught the 2-week unit on electricity and magnetism to five classes. Three classes played the game in the experimental condition and two received traditional lectures and assignments in the control condition. We wanted to see what conceptual understandings emerged and how learning in a game-based class compared to learning in a traditional one. Considering everything, the experiment was a success; going from design to a classroom implementation in under a year is no small feat. Our findings (reported in Barnett, Squire, Higgenbotham, & Grant, 2004) follow.

The Floor Versus the Ceiling

Educators have debated whether educational games can succeed because "they can't compete with *Grand Theft Auto*." Commonly called the "floor or ceiling" debate, the question it poses is, do commercial video games create such a high *ceiling* that educational games can never succeed? Or, is the *floor* of standard school curriculum so low that halfway decent games will be welcomed?

Supercharged!, when brought into school, proved very engaging. Kids compared it to "what they did at school" rather than "the games they played at home." We saw no evidence of kids rejecting *Supercharged!* because it wasn't *Grand Theft Auto*. There was not one complaint about the graphics or lack of violent content. We presented *Supercharged!* as a game, and students played it.

These kids *were* critical of bad design. Poorly arranged levels that didn't match the ship's controls (e.g., levels that were too big or too small) were criticized. Likewise, when the pacing was off—when new levels did not introduce new challenges or challenges graduated too quickly, students tuned out. Finally, sometimes the collision detection clipped or players got stuck near a wall, which was deadly for engagement. I couldn't help but wonder how often we say, "They didn't like my game because it's not *Grand Theft Auto*," when in reality they didn't like the game because of its lack of polish.

These experiences solidified my take on the "floor or ceiling" debate: Kids don't expect educational games to be *Grand Theft Auto*, but they *do* expect good design. This means clear, compelling objectives; intuitive controls; clean interfaces; aesthetically pleasing worlds; and difficulty curves that ramp well—the same kinds of things that separate Sid Meier's *Pirates!* from *Sea Dogs*. As kids grow up awash in software, their expectations evolve. Twenty years ago, when I was a kid, the computer was so interesting it really didn't matter what we did with it. We were happy just to be on the computer. Now, almost every kid has access to an iPod touch, gaming console, and personal computer. They are sophisticated consumers who expect good design.

Accommodating Diverse Play Styles

We saw a wide range of play styles, even in a "targeted" game as straightforward as *Supercharged!* Some kids burned through levels trying to "win" as quickly as possible. One kid even spiked the controller afterward, declaring, "Ha! I beat your game!" I gravitate toward games that are "unbeatable," so this struck me as odd behavior, even though it's quite common. Other players, many of whom were girls, replayed levels and sought more elegant solutions. I also replay levels, obsessing about how to do it "right" at the expense of ever finishing.

The "playing to win" kids beat our original levels the first day. I suggested they replay, but I might as well have suggested that they go read *War and Peace*. They had won, and to them that was the point. I told them I'd bring in more levels the next day, that they had simply beat the first chapter. This type of highly competitive student never enjoyed *Supercharged!* as much as the others. The teacher was careful to remind us that these same kids generally paid "no attention" during normal school activities. For her, the game was a godsend.

In many respects, we hadn't honored the genre. Our levels didn't sufficiently build players' understandings, teach them new abilities, extend their skills in new directions, and then let them be creative in their problem solving. In fairness, many *entertainment* games make this mistake. *Full Spectrum Warrior* (a great game otherwise) teaches the player all their skills in the first hour and then spends the next 7 hours simply applying these skills in new contexts. Reviews said that it "got boring." More precisely, good games don't throw people in over their heads with an hour-long tutorial and then say, "Go practice." They build skills over time.

Observing the "control" curriculum in this context was enlightening. Mike created an excellent curriculum that mixed hands-on demonstrations (such as using balloons to create static electricity) with videos, experiments, and the occasional lecture. As good as it was, you could see that for many kids the big question was, "Why do I care?" Few students participated in discussions. When asked why, one responded, "We're not used to talking in school. You're supposed to just take notes." Memories from junior high school flooded back. Sure, it was important not to look dumb, but you also didn't want to look *smart*, lest you get beaten up, teased, or picked on. The social game in junior high is how to attract as little attention as possible.

The results were positive. Kids in both the control and experimental conditions did about 20% better on the post-tests than on the pre-tests. Surprisingly, the only statistically significant effect we found between the control and experimental groups was for the girls. Girls did about the same in the control pre- and post-tests but did about 10–20% better in the experimental condition than the control. We weren't totally sure why, but we had some theories. First, the girls played reflectively, as we'd hoped. They were our model user. They didn't play to win, but rather to understand. Second, many girls shied away from the collaborative activities in the control condition. Maybe they didn't want to "look too smart" in science, something that's an issue for some girls at this age (although the girls did better than the boys across conditions). Video games enabled girls to dig in and play at their own pace, and many took pride in their work.

Being labeled as a "gamer" wasn't an issue for *any* girl we studied. The girls all reported playing *The Sims*, and most played console games. Many girls also reported liking fighting games. I found it *more* interesting that our data suggested that "participating in class discussions to show what you know about science" was *not* a game many girls liked.

Figure 5.4, taken from the pre- and post-tests, illustrates some of the learning gains. On the left (from the pre-test), the student is asked to draw the field lines around a single positive charge, and he draws a baseball bat and ball. (It is springtime in Boston, after all.) On the right (from the post-test), he is asked to draw the field lines between charges and does a pretty good job. It's not a perfect response, but it's not bad. This was typical for many students. Dramatic differences between groups emerged in the interviews—even among those who got the answers "right" in the control. The following excerpt comes from a student in the control group who scored well on the post-tests.

Interviewer: What do you think the electric field looks like around a positive charge?
Alex: It has lines going outward from it like this [drawing lines with arrows
    pointing outward].
Interviewer: Why?
Alex: I don't know. The teacher said so and showed us a picture and that was what
    it looked like.

Compare this response to the student from the experimental condition.

The electric field goes from the positive charge to the negative charge like this [drawing a curved live from a positive charge to a negative charge]. This is what it looked like in the game, and it was hard to move away or toward it because the two charges are close together, so they sort of cancel each other out.

The control response recapitulates familiar findings across the learning sciences. Just because students copy back the correct answer on a test doesn't mean that they *understand* the concept (see Bransford, Brown, & Cocking, 1999).

Second, it's difficult to understand *why concepts are important*. In physics, we don't want students simply to draw field lines correctly; we want them to understand that these representations show force. Some students in the experimental condition "got" this in a visceral way. They understood that the field lines showed force because they were tools in the game. *Supercharged!* was particularly good at tying academic ideas to *action*. It helped students understand *movement* via cause and effect.

We struggled to make *Supercharged!* relevant to average 8th graders. We tried—through cut scenes, lectures, and presentations—to connect our representations of

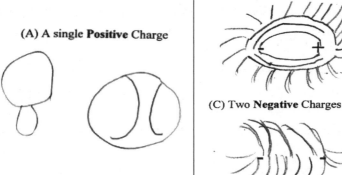

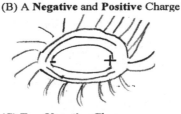

(A) A single **Positive** Charge

(B) A **Negative** and **Positive** Charge

(C) Two **Negative** Charges

**Figure 5.4.
Pre- and Post-
Test Images of
Learning Through
*Supercharged!***

electrostatic forces to the real world, but it was tough. The abstract world of *Supercharged!* (even when we included wires and magnets) was a huge leap from the world around them. These kids needed more connections to see science as important to their lives. They needed to see themselves as scientists, actively solving problems. For these kids (think of the girls who may not want to speak up in class), science wasn't something you cared about; it was something you did for a passing grade to stay out of trouble. Maybe a game in which they used knowledge to act in the world would be more successful. Our attention turned toward *Environmental Detectives*, another Games-to-Teach game.

INVENTING NEW GENRES: *ENVIRONMENTAL DETECTIVES*

Environmental Detectives began by our team scouring chemistry textbooks and arriving at a simple, but ultimately doomed, concept.

"I've got it! A lot of chemistry is about how chemical processes can hurt you! What if we simulated a chemical spill right here on campus?" In a post–September 11 atmosphere, these scenarios were easy to imagine. A series of gruesome game scenarios could tie together environmental science and chemistry standards and be used across a variety of areas. This had promise.

Wally begged us to reconsider.

"Please! Let's not have a game in which we faithfully re-create the MIT campus in glorious 3-D." With the infinite possibilities for what artists *could* do in virtual worlds (travel to other planets, nonrepresentational art), surely we could do better than building 3-D classrooms.

Eric Klopfer suggested a way out. Why not build the games on handhelds and run the simulation in the background? Eric, who is director of the MIT Teacher

Education Program, joined the Games-to-Teach team during our first year. Eric is a gifted educational technologist who understands the affordances of technology and builds systems that leverage them smartly. Eric also might be the kindest, most generous collaborator I've known.

Immediately, the room reverberated with ideas. We wanted to make a game using the Global Positioning System (GPS). Soon, GPS devices would be available for pocket PCs. If we could write software that tied the device to the player's GPS location, we could model how a toxin moved across campus in real time and enable players to interact with characters, pass diseases, and investigate events based on where they were standing (Klopfer, 2008).

So, once again it was back to the research literature. At MIT, we found Dr. Heidi Nepf, a hydrologist who does problem- and case-based learning. Nepf argued that trichloroethylene (TCE), a common degreasing agent, was the perfect chemical for the game. TCE is found everywhere and is cancerous. A number of high-profile TCE spills are causing the Environmental Protection Agency (EPA) to re-evaluate TCE safety levels. It would make a great foil, in that we could build a story around the scare of a terrorist attack, but it would actually be an accident with a common toxin.

Building an Engine for a Game Genre that Doesn't Exist

We began coding *Environmental Detectives*, but because we had no idea how it would work, we went through several cycles of building prototypes, repeatedly throwing them away and starting over (see Klopfer & Squire, 2007). Although it was technically *feasible*, no one was doing GPS positioning outside of custom dedicated hardware devices. Eric led the team and ran the code base. A trusty undergraduate, Gunnar Harboe, did the brunt of the work. If *Supercharged!* was an exercise in rapid development using known tools, *Environmental Detectives* was the exact opposite. Working in C# and .NET (new tools at the time), we encountered an insane number of bugs and setbacks.

I remember looking out the window and seeing Gunnar standing on the roof with his laptop, a personal digital assistant (PDA), and some sort of blanket. An extension cord ran through the window to charge his tools. I asked if he was camping. No, he wasn't camping. It took 4 to 8 hours to get a GPS fix. While running a GPS device, Pocket PCs had 3 hours of battery life. He plugged the GPS into the laptop, but it drained that as well. The alarm clock reminded him to look for a GPS signal every few hours, while he coded from the roof.

It was thrilling to play with these technologies and worry about the next *decade* of education, rather than next Monday. It was a stark contrast to the current fixation upon "use-inspired research." Although politically expedient, use-inspired research was strategically designed to ensure that we don't disrupt the system and miss key technologies (such as smartphones; see Chapter 10).[13] A point of educational technology research should be to anticipate and study these developments as they unfold.

As I looked out the window and saw Gunnar with his setup, I feared that we were completely crazy. None of this technology was tested. If we couldn't even get a device to find its location in under 2 hours, it would be *10 years* before we got into schools. My fears were misplaced; sure enough, these learning technologies went from cutting edge to commonplace in about 5 years. Today, our group works in nearly 40 classrooms with thousands of kids, albeit in a research context. By the time this book comes out, GPS may be standard on just about every cellphone. Cellphones might not be commonplace in *schools*, but they are commonplace in people's *lives*, and if students start bringing them to schools on their own, schools may face pressure to respond.

Our educational goal was to communicate the idea of science as a social enterprise. Students enter college with an idealized vision of science as the pursuit of perfect answers free from context. In reality, scientific investigation is imperfect. Investigators *always* make trade offs between the quality of data and the time and resources it takes to obtain these data. For example, when an investigator learns about a rash of illnesses, he or she considers, do we immediately notify local law authorities? If so, will it cause unnecessary panic? Or will people die if we take 6 months to order evacuations?

Science Mystery Games

Environmental Detectives' core mechanic was deciding between desktop research and fieldwork. Investigators told us that, in general, "an ounce of desktop research is worth a pound of fieldwork." They often rule out causes simply by researching what chemicals are used in the area. Some investigations require gathering little "hard" data at all. Our science education partners hoped that if students conducted an investigation, they might be prepared to understand these ideas in class.

---

13. Maybe it's my Montessori background, but it seems odd to direct future innovations by what is happening now in schools, given that they are just one social configuration. Seymour Papert called this the horse and buggy problem; you can't design a car by studying the horse and buggy. Moving to the automobile from the horse and buggy was revolutionary and required new values and new infrastructure (roads, service stations, etc.).

Consider the following fictitious scenario in *Environmental Detectives* (see Figure 5.5). On the MIT campus, a TCE spill was uncovered during routine testing during construction. MIT's president is anxious. What does the spill mean for residents' health? The water supply? The environment? When the public learns that MIT dumped tons of toxins into the watershed, they will demand answers. Is their drinking water safe? Is it safe to continue eating Atlantic fish (such as cod)? Who is to blame? Can we keep this from happening again?

This is the scenario that we posed to students. To give away the mystery (again, this is fiction), TCE was spilled in an engineering machine shop but wasn't reported. TCE is a carcinogen and if inhaled or ingested, is damaging to the liver and kidneys. The TCE plume flowed through the groundwater and into the Charles River. Then, it flowed into Boston Harbor and into the Atlantic. However, because no one drinks the groundwater or swims in the Charles, there were no anticipated human health effects. Still, having a toxic chemical flow off the campus is bad for PR, if not against EPA regulations (depending on the concentration as it leaves MIT property).

The game started with a dramatic, secret video transmitted from MIT president Chuck Vest, shot *X-Files* style. Teams had 60 minutes to brief the president, who was about to face reporters. He demanded that players brief him on the health consequences, the EPA limits for TCE, how TCE moves through groundwater, and remediation strategies. Players' proposals needed to include an analysis of the cause, the anticipated severity, and a solution.

At every key point, players must decide what information is good enough to meet the investigation's goals. Whereas pinpointing the exact source of the pollution

Figure 5.5.
Environmental Detectives
Data Analysis

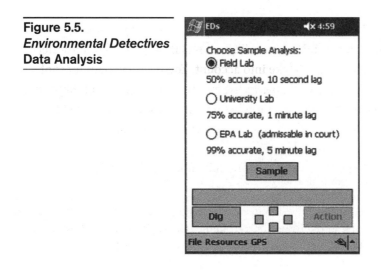

could take a few hours, if one discerned the general size, location, and age of the plume, one could use the process of elimination to discern the location in about an hour. The first version enabled players to place up to three wells at a time to sample the groundwater, and they could talk with characters to get information about TCE, its health effects, and so on. We included a branching narrative path in which the player *could* discover the culprit. To unlock this chain of events, the player had to find the general location of the spill, confront a virtual character, and then chase the culprit across campus.

Results

That fall, we ran *Environmental Detectives* with 25 first-year environmental science students. We hoped it would dazzle them, cementing forever their desire to become environmental engineers, but it wasn't quite *that* successful. It did, however, teach us about using this platform for education. The following excerpt details one related conversation (edited for readability). Jenny begins by interpreting a read-out.

Jenny: The results of the lab said "30," so it [the concentration of TCE] might be 30 parts per cubic feet.
Steve: That is not as bad as the military base in Cape Cod. So just remember that it *can* be nasty or something.

Steve had read about TCE at Cape Cod, and he used that information to puzzle through this problem. Next, Steve has a breakthrough. He realizes that they must use their data to construct a model of where the spill occurred. As he reads the text, he synthesizes its implications for their team.

Steve: We need to build a model of how TCE moves through the groundwater. [There are] lots of things to take into account. You have a certain mass of stuff that's been spilled, and it's covering a larger and larger region every day because of spread. As a rule of thumb you might assume that it spreads at a rate of 150 feet per year.

Bill started building the model, and thought aloud for his group.

Bill: 150 feet per year. OK. So, decaying at about half of its concentration. So if you start with 100 parts per billion, that's . . . 50 parts per billion at 150 feet per year. The 30 and 70 could be possible.

This exchange was typical as groups modeled the spill. They were initially skeptical of desktop research, just as the teacher predicted. Many students—the males in particular—thought, drill first, ask questions second. However, the game forced them to build crude models of the spill on the fly. This kind of model-based reasoning is quite sophisticated and hard to engender. We didn't overtly teach them this model-based reasoning, but they "constructed" it to play the game. In playing the game, it made sense to build models. Games excel at creating teachable moments for teachers to explain investigative and model-building skills. Students frequently used personal knowledge about the location to solve the problems, as in this exchange:

Bill: We know that it's in the Charles, which is already disgusting. It's possible that TCE is such a ridiculously small effect compared to the big mess of the Charles—and I have friends by the way who study the Charles River and are not impressed. We also know that the water isn't used for drinking.

Jenny: We used to go canoeing on the Charles River. And we always had to watch out. People fell out of their canoe; their eyes were stinging and stuff.

Students spontaneously connected background knowledge to their game experiences, which was exciting. Bill's knowledge of the Charles became a tool for anticipating academic concerns such as *concentration*.

Players were forced to ask what they knew, what they needed to know, and then predict the quality of information they would get from data. Almost every group "invented" triangulation as a sampling strategy to maximize the information gained from their samples. Students even built back-of-the-envelope models in the field. Everyone naturally started asking about the ethical and legal consequences of the spill. These pilots encouraged us that this sort of environmental mysteries scenario had potential for connecting game play and scientific thinking, and this led us to develop future projects such as *Saving Lake Wingra*, described in Chapter 9.

THEORY AND PRACTICE

This chapter opened by asking how we might design games for learning that meshed the content and the game play so as to reflect contemporary learning theory as well as best practices in game design.

- After building and researching our prototypes, we generated existence proof for meshing compelling game play with meaningful academic content and ways of thinking. *Supercharged!* showed that even an imperfect game can be compelling for classroom use. We became even more convinced of the importance of honoring good game design techniques and processes. Our design process uncovered three key themes for educational game design: (1) respecting the importance of art design, (2) focusing on experience rather than content, and (3) making explicit connections to existing learning theory.

- Genres, or family resemblances among media that use similar techniques to achieve similar goals, are a good way to think about next-generation games. Some games will build on existing genres (just as *Supercharged!* built on puzzle games), but we also need to create new genres of experience (e.g., *Environmental Detectives*).

Table 5.1 highlights five genres of educational games, which are clusters of games that share some family resemblances. One might imagine different organizational schemes, but this framework, which mirrors genres in entertainment, ties them to key educational issues. For example: How long is the game meant to be played, both in and out of the classroom? How open is the game and its meanings, and is it flexible for supporting many learning goals (see *Civilization*, next chapter) or is it relatively fixed, as in *Supercharged!*, and designed to teach specific objectives?

A key question for educators is, "In what ways can players be creative?" Games like *Supercharged!* afford fairly constrained opportunities for creativity, most of which are centered around how players complete levels. Action games add to this the capacity to solve problems in meaningful and varied ways (see Chapter 7). Role-playing games enable players to *affect* or change the world, and open-ended games allow players to *build* worlds. The collaboration opportunities available in persistent world games (games such as *WoW*, which are online worlds that are open 24/7) are among the most interesting to educators because they enable players to be creative through social engineering.

We are still exploring how to build educational games, put together good design teams, and construct processes, but we learned from Games-to-Teach. At this point, we know that:

- *Teams should integrate learning scientists, game designers, and subject matter experts.* In the best cases, a producer understands aspects of *all three* areas. Educators must appeal to all learners (not just those who enjoy that genre, such as the girls who like *Supercharged!*). Similarly, educators can't be allowed to make decisions at the expense of game design, and game designers can't make decisions where they are entertaining at the expense of learning goals. These game design teams should include, not just programmers, but artists and interface designers as well.

- *Development should be iterative, with frequent prototyping and testing.* This means favoring lots of quick builds and test plays with users rather than excessive storyboarding and preproduction. We recommend building playable "toys" very early in the process so that teachers, students, subject matter experts, and learning scientists can all play with the basic interactions. This is benefical because, first, there are few established models of educational games, so educational game designers are always negotiating multiple unknowns. Second, and most important, educational game designers have to create, not just compelling *game play* experiences, but compelling *educational* experiences. Extensive user testing can help ensure that players are gaining the kinds of insights that educators desire.

Table 5.1. Emerging game genres

Genre	Time (hours)	Timescale	Openness of Goals	Creative Expression	Examples
Microworld	1–4	Days	Low	Style of completion; Level creation	*Supercharged! Surge Immune Attack*
Linear Action	6–20	1–4 weeks	Low	Solution paths; Machinema	*Environmental Detectives Full Spectrum Warrior Dow Day*
Role Playing	12–80	3–12 weeks	Medium	Solution paths; Character progression; World outcome	*Citizen Science River City Saving Lake Wingra WolfQuest*
Sandbox	1–4	2–24 months	High	Solution paths; World state; Modding	*Civilization Sim City Virtual University*
Persistent World	1–4	6+ months	High	Social engineering	*Hephaestus Whyville Quest Atlantis*

LEARNING TO BE A FULL-SPECTRUM WARRIOR

by Kurt Squire and Henry Jenkins

Full Spectrum Warrior, the "Military Operations in Urban Terrain Simulation" (MOUT) developed by USC's Institute for Creative Technologies and Pandemic Studios, is a fascinating test case for educational games. The game's roots are in a military simulation that has been revamped for commercial release, creating a number of interesting paradoxes.

On the one hand, proponents laud *Full Spectrum Warrior*'s realistic graphics and original game play for reinvigorating the atrophying military-strategy genre. Critics argue that the tutorial, which takes about an hour, is too long, and the game grows stale. They complain that there is little room for exploration, and players must (almost) always do as they are told.

Some learning tool! Most players learn through trial and error, experimentation, and information presented just in time and on demand, in levels that build upon one another. With its PowerPoint-ready bullet points that recap each mission, *Full Spectrum Warrior* has the feel of being designed by instructional designers who don't trust the medium. Games "teach" players by building systems in which players can experiment and infer from game play what strategies work. We don't need anyone to tell us that the corners of buildings are the best places to stand in a game; let us run into the street a few times, get our butts shot off, and then realize we need a better tactic. Learning through such experimentation is a powerful experience because we learn why we need to do something instead of just taking it on faith.

Aesthetically, this is why *Full Spectrum Warrior* is interesting: Everything in the game communicates, "You're in the army now." The barking voiceover demands 100% perfection. *Full Spectrum Warrior* invites the player to inhabit this identity of a combat soldier, thinking, acting, and evaluating the world from that perspective. After playing for a few hours and realizing that you are now diligently waiting to press buttons only after you are told, you start thinking, "Hey, I'm a regular soldier."

Playing *Full Spectrum Warrior* provokes us to reflect on what doing a *real* MOUT mission might be like and whether we would submit our will to military discipline. Such a game could function as propaganda if we accepted its demands for our obedience, but it might also encourage us to reflect on what it means to be in the military.

Some may counter that these games are making entertainment of war, something called *militainment*. Yet, in World War II, psychologists recommended that children enact the horrors of war through play in order to bring their fears of death and destruction under their own control. Used wisely, such games can be employed as tools for reflection on the situation confronting our nation. For some, these games may be a call to arms. For others, like me, dying in *Full Spectrum Warrior* is a reminder that war has enormous human costs and I'd rather play soldier from the comforts of an overstuffed couch than on a hot dirty street in the war-torn Middle East.

CHAPTER 6

Games in Classrooms: Replaying History

As we build new games for learning, it makes sense to study what happens when existing commercial video games, full of transgression, competition, complexity, and learning through failure, enter a classroom. Until recently, very few people had observed everyday gaming in *any* context.[1] *SimCity*, which has been played by more people than almost any other educational software, has been the subject of much academic debate, but no academic had actually studied what people learned (or didn't) through *playing* it. This chapter asks:

- What happens when you bring complex games with features such as learning through failure, competition, and opportunities for transgression into the classroom?
- What teaching practices are useful in game-based learning contexts?
- What kinds of learning occur through participation in a game-based curriculum?

This chapter considers these questions via a case study of what happened when I brought *Civilization III* (*Civ3*) to one class of marginalized students in Boston.

TEACHING WORLD HISTORY

Interviewer: Do you like social studies?

Andrea: I never really liked social studies. I don't like learning American history every year. Why don't we do something else? If you're going to have social studies class, make it [about something] besides wars. Like the Holocaust.

---

1. The findings are interesting. Mitchell (1985) gave Nintendos to families and found that, rather than destroying all that is good in the world, the Nintendos had a positive impact. Families played together in the same manner that you would expect with a board games or charades. Many described it as one of the best things they ever did.

Why should I learn about the Holocaust *every year*? It's boring. And they only talk about the Jews when they talk about the Holocaust. That makes me upset too. You know, if I was alive back then, I'd be dead. I was like, "Can we talk about *me* for a second? I'm a Jehovah's Witness, so I would have been dead anyway because of my religion."

And we have to learn about American history from the same textbook. I just now realized that there's a whole bunch of stuff that they don't even write in the textbook. So they should have us do projects on what we think *isn't* written in the textbooks. We should do a huge project on that or something.

I think it would be better if you did a lot of hands-on stuff instead of reading and taking tests, because basically that's all that social studies has been. It's not like science or English where you can be creative. [In social studies,] you read it, you memorize it, and then it's over. If you did projects, like build landscapes or build what you think the world was like back then, it would be more interesting. If it wasn't so boring, I would like it.

Interviewer: So it's not social studies but it's how it's taught in schools?

Andrea: Yeah—how it's taught in school is boring. I think African American history is left out of schools. I think Hispanic history is left out of schools. And I think that for schools that are so diverse in culture, they only teach one side of history, and I think that's wrong. So if you're going to have schools all filled with a bunch of people, why are you going to teach them all about White history and not teach them anything about Black history? Why have a school all about White history? That's why people don't like social studies. Social studies is boring.

Reality and Myth in World History Education

Andrea's observations jive perfectly with the research literature. U.S. social studies education is dominated by U.S. history. Little attention is given to *anything* else, even though the standards cover a *broad* range of topics (such as how to tie economics to geography).[2] What is *left out* is as important as what is included (see Loewen, 1995; Stearns, Seixas, & Wineburg, 2000). Andrea summarizes her feelings flatly: "Social studies is boring."

---

2. Note the conflation of multiple, unrelated meanings of the word *standard*. Academic standards refer to things students should know and do (and are usually good). High standards suggest benchmarks. Standardized tests refer to a statistical procedure by which scores are normalized, or graded along a curve. Standardized tests have nothing to do with actual academic standards or high standards of learning and may be inherently contrary to them.

The commonalities between Loewen's (1995) critique and Andrea's are striking. Loewen begins his book *Lies My Teacher Told Me* with: "HIGH SCHOOL STUDENTS HATE HISTORY. When they list their favorite subjects, history invariably comes in last. Students consider history 'the most irrelevant' of twenty-one academic subjects commonly taught in high school. Bor-r-ring is the adjective they commonly apply to it" (p. 12). Marginalized students (from around the globe, not just those in the United States; see Wertsch, 2000) are especially alienated by school-taught history; they see it as irrelevant, oppressive, or just plain wrong. The dominant narratives of progress taught in world history classes—Western cultural domination, Western intellectual superiority, and colonial expansion—are questioned by historians (see Dunn, 2000) and openly mocked by students like Andrea. Not every student would agree with Andrea, but her ambivalence toward traditional, school-taught history is common.

Patterns of Change Approach to World History

History education is highly politicized. The main debate is whether to teach history as narratives in which evidence is mobilized to make arguments or as heritage (myth or fiction). As detailed in *History on Trial: Culture Wars and the Teaching of the Past* by Nash, Crabtree, and Dunn (2000), a large, mobilized group of people are more interested in promulgating myths to reinforce cultural values than in teaching what actually happened.

Within world history, this plays out in the teaching of the past 6,000 years of global history, or Western civilization. "Western civilization" is not a field of study at all, but a survey course invented to enculturate U.S. immigrants in the early 20th century. As Patrick Manning (2003) describes, educators feared Bolshevism, so they invented Western civilization as a unifying concept rooting the United States' greatness in Greco-Roman law, Enlightenment rationality, the Renaissance, free-market capitalism, and Protestant Christianity, among other things (particularly opposed to southern and eastern European Catholicism, which was linked to Bolshevism; see also McNeil, 1998). In fact, until 1900 no one had any concept of Western civilization; most thought in terms of specific cultures.[3] Even when people talk about "Western culture" today, they usually cherry-pick which

---

3. It is true that the idea of East vs. West was helpful in describing the long-standing Greco-Persian, Roman-Persian, and Islamic-Christian split. At the same time, because Islam comes from the Judeo-Christian tradition (as opposed to Hindu-Buddhism, Taoism, or Confucianism), it fits most definitions of Western *Civ* (as does, oddly enough, Roman-Italian Catholicism). See the problem?

parts count; Greece's government is good, but its religion and sexual practices are bad. Had educators just said, "U.S. government and culture is based on some ideas that I want to teach," it would be easier, but I digress.

As I researched the feasibility of using *Civilization* (the game, now in its third edition) for teaching history, world historian Pat Seed explained to me that teaching with *Civilization* could move beyond this mythical narrative of Western progress. *Civ*, with its geographical orientation, lays the world out in 4000 BC and then lets players experiment with how civilizations "advance." It could be taught like an interactive version of Jared Diamond's (1999) Pulitzer Prize–winning *Guns, Germs, and Steel*. I started building a world history mod based on Diamond's work, which became the design bible for the unit I brought into test classrooms.

This approach fits with what Ross Dunn (2000) calls the *patterns of change* approach to history. Dunn argues that students should understand the processes that pull people together (e.g., trade networks, religion, and culture) or create differences (e.g., geographic isolation, political units, or culture). Dunn argues against teaching a parade of civilizations (Egypt, Greece, Rome, then on to Renaissance Europe) and instead favors organizing learning through interesting, engaging questions. Encouraged by my partner teachers (see next section), I used Jared Diamond's driving question "Why did Europeans colonize the Americas instead of the reverse?"

Finding Teaching Partners

I found partner teachers in two Boston areas: the Media and Technology Charter School (MATCH) in Brookline and an after-school computer program in Revere. For space considerations, I'll cover just the MATCH school here (for the full study, go to kurtsquire.info).

The MATCH school served unengaged, underserved kids, 95% of whom identified as African American. The teachers saw their kids' fascination with video games and wanted to leverage it for learning.

Plus, their school didn't actually *teach* world history anymore. World history wasn't on the MCAS (the Massachusetts Comprehensive Assessment System, which is the state's high-stakes test), so, shockingly, the school dropped it outright.[4]

---

4. To prepare for the MCAS, MATCH hired testing tutors, and then paid kids for every hour of test prep they attended. If paying students seems crass, remember that legislators, not teachers, brought money into the equation. If we are going to have a system in which students' and teachers' lives are so deeply affected by a test that can be "played," paying

This presented an opening for my course. I wanted to use the game as the context for large, extended projects in which students made maps, constructed time lines, and produced a major project inspired by their games. The teachers looked at me kind of funny and said that if students could locate Egypt on a map, the project would be a success.

INTRODUCING *CIV3*

The first class was chaos. We tried an introductory activity, but many students refused to even give their names, and we abandoned videotaping entirely. The *entire class* had failed 9th grade. There were sharp cultural divides between the students and me, and I soon felt like yet another "drive-by researcher." I quickly fired up the game, hoping it would enthrall them. Andrea was *really* interested, but she was immediately annoyed. She shouted, "Where are the women in here?!" The units represented both men and women, but Andrea was unconvinced. "They don't *look* like women" (see Figure 6.1).

The students who had played strategy games were enthralled. Tony was typical. He read each screen carefully and weighed whether to build military units, granaries, temples, or workers. Dwayne, who was one of the brightest students in the school but wasn't advancing to 10th grade for the third year in a row (making him a 17-year-old sophomore), also played intently. Soon, most players navigated the interface without problems, and several played after dismissal.

Still, a few were *completely* confused. For example, Kathy was starving her civilization and was completely bankrupt.[5] Kent strolled about the room, looking over shoulders. The teacher threatened him with detention, and he replied, "Kent will go home when Kent wants to go home." That about summed it up.

After class, I debriefed with the teachers. Classroom management was killing us. We divided into two groups. On alternating days, one would play while the other did related activities. The first activity was for students to research which civilization they wanted to play. I made reading packets on the civilizations.

---

students for test prep courses is the logical endgame.

5. Kathy ordered her laborers to become entertainers because entertainers are represented by colorful icons, and so the visual feedback suggested it was a good idea to turn a laborer into an entertainer. Meanwhile, her civilization starved and went bankrupt as they entertained one another rather than producing food, gathering natural resources, or engaging in commerce.

**Figure 6.1.
A look at *Civ3***

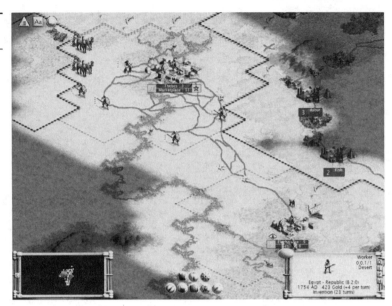

Dividing into Groups

The third day began with group discussion. I distributed readings covering a variety of historical and philosophical perspectives on civilizations, hoping to interrogate the notion of "civilization." The definition I promoted was that *civilization* essentially means intense, permanent human settlements, or cities. Within 5 minutes we had lost them. Three students were removed from class for disciplinary reasons.

In case things weren't shaky enough, we administered the pre-test next. Andrea asked, "What's the difference between BC and AD?" I asked her to guess, and she said, "Maybe that's why we're doing this unit!"

Next, the teacher led a discussion. She asked, "In what grade did you study Egypt?" Jason replied, "All my life!" There were groans as they began a ritualized recapitulation of all things Egypt. These kids learned about Egypt just about every year under the guise of multiculturalism. Most saw no point in this because they viewed themselves as no more Egyptian than Roman or Russian. Andrea grabbed the chalk from the teacher and drew a concept map at the board. The others yelled out random facts about Egypt: Egyptians were the first do brain surgery, Egyptian gods were part animal, Egyptians invented hieroglyphics, Egyptians made beer, Egyptians pulled the brains out of the nose of their dead during mummification. They had forgotten more Egyptian trivia than I'd ever learned. Still, most couldn't find it on a map.

Although class morale was improving, I was panicking. Only a few grokked the game; the others wanted little to do with it, or with me, for that matter. I reached a point that I've since recognized as being critical in all teaching, reflected in the question: When do you throw away your plans and follow the needs of your students?

Engagement Through Historical Play

The next day, I started over. Until now, I had team-taught with the MATCH faculty, but it was clear that *I* needed to teach. I reorganized the classroom so that students faced me. I drew a map of the Earth on the whiteboard to use for a mini-lecture.

As the kids entered, the map grabbed their attention. Jason and Chris couldn't believe that I had drawn it freehand. Tony, who was from Puerto Rico, noticed that Puerto Rico was missing. Ironically, of all the technologies in the classroom, it was a hand-drawn whiteboard map that piqued their interest most.

I asked, "What was the Earth like 1 million years ago? What about 15,000 years ago?" I illustrated Native American migration patterns and introduced debates about life in North America prior to the last Ice Age. I was losing them again. Engagement slipped whenever activities were not directly related to game play, so I went back to the game.

"Let's share the results of the civilization tally," I suggested. The winners were Egyptians, Aztecs, Iroquois, and then Bantu. I called on volunteers to identify where each civilization started. There was at least one student in the class who could pinpoint these civilizations' origins but none could place China, India, or Babylon.

The discussion shifted to "replaying history"—using the game to explore hypothetical historical scenarios. I asked, "If you wanted to play in the Americas, who would you play as?" The students announced, "Europe." I explained that within the game, the *player* determines who settles America, not real-life history. The player can try to "replay history" just as it happened, or they could play as the Iroquois and fend off Europeans. They could even play as the Bantu to try and settle the Americas or colonize Europe.

The teacher reframed it: "What languages do they speak in South America?" The class responded, "Spanish and Portuguese." Lisa continued, "Exactly. Why? That's where the people who settled there came from. You could play as any civilization and settle North America. Or, you could try to settle Europe with Native Americans." Until this point, students had been treating the game as a fixed narrative with predefined, scripted events rather than as a simulation for exploring hypotheticals.

A chorus of "cool!" and "awesome!" erupted around the room.

FAILURE, TRADE OFFS, AND JUST-IN-TIME LECTURES

Finally, students' questions were related to world history. Dan asked about the barbarians attacking him. Andrea asked about the Colossus. Kent asked what *irrigate*
meant. Everyone wanted to know about different civilizations and where they originated. Many asked about what was *happening* in their games—questions about
interpreting the game model.

Each played for unique reasons. Dwayne was motivated to "reverse thousands of
years of Chinese oppression on the Japanese peoples." He used embargoes, treaties,
and trade to play civilizations off one another in an impressive display of Machiavel-
lian tactics. Dwayne's civilization was easily the most advanced in the class.

Game *failures*, such as preventing civil unrest and balancing budgets, dominated the discussion. Several students, particularly Deborah and Andrea (defying
gender stereotypes), were constantly at war. Indeed, few students had *built* much
technology, managed military spending, or traded goods, instead focusing mostly
on military. Making connections across economics, politics, and geography was
difficult for them. Despite—or perhaps because of—these game challenges, 16 of
the 18 students were now deeply involved in playing.

Balancing Guns and Butter

Balancing a strong economy with a strong military was the defining game issue. Norman (Iroquois, 500 BC)[6] proudly held off the barbarians and showed off his
defensive network, but this crippled his economy. So he restarted and built roads
to strengthen his economy and make his people happy. I introduced mini-lectures
"just in time" when students became frustrated, presenting example games from
students to the full class and discussing formulas and strategies.

Recursive Play to Investigate Geography

Game failures led to *recursive play*, wherein students devised a strategy, observed its consequences, and then tried another strategy, learning the properties
of the model as they played. This process is a form of hypothesis testing in which
players observe phenomena, analyze their causes, and implement solutions. Jason
began playing as the Egyptians and was quickly concerned about the encroach-
ing Babylonians. So he restarted his game as the Iroquois. He explained, "I think I

---

6. The (civilization, date) notation indicates who they are playing in the game and
what year their game is in.

declared war too early, and my cities were too close together and too close to other civilizations. I want to play in North America where I can spread out."

I asked Jason about his location, but he only had a vague sense that he was in Canada. We studied the map together. This helped him connect the game map to other maps, and he started to use his knowledge of geography as a *tool* for game play. His first step was to consider colonizing Alaska or Greenland for resources. In post-interviews, Jason said this was his favorite part of the game.

Two major themes arose. Those in North America were isolated and developed slowly, while those in the Middle East constantly feuded. Jason couldn't decide which was worse, so he switched back and forth between Egypt and the Iroquois. Every student who played as Egypt dealt with Greek or Roman settlements in modern-day Libya, an interesting simulation of ancient Greek and Roman expansion.

"THIS GAME ISN'T SO BAD": FRUSTRATION, FAILURE, AND APPROPRIATION

After a week off for MCAS testing, we resumed, but everyone was punchy from the standardized testing. Immediately, several kids were kicked out of class for flirting. After class, a group of girls asked to withdraw from the study. The teacher agreed, but on the condition that they wrote a letter explaining why. They gave me permission to use their data.[7] All five letters said that the game was not interesting, too complicated, or too frustrating. In the post-interviews, I asked Andrea, who was friends with them, about what had happened. She responded,

> [At first] I wasn't interested because I didn't know how to play the game. I think the only reason that I became interested was because I learned how to play. I think that's why a lot of people gave up on it. They were like, "I don't know what I'm doing; I don't want to play this no more." But since I had to be there anyway, I just learned how to play the game. It's OK when you get used to it.

---

7. This is another example in which IRBs (Internal Review Boards) aren't set up for research in schools. Teachers wanted to remove the phrase "You can withdraw from the study to do an alternative activity" from the forms, because they believed that students would withdraw just to be difficult. They saw the option to withdraw as a classroom management disaster because students don't have to commit beyond their initial frustrations. Sure enough, several withdrew. I could have (and indeed, according to the IRB, was ethically obligated to) pretend they never participated. This struck me as less ethical, in that if there was something frustrating about their experience, then their voices should be heard.

The results were consistent. For a subset of students, *Civ* held little immediate appeal, was frustrating, and was complicated. They had never played games like *Civilization*. This reminds us that although games (especially award-winning ones like *Civilization*) are generally entertaining, few games are entertaining for *everyone*. Failure was very frustrating for these girls—especially when it was tied to the high consequences of school. These were the most school-affiliating students in the group, and they would rather learn history through reading historical fiction or literature. Whether these students should have been forced to persevere and have new experiences makes an interesting debate (imagine a boy labeled ADHD claiming he would rather play games than read *The Diary of Anne Frank* and not being encouraged to broaden his interests). However, given my commitment to supporting students in following their interests (see Chapter 4), this strategy made sense.

Sensing my disappointment, a teacher shared that she overheard three students *raving* about the unit. She thought it was going *great*. She commented, "For someone like Dwayne or Kent, this may be the only reason they come to school. There is at least one thing that they can look forward to in the day. Keep in mind that most of these kids are flunking several classes. Some of them are flunking *all* of their classes. These are *all* students who flunked 9th grade." In this light, the frustration of the girls who withdrew was not surprising: It's hard to start over when you've failed so often in school.

I wondered what was happening with these low-achieving boys who thrived playing *Civ*. Working-class, non-school-affiliated boys are way behind girls in almost every subject area and represent one of the biggest educational problems we face. They are far more likely to be in trouble in school, to be truant, and to be diagnosed with learning disabilities. These boys take up teachers' time, gum up principals' offices and special education rooms, and trail way behind girls in tests. This unit was reaching these struggling students, and the teachers were impressed.

THE EMERGENCE OF A GAME-PLAYING CULTURE

With the five "difficult" students (all girls, none of whom were truly all that difficult in general) gone, the class immediately ran smoothly. Thirteen students (9 boys, 4 girls) participated for the remainder of the unit, and I took on primary teaching responsibility.

Students all had clear individual goals (such as colonizing a continent), although the experience was profoundly social. Dwayne, who was charismatic and popular, was by far the most successful player and completely absorbed in the game. Bill, Kent, and Chris constantly compared their games with Dwayne's and simply liked being around him. Meanwhile, Dan, Shirley, and Sheila talked among themselves. Andrea played alone, fighting her dreaded Greeks. These clusters emerged based on a combination of game-playing goals and existing social networks. In some cases, game play enabled new friendships to emerge.

Building Civilizations in the Americas

With the games "taking off," the class became a gaming community of practice. Students discussed strategies between turns. Children playing as the New World civilizations studied maps to identify natural resources and sought to build trade routes with the Old World. Jason was a "min-maxer" who wanted to optimize his infrastructure. I explained how to create cities that are production centers for resources (much in the way that Kansas City was a cattle hub). Jason, whose favorite class was mathematics, turned the game into an optimization exercise of mastering the game system as a formal set of rules.

Tony was an *explorer* who traversed all the Americas and walked about the room to explore others' games in between turns. Jason taught Tony to exploit mineral resources in the western United States, so Tony restarted his game to expand westward first. In post-interviews, Tony described what he learned from losing: "Playing the game forces you to learn about the material. It actually *forces* you to learn about other civilizations in order to survive."

Transgressive Play

As players shared strategies, "taken-as-shared understandings" emerged. Paul Cobb and colleagues (2001) use taken-as-shared meanings to describe ideas that groups use for future action and as evidence for learning. For example, Norman, Chris, and Tony all met the Inca civilization. At first, they wanted to trade, but soon they decided to conquer them.

The moral justification for imperialism started with Norman. Norman saw that South America was full of minerals, but the Incas lacked the technology to exploit them. So, he attacked. He explained, "It is for their own good, really. Look how much more I have. They will be *happier* living as Iroquois." Chris and Tony laughed at this rationalization and then soon followed suit.

I expressed uneasiness seeing such transgressive, imperialist behavior in school, but they scoffed at my naiveté. Like Andrea, *none* of these kids harbored fantasies that U.S. expansion was anything but imperialism. They were just replaying it. The recent outbreak of the war in Iraq had only further reinforced these views. Briefly, Tony *did* try to trade with the Incas, but he decided that it was "safer" just to take over their city and defend their people as a benevolent imperialist force. The *transgressive* play of appropriating colonial rhetoric in the service of *Native American* domination particularly delighted Tony. I smiled at his mock concern for their well-being and joked that he had a firm grasp of American foreign policy.

Geography as a Tool

Chris (Aztecs, 1700 AD) wanted to contact the old world. He sailed about the Americas, looking for civilizations to trade with. As his game approached 1814 AD, he was shocked that no Europeans had arrived yet. He sailed a galley across the Bering Strait into Siberia looking for Asians. He called over, "Kurt, I found it! I'm in Asia!" I suggested that, as bizarre as it seems, it was theoretically possible. The unrealistic part was that Chris had a *reason* to row from Mexico to Alaska, as he had historical foresight, an awareness of China, and a sense of a unified fate for the Native Americans. The idea of using geography and history as a *cheat* in the game quickly caught on across the group.

Changing the Course of History

A friend came in and asked Dan what he was doing, and he explained, "Changing the course of history." Dan's goal was to "build a huge empire and hold off all the Europeans." When I told Dan that the Egyptians were making discoveries more quickly because they could trade with the Romans, Babylonians, Bantu, and Carthaginians, he became worried. Dan finally understood that his fate lay not just in building a large military—40,000 spearmen could be demolished by 200 cavalry, as was the case historically. As time wore on, Dan's civilization crumbled under the weight of his military spending.

Gender Wars

Andrea, on the other hand, was *always* at war, and she fought everyone from the Babylonians to the Greeks to the Carthaginians. Any time a city formed near her, she would shout, "You can't just come in here" and declare war. Andrea's play style reflected a pattern common to *many* female *Civ* players (and myself). She would never *start* a war, but hell hath no fury like a leader being unjustifiably attacked.

Sometimes, that "attack" was no more than a neighboring *Civ* peacefully expanding, but "you *know* what they were thinking."

After *5,000 years* of war, things looked bad for Andrea. The Romans encroached on her capitol. She realized that she had no economy and no infrastructure. So she started over and this time asked me, her teacher, for advice. Now that Andrea *needed* to know history, she listened closely. Her plan was to attack the Romans, so she studied maps to plan her attack. She asked about naval technologies such as mapmaking, harbors, and galleys. This was the first time that Andrea had shown any interest in learning game concepts, reading the *Civilopedia* (the in-game encyclopedia, which contains hundreds of entries), or building city improvements. *Failure* motivated her. These concepts were *tools* for her to solve problems that she cared about; namely, this was protecting her people.

Teaching Practices

The end of class was saved for debriefing. I drew a chart on the board listing students' civilizations and key variables. I polled students as they played, filling in the chart with data. We used these aggregated game statistics (see Table 6.1) to identify game play patterns.

Those playing as the Iroquois saw that they were severed from the North African, European, and Asian trade networks. In fact, they couldn't *help* but see the trade networks that Diamond describes. We compared the advantages of trading versus remaining isolated on the board. Trading helped them learn new technologies, but also left them at risk of being attacked by those very technologies. Isolationism was safer in the short run, but ultimately left you *more* vulnerable.

Detecting Bias

Although structured activities worked when they informed game play, they also helped students vent frustrations. We turned complaints about realism into an exercise in which each student made note of three unrealistic things about the game. Many critics claim that students will blindly adopt the properties of the game model, but we found the opposite to be true because the game *forces* you to understand its rules (see Table 6.2).

Most students focused on *factual inaccuracies* rather than *underlying biases*. Students quickly identified incorrect emergent events, such the failure of the Portuguese or Spanish to explore the Americas in the 15th century. Jason's observation that the Iroquois' harbors were unrealistic has some validity, although his questioning the Iroquois Republic is less so. Kent questioned the game's bias toward a conflict-driven theory of diplomacy, complaining that it was impossible to survive while "staying neutral." Curiously, students also thought that some realistic products of the simulation, such as Celtic French settlements in Canada, were unbelievable. Students tended to detect those biases that had a direct impact on their game play, such as civilizations' tendency to attack them.

Table 6.1. Sample Aggregated Statistics from Students' Games in *Civ3*

Student	Civilization	Year (AD)	Government	Technology	Horses	Luxuries
Jason	Egypt	760	Republic	Engineering	Yes	Incense
Andrea	Egypt	1040	Despotism	Mathematics	Yes	Incense
Tony	Iroquois	1020	Monarchy	Monotheism	No	Iron, furs

Table 6.2. Students' Perceptions of Unrealistic Game Features in *Civ3*

Name	Unrealistic "things" about the game
Shirley	1. Can they really burn your town?
	2. If this game was true, can it start world peace?
Norman	1. French are building cities next to my city in North America.
	2. People love me one year, burn my city the next.
	3. My people are starving.
Jason	1. The Iroquois learned republic.
	2. The Iroquois had harbors.
	3. The Iroquois were about to take over South America.
Tony	1. The years are off.
	2. The colonization is off.
	3. The amount of people (is unrealistic).

RECURSIVE PLAY

Testing Geography

Many students started new games to test theories of geographical advantage. Chris and Jason switched to the Egyptians, being technologically behind the Europeans. They tested hypotheses about which civilizations stood a better chance of surviving through history.

Players often restarted games to simply improve on their work. In these games, players demonstrated mastery over the game's basics. For example, Andrea restarted to get out of her war with Greece. Within 5 minutes, she had created two cities, irrigated the flood plains, and built roads for incense. Likewise, her cities were perfectly placed to balance food production, trade, and resource attainment.

Systemic Understandings, or Here Come the Celts!

The impending clash of civilizations haunted those playing as the Iroquois. Each player tried a different strategy: Tony built a robust infrastructure, Dan had a massive army, Chris explored China for trade routes.

Finally, in 1914 the Celts reached the shores of Nova Scotia and trans-Atlantic contact was made. Dan screeched in horror as the Celts moved toward the St. Lawrence. "How did they get here?!" Waves of cavalry disembarked from Celtic frigates, and Dan knew he was in trouble.

This emergent phenomenon of the Celtic French settling Canada was intriguing. It was odd that the computer-controlled civilizations (also called artificial intelligence, or AI) took so long to reach the Americas (probably because of the difficulty-level setting), but the French settling Canada was eerily accurate. Within moments, the Carthaginians had also landed along the eastern shores of North America (a hypothetical historical scenario that's really mind-bending to think about. Go ahead. I'll get back to you). I'm not sure what happened to the Spanish.

Dan fell behind because he wasn't trading technologies. He would need to trade resources quickly to avoid being overpowered. Dan's first goal was to trade for horses, but no one would, so he built a galley to sail to Europe. We wondered, "What if the Native Americans had done something similar? Could they find navigation technologies and start trade missions (or raids) on Europe?" It was an authentic question. Under what conditions might the indigenous populations have explored Europe? (The answers include maybe if there was no disease, a sense of unity among Native Americans, and a sense of perspective over time scales). Given the Viking exploration of the Americas and Polynesian expansion in the South Pacific, there don't seem to be any inherent technological reasons they could not have sailed to Europe, although such a civilization would probably be a seafaring one.

Dan, Tony, Chris, and I discussed this hypothetical. They saw the primary issues as population density and struggles for resources. On their maps, the European and Asian countries battled over resources while the Native Americans had no incentive to expand beyond North America. These responses, while more abstracted than traditional historians might frame them, are consistent with many modern readings of colonization.[8]

Historical Interpretations from Game Play

In the post-test interviews, I asked Dan about the colonization of the Americas.

Interviewer: Why did the Europeans colonize the Americas as opposed to the other way around?

Dan: Because the Europeans had more [material goods] than the Native Americans did. [The Native Americans] weren't as civilized. I'm not going to say civilized. But they were pretty much peaceful. They were focusing in on their land for themselves, not going around the world trying to focus on everything else . . . having everything nice and calm.

Dan's response was basically *uninformed* by his game experiences. He described the Native Americans as less "civilized" but ultimately attributed European colonization to European greed rather than Native American pacifism. I probed this tension between cultural and philosophical readings of history:

Interviewer: So were their reasons behind colonization more a matter of philosophy or geography?

Dan: Probably more philosophy. They didn't want to go anywhere because they were happy with where they were. They didn't have any troubles with any animals. They were killing them, using them for fur or food or whatever. They had everything they needed, whereas Europe got overpopulated and needed more land.

Dan distinguishes between Native American and European civilizations in terms of "philosophy," before reintroducing geography—namely, food and the shortage of land in Europe. I pressed on.

Interviewer: Do you think that natural resources had anything to do with it as well? Horses, iron, gold, diamonds?

---

8. Many scholars believe that Native American civilizations were quite large, rivaling European cities (e.g., Diamond, 1999). That said, it's fair to believe that there was still plenty of land in North and South America, compared with the giant contiguous land mass of Europe, Asia, and Africa and the tens of thousands of years' head start that Europeans, Asians, and Africans had had in exploring it.

Dan: It probably does. But, like I said, the Native Americans probably didn't pay any attention to it because they were happy. They didn't have anything to worry about. They were pretty much peaceful. The only people they had to worry about were enemy tribes. No disease, nothing like that.

I suggested natural resources, but Dan wanted to talk about culture. He struggled with whether Native Americans were peaceful or if they *could* have been expansionist but just lacked the motivation. He describes the infrequency of diseases in Native Americans, meaning that he basically covered the "top factors influencing colonization."

I followed up by asking about Asian colonization. I wanted to see how Dan compared Chinese civilization with the Europeans.

Interviewer: Why do you think China didn't settle North America?
Dan: I have no idea. I was going to say the same thing I said for Native Americans, then I thought about it. But they were probably just not prepared to actually settle somewhere else.

China posed a problem. Dan's explanations so far were population density and cultural pacifism. However, the Chinese did not fit either condition, leaving him with little basis to theorize why the Chinese would not have colonized the Americas. He speculates that the Chinese perhaps were not "prepared" for explorations.[9]

Dan's interpretation of historical forces was sophisticated. At times he drew from earlier readings of history, particularly descriptions of Native Americans as peaceful peoples. At other times, he used more materialist, geographical concepts. Dan's model of colonization has several interacting variables. Clearly he did not uncritically adopt the game's materialist, geographically based theory. Rather, he read the game in terms of his understanding of history and personal experience. For Dan, the game was a useful simulation for *material* processes but less so for *cultural* ones.

This finding should give educators some encouragement that game-playing students do not necessarily buy into one particular model wholesale, but use existing understandings to interpret game play. These students don't play one game and then forget everything that they knew about the world beforehand.

---

9. Some scholars believe that China did in fact visit America. Prior to the closing down of the Chinese in the 15th century, the Chinese navy was large and traveled to India and the coast of Africa. This exploration was shut down for political, cultural, and economic reasons, much like a *Civ* leader shifting priorities.

Experimentation

Much like a scientist runs multiple simulations to infer emergent patterns, students used one another's games as data. Those playing as the Iroquois watched in horror as the Romans and Celts sailed into Norman's territory and took action. Tony immediately set out across the Bering Strait to find Asian civilizations. "If they are not going to come to me, then I'm going to them!" he said.

Next, players took an interest in the model itself. Chris's Iroquois nations struggled to grow, so he asked about the game's agricultural model, and he wanted *details*. Chris, like most, understood the general game systems (e.g., irrigation causes more food) and used rules of thumb (e.g., build roads everywhere), but this was no longer sufficient. In fact, many players start with general understandings, and then unpack the model mathematically when general understandings no longer suffice.

Jason was troubled that the computer-generated AI civilizations were not colonizing the Americas sooner, and he began to question *Civ*'s accuracy. I re-explained how *Civ* is a simulation based on initial conditions, so that any action in that 6,000-year history could radically change its course. Jason became captured by a historical hypothetical such as "What if Native Americans sailed across Greenland to Europe?" Jason wanted to make Greenland "Seward's Folly version 2.0" and peppered me with questions about Greenland that I couldn't begin to answer: "Is there oil in Greenland? Are there other resources there? Do people live there now? How many?" Game questions often motivated historical ones.

Jason periodically played as Egyptians to test the differences between the northeastern United States and the Nile River Valley. "Look how fast Egyptian cities grow!" he shouted. I asked if he knew why. He commented, "Well, yes, the Nile River Valley." He went on, "Before, I didn't like the Egyptians because they got all trapped up here," pointing to the Mediterranean, the Sahara, and the Red Sea. Renewed with hope, Jason read the *Civilopedia*, which led him to experimenting with new game systems such as government.

Africanizing the Americas

After winning a costly war with the English, Dwayne (English 1682) restarted as the Bantu. He wanted to see if Africans could conquer the world. By the second day, Dwayne made it to 790 AD. He had quickly mapped Africa and sent emissaries as far north as Germany. He bragged about his plan to make the Americas African. He would build cities along the shores of Africa, gather its resources, establish borders in sub-Saharan Africa, and then build an empire inward.

I complimented Dwayne on his strategy because playing as the Bantu was particularly difficult: The capital city was surrounded by jungle, leaving no farmland; the Sahara Desert cut off northern expansion; and the south brought more jungle, the Kalahari, and rival tribes. Dwayne had avoided each of these pitfalls by planning to span the entire continent from the beginning.

"Wow," I commented. "It makes you wonder, What if Africa unified?"

Dwayne said quietly, "Well, we'll find out, won't we?" He reminded me that he had read Sun Tzu's *Art of War*. Who was I to doubt him?

By 1310, Dwayne had built up the interior of Africa, and by 1545, he had colonized South America. Dwayne proudly showed off his work to the class. His was the first civilization to cross the Atlantic, make a permanent settlement, and have any chance of winning. And he did it as the Bantu. Sandy, a teacher who had lived in Mozambique, approached Dwayne to discuss African civilizations. Recall that Dwayne attended school 50% of the time and was deeply antagonistic to authority. He was opening up in front of us.

WHAT STUDENTS LEARNED

By the close of the unit, each student pursued unique goals with little outside help. In post-interviews, students reported that playing *Civ*

1. required them to pay closer attention and think more deeply than was typical;
2. led to learning geographical features;
3. helped them understand how geography affected civilizations;
4. provided background information about technologies and civilizations;
5. produced understandings of ordinal relations among historical events (like what came first, the Pyramids or gunpowder); and
6. was unrealistic in how it portrayed leading a civilization.

As Deborah summarized it, "Playing the game made you pay attention and read everything." Our observations confirmed this. Students frequently read passages, asked the meaning of words, and debated the meanings of texts—particularly during diplomacy. Compare this to the average day, in which 10 to 20% of the class was kicked out for behavioral issues.

With fluency, each student discussed how geography affected civilizations, including noting where civilizations (among them competing civilizations) started, fulfilling teachers' hope that they "find Egypt on a map." They did best in areas they attended to most closely because it applied to their unique game-play styles. Andrea learned the most about military history. She discussed the catapult, war chariots, musketmen, and aqueducts. Dan discussed the strategic importance of resources and technologies. Jason read the *Civilopedia* most extensively and had the best explanations for historical events. He described colonization as driven by European trade with global trade networks, the production capacity of European cities, and naval technologies.

Students also *all* described how their games were unrealistic in that there was no historical analog for their perspective; each also described in detail how they micromanaged their civilization in ways that kings, republics, or presidents never would. There was no evidence of confusion about roles.

Each student had different ways of interpreting the game as a historical text. Most students showed general increases in understandings on time lines. They knew that mathematics, bronze working, and the alphabet were ancient technologies, and many could pin down ancient wonders (e.g., the pyramids) to ancient eras. On an individual level, it was more complex. Jason drew analogies to history all the time, while Andrea was not sure how her game compared to history much of the time. She couldn't describe how her borders compared with the historical borders of Egypt.

The biggest gains were in students' *interest* in history and geography. They regularly asked dozens of questions about far-reaching topics. Chris's game became an inquiry project on the impact of geography on civilizations. Others asked about religion in history and wanted to know more about the terms they were using. By the end of the unit, asking questions was the predominant class activity.

One of the biggest questions to emerge was "Can we have just one more turn?" Several students asked if they could play next year, and they offered suggestions for how to integrate it in courses.

CIVILIZATION CAMP: DEVELOPING EXPERT GAMERS

We invited students to participate in a summer *Civ* program for the school's Media Week. Media Week was a hands-on opportunity to produce media. Five students—Kent, Dwayne, Chris, Tony, and Norman—signed up. Others wanted to, but were committed to a youth peace leadership camp—not something I wanted to fight. It's worth reiterating that this camp—like the class—is *not* "just a group of kids playing *Civ*," but rather a *particular* gaming community with its own culture. My goal was to leverage these emerging understandings to draw deeper connections to world history. The students mostly wanted to finish their games and participate in an expert gaming community. The teachers hoped to nurture their burgeoning school affiliation and interest in history.

CREATING A NEW GAMING CULTURE

Immediately a new culture emerged. These kids were *serious* about *Civ*. They arrived early the first day, installed the game in the teacher's lounge, and played independently. An angry mob confronted me, demanding that I locate their saved games. Compare that to 6 weeks earlier, when Dwayne had refused to share his name. Every student, including Dwayne, agreed to be videotaped. I'd finally earned their trust.

The point of the camp was for *them* to examine if *Civ* could help them learn world history. They would present their analysis to other campers. The primary social activity remained asking questions. In one 21-minute period, they asked about coastal fortresses, mutual protection pacts, the corporation, oil refining, espionage, cavalry, diplomacy, theology, steam power, free artistry, and what happened when the game ran out of names for new cities. Kent also wanted to know if he could stay at peace without giving away money. "These civilizations ask for too much freaking money," he complained.

We rearranged the room to facilitate knowledge sharing. Students sat in a small circle and could lean over to see anyone's game at any time, and students took advantage of this. For example, Dwayne built a frigate and was trying to colonize Japan as the Bantu. Kent overheard and wanted a frigate to trade with Iroquois. He needed magnetism and navigation, which would take *hundreds* of years the rate he was going.

"Why didn't you tell me this before, Kurt?"

"Because you wouldn't have listened," I chided back. Everyone laughed, confirming that no one paid attention unless a question was being answered. Kent thought about it, then asked, "Can my guys swim?" He was frustrated that fully equipped spearmen could not swim across the Mediterranean.

As the only link between the game simulation and history, I answered many questions. I had a historical time line and a globe available, but the students rarely, if ever, consulted them. Although they all showed curiosity about history and geography in general, they wanted resources *specifically tied to their game goals*.

DEVELOPING GAMING EXPERTISE

As they entered the industrial age, students encountered new concepts (such as democracy, espionage, or replaceable parts). Tony switched to democracy, and observed how this transformed his economy. In the post-interviews, Tony recalled these effects in great detail. He believed that *Civ*'s capacity to tie together disparate ideas and provide a context for caring was its primary educational value: "*Civ* is perfect for learning. It should be used. This game has everything in a history class all at once. While you play the game, the teacher can tell you about things that happened in real life. Then, you use it to take advantage in the game."

Lifting the Hood

I introduced *Civ*'s editor in an attempt to improve understandings of *Civ* as a simulation. Educators have long argued for the importance of making simulations transparent so that players can understand their underlying rules (see Turkle, 2003), and through *Civ*'s editor, players can "lift the hood" to see how it models population growth, happiness, economics, and so on. The point of this exercise, to expose them to properties of the model (e.g., Starr, 1994), was lost on them. I explained how they could modify anything on screen—even convert the entire game to a *Star Wars* universe. Surprisingly, no one was interested. So I turned to our scenario and demonstrated decisions I made in improving its historical accuracy. They looked befuddled.

Next, we opened a map to ground the discussion, which worked better. Immediately they asked about the icons involving future resources that they hadn't seen. Norman asked about oil in Alaska; Chris asked about aluminum and saltpeter. I pointed out that they could add horses to North America and see what happens. They experimented intently.

Seeing the map uncovered was like seeing the "answer sheet." Abstract discussions of simulation bias didn't capture them, but exploiting natural resources did. Seeing the map grounded the discussion and enabled them to discuss unrealistic geographic features, although they still struggled with advanced game ideas like revolution. Chris and Kent both made mini-scenarios that they wanted to play.

Although there is value in showing students the rules underlying the game, we should be cautioned against doing so too quickly. Games like *Civ* are *very* complex. Simply learning the game's "grammar" (interface, terms, underlying logic) takes hours. Indeed, most games' rules make little sense until you've played them, and even then it's most often the *emergent properties* of events that the rules produce, not the rules themselves, that are interesting. As Gee (2003) points out, try reading a game manual before you've played it, and it's incomprehensible. However, once the player has a situated understanding—once he or she has sufficiently experienced rules and can predict what changing them might mean—seeing the rules allows for concretizing abstract phenomena (such as war weariness). However, even then, seeing the rules doesn't necessarily lead to seeing patterns that emerge across games, such as the Iroquois civilizations struggling to grow while Egyptians thrived in the Nile (before facing an over-crowded Mediterranean).

Game Play as Identity Performance: Beware of the Damned Russians

As *Civ* Camp closed, new friendships formed. Tony and Dwayne, who weren't ordinarily friends, both ran large, democratic civilizations and played collaboratively. Dwayne was normally antisocial but regularly asked Tony for help, which Tony enjoyed. In fact, *Civ* enabled a variety of unique social interactions, suggesting that games may be *more* social than many traditional pedagogies. This evidence conflicts with the "bowling alone" theory that digital media isolates us and that video games are driving this change. Video games can, in certain cultural contexts, be deeply social (much in the same way that book clubs encourage social interaction).

This peaceful building was interrupted by the Celts, who built a city in Tony's backyard (Nova Scotia).

"Bomb them," Chris said.

Tony tended toward pacifism, so he objected: "They're just building little towns!"

"Hello! They may be little towns, but they could grow."

"Who cares? They're real people, man," Tony said. "Besides, I'm the strongest *Civ* anyway." Tony brought a deep sense of morality to his play, but he felt compelled to back up this pacifism with braggadocio. This brief interaction reveals just how comfortable they were observing games, collaboratively analyzing problems, asking for help, debating solutions, and negotiating values.

As games entered the modern era, more questions arose. For the partnering teachers this was the best part of the unit.

"I can't believe what I'm hearing," one commented. Within 20 minutes, she heard questions ranging from the conceptual (e.g., What are barracks, catapults, the Colossus, treaties, the forbidden palace, embassies?) to deep questions about the game system (e.g., How does artificial intelligence work?). They were developing theories about how the game worked, and they could articulate and defend these theories. Debating about the merits of building embassies or espionage was enjoyable.

Tristan, a student in another class, walked in and started asking questions. Observing that Dwayne was in 2003 and Tony was in 2020, he started pestering Tony: "Why is Dwayne going into space and you don't even have battleships? And wait, they're still riding horses. That makes no sense. Why don't you have jet fighters? Why don't you bomb a neighboring country? Damn, I'm sweating in here. Why don't you build tanks?"

"Tanks? I don't need tanks," Tony responded. Once again, Tony had to defend his pacifism. But Tristan wasn't done yet.

"Tony, Tony, Tony. Why don't we go by *America's* principles? Build as many weapons as you can even though you don't need it, just in case war breaks out," he said mockingly.

"Isn't that overkill?" Tony tried to stick to his game. Tony knew firsthand the perils of maintaining a bloated military, but Tristan leveraged the occasion for his *own* just-in-time lecture about the Cold War.

"What was the Cold War about? Building as many weapons as you can, just in case Russia starts something. Build enough weapons to destroy the Earth 10 times over just because." I'm not sure if Tristan had just returned from a Chomsky lecture or what, but he was on a roll.

Kent hadn't discovered gunpowder, much less tanks, but he joined Tristan in barbing Tony. "Always have tanks!" Goading Tony into war was a favorite pastime.

Dwayne punctuated the discussion. "And, always beware of the damned Russians."

Tristan looked on. "Tony, you still haven't reached Africa yet? Isn't the object to take over people with the military and rule the world?"

"Yeah, but it's almost *impossible* just with military." Tony didn't want to explain to a newbie the foolishness of building military and ignoring economics and politics. Tony had developed systemic understandings of *Civ's* economic, geographic, and diplomatic models.

Interdisciplinary Connections

It was time to revisit their final presentations. I asked Chris what his most important findings were.

"Well, the game depends on where you're sitting. In Egypt you become rich because their geography has a lot of gold."

Chris described not a particular technology or unit, but rather the *idea* of the interplay between geography and civilizations. For days, Chris's play was a study of how geography affects the growth of civilizations. Chris was discerning the materialist orientation of the simulation and unpacking it.

I asked Kent, who hadn't had much success, what technologies were important for him.

"Location is important. Playing in America was easier." Although Kent struggled with specifics, he too had rudimentary understandings of the game's model. He acknowledged the importance of scientific discovery, particularly his own lack of it, and that the scenario ultimately depended on geography.

Reviewing the Underlying Game Variables

The unit was almost over. I pushed the students to critique *Civ3* and used these discussions to also assess what they had learned. Everyone identified the three main variables (food, resources, and commerce) as the basis of the simulation. Further, they all could discuss what affected these basic variables (irrigation, mining, roads, and geography). Through playing as different civilizations, they *all* knew that river valleys generated the most food, and tundra the least. Their understanding of industrial production, an abstract concept we discussed little in class, was weaker.

Norman interrupted to ask, "Are North and South America considered the same continent?"

"Umm . . . no," I answered.

"Doesn't a bridge separate them?" Norman asked.

Tony, our resident expert in geography, offered his answer.

"No, I don't think they're connected." Moments like this reminded me of how little background knowledge most brought to the unit. Although they had probably been taught the continents since at least 4th grade, it hadn't stuck in any meaningful way. Maybe the teachers were right. If *Civ* could provide background knowledge and pique their interest in learning, it would be a success. I demonstrated how to build a port in Central America to re-create the Panama Canal. I hoped that connecting geography to specific strategies would make it meaningful.

Students wrote what they had learned on note cards. We hoped to organize them by theme, but this activity broke down, revealing the ultimate lesson of the unit.

I read a post. "OK, democracy makes more money and science."

"That's bias," Tony said. "Some people believe that technology will win the game."

I continued, "Cities grow slower in mountains and forests."

"Geography," Kent offered.

"Discovering democracy helped my civilization." That was Tony. "Politics."

"Technology of flight. How did that help?" I asked.

Dwayne, who had written *flight* (perhaps as a "brag fact") said, "Military superiority."

Tony also showed off his progress. "Discovery of flight helped my military."

"So are you saying politics?"

"Yeah, but it could also be history," Tony said, as he paused and thought. As he tried to categorize themes, Tony saw multiple ways to understand technological advances. I read a card about the strategic value of the Nile River, and Tony responded.

"Money allows me to buy technology, so politics. When you have a lot of money you can do whatever you want. When you're rich you can buy off other countries." Soon, Tony saw the problem with this activity: Because geography, politics, economics, and history are all connected (in *Civ* and in life), it is difficult to know where one domain begins and another ends. It was impossible for Tony to describe the importance of the Nile River without discussing economics, which then had political implications. This became clearer as the discussion turned to amphibious warfare.

"Could be bias. It could be history and politics. In a way it's history . . . It allows you to bombard other countries. But politics-wise you can demand stuff now," Tony said.

After a few minutes of conversation, Tony stood up, obviously thinking, and said: "Well, in some ways, they're all related to each other." There was general nodding.

Tony synthesized. "Well, money is the key. . . . Money is the root of everything. With money you can save yourself from war, and that also means that politics . . . With money, that ties everything together." By tracing everything back to money, Tony is picking up on the materialist nature of the game.

The *majority* of our stick-on notes—amphibious warfare, luxuries, geography, uniting Africa—were all in the middle of the chart connecting history, geography, and politics. I connected the dots: "I want to suggest a change here. Maybe what we learned is that history, geography, and politics are all related. Why?"

Tony was on fire: "Luxuries buys you money, and money buys you everything. The right *location* gives you luxuries, which gives you income. More income gives you technology, which effects your politics. It all connects."

"Yes," Chris concluded.

Kent elaborated, "Geography effects your diplomacy because it gets you more resources and determines how they treat you." Kent had struggled with specific strategies, but his failures also taught him core lessons of the game.

Tony chimed in with a more obvious link: "Geography can effect the growth of your civilization." The class was honing in on the chief lesson of the game. Geography (and, of course, decision making) could explain the story of civilizations: Why some civilizations "succeed" and others do not.

In closing interviews, Tony expounded further on these relationships. He was asked, "Do you think that playing *Civilization* taught you anything about social studies?"

He answered, "I think it did. I always knew that certain locations helped certain people, but with this, I have a better understanding of it. I have a better idea of—like, if you're in the middle of a forest—sure there's a lot of things there, but your civilization doesn't grow that quickly and money is hard to come by. That affects population, the mood of your civilization and food . . ." Tony trailed off, thinking, with a smile on his face.

"In class," I asked, "you said that geography affects politics, which affects history. Could you talk more about that?"

Tony answered, "Well, if you're next to the ocean, that's a good place for any city to be. It has food, water, a moderate climate, and that's a good place for a city to flourish. If you have luxuries and are around water, that brings in trade. That brings in money that you can use to talk with other civilizations. If you have enough money you can buy a lot of things and you can sell a lot of things."

For Tony, the most educationally valuable aspect of playing *Civ* was how it helped him see connections between domains. When Tony says, "I always *knew* that certain locations helped certain people but . . . I have a better *understanding* of it," he articulates a critique of education from the situated-learning perspective. Tony had read, been told, and had even seen in videos that "river valleys produce more food," but now he had *experienced* this playing out. More significant, he knew why this was important—why this is the sort of fact to include in a textbook. The fate of his civilization depended on his understanding it.

Next, I asked Tony if he detected any biases in the game. Tony immediately gravitated toward government. Tony recalled the dramatic impact that shifting to democracy caused in his game:

> The form of government, democracy, has been the best. Any form of government could work for any *Civ*. In some ways, the ways technology works in the game is very true, like how we are now. I remember in history books they talk about how there was an arms race.[10] The more technology we had, the more powerful we should be, and there was a race to go to the moon or outer space, at least. I guess the more power you have in technology, the better you are in the game.

"So it might be realistic?" I asked.

Tony replied, "Yes, close enough. Geography is the main game. In my other game I started next to the mountains and next to the water, as well. The water was the only thing sustaining me. I'm secluded from everything. Everyone else hates us because we're weak. They won't share whatever they have. They only come in when I find something good. Then they start calling me: 'Do you want to trade this?'" Here, Tony expresses frustration with how the artificial intelligence has no interest in peaceful negotiations and is ruthless in extracting what it wants. He's detecting its bias toward power.

"Is that an unrealistic bias to you?" I asked.

---

10. Read about the arms race in a textbook? I'm getting old.

"In some ways, yes." Tony, like Norman and Dan (and unlike Dwayne), was optimistic that civilizations could coexist peacefully. He did not believe that other civilizations should only trade for their own material gain, which also might be considered a materialistic game bias. For Tony, the game's power-driven political negotiations felt unnecessarily harsh.

Game Play as Analysis

Norman started the PowerPoint presentation while everyone else worked. Between turns, Tony gathered screenshots on a second computer (meaning he was playing two games at once; compare that to the first day). He took his second game to 1000 BC without even paying full attention. He wanted images of thriving cities, wars, and multiple cultures, and he manipulated events to make those happen.

Chris spent the last day starting games in different areas and testing the relative advantages of each. Chris described what he learned through these experiments:

> For Egypt it wasn't a really good idea to have war with other cultures. They grew fast but there were so many around you—the Greeks, the Babylonians, the Romans, and the Bantus—they surrounded you. The Egyptians had a lot of gold, so others might try to gang up on you. As the Aztecs, it was harder to be rich, but it was good to trade with other countries. They had fewer reasons to invade you.

By examining multiple cases, players saw deeper structural patterns in the simulation, a feature of deep learning (e.g., Bransford & Schwartz, 1999).

The Medium Is the Message

I asked what changes they would make to the game.

"Yeah, they (nomadic groups) are barbarians, but they're still people," Tony said. "They should still be learning technologies." Tony struggled with the representation of nomadic groups and the ethics of attacking them (whereas for most it was decidedly a *game* and not something you would think about ethically).

I asked what it was like to be geographically isolated, and Tony eagerly responded. "Well, when you're isolated it's good and bad. In some ways it's good because you don't really have any enemies, you flourish. But it's kind of bad because you develop at a slower pace." I asked the class if this made sense, and they all nodded in agreement.

"Really, we're learning about managing civilizations," Norman offered. Different social policies, over the long term, lead to different outcomes. However, there are still legitimate concerns that students might think that any *one* person could change the system (much as we might naively think that one historical figure—a President Bush or Obama—can alter the U.S. political and economic system). I wanted to see if students saw themselves as a president, a god, an emperor, or something different.

Kent picked up the thread. "Resources . . . money, treaties, alliances . . . You know . . . politics." Again, Kent wasn't good at playing *Civ*, but he grokked the basic systems.

Norman got more specific: "You worry about how much you spend on science compared to how much on making money." We discussed guns versus butter and wrote that down.

Whereas the "management bias" has been a critique, these students valued the lessons they learned as civilization "managers." They valued opportunities to experience trade offs between trade and isolation or short-term spending and long-term investment in scientific progress. These understandings make good analogies to contemporary policy agendas, such as comparing investment in military spending versus basic research. They were identifying patterns that are central to world history (see Dunn, 2000).

I was concerned that they might overgeneralize toward history based on one game experience, so I asked, "What did we learn about history?"

Tony responded, "No matter how history plays out in this game, it's all based on the same rules—like in real life."

Marshall McLuhan famously wrote, "The medium is the message." Here, we see evidence for two ways that *Civ* changed students' thinking about history. In both cases, what's interesting is how it subtly colored their thinking.

1. *World history as patterns of interactions*. These players all described their learning as the broad trade offs facing civilizations (which is the core game play). They were less concerned about the "management" bias (poor management is just stupid) and more concerned about broad policy directives (technology vs. military).
2. *History could be represented through rules*. History is usually organized by narratives. Yet these students felt that history could also be described by rules determining the effects of geography, policy decisions, and so on.

THEORY AND PRACTICE

So what did we learn about teaching with games? First, that games *can* be deeply engaging for some (these students were low-achieving, struggling students), but not all will be engaged. There were classroom management challenges, particularly when students experienced failure. Second, the learning that occurred reflected particular gaming and teaching practices, reminding us that we never test a "game" but rather how we teach with a game in a certain context. Each student showed a more robust understanding of geography and its effects on history, although the extent of this varied across students. Whereas Tony and Jason compared their games to history quite frequently, Andrea did not. Students all developed *systemic understandings* (albeit with varying depth) about how relationships among variables within one subsystem (e.g., geography and food production) relate to another subsystem (e.g., money and diplomacy).

Specific teaching strategies emerged that might be helpful for teaching with games:

- *Know thy game.* It is imperative that teachers know the game. Students benefit from assistance interpreting the game's model. Students like Andrea did not readily identify pattern themes (such as the historical qualities of the Nile). Mini-lectures help students draw causal inferences about the game's underlying mechanics.
- *Game play drives learning.* We tried many teaching approaches, but found the most success when teaching and learning activities were in direct response to game play challenges. Managing failure and frustration was a constant challenge, and facilitating students' learning as players minimized these challenges. Additional resources, texts, and experiences were embraced when directed toward helping students reach in-game goals.
- *Just-in-time lectures.* We gravitated toward just-in-time lectures pertaining to players' issues at hand. We found it useful to give specific, detailed instructions about the game to minimize failure early on. These shifted toward historical or geographic discussions tied more closely to academically valued content. These lectures helped students understand the game's model, connected students with useful resources (such as maps or the *Civilopedia*) and used historical micronarratives to illuminate strategy decisions (such as isolationism vs. trade).
- *Supporting gaming communities.* Participating in a community transformed students' experience from focusing on their game, to studying games, to

understanding the underlying game model. This positioned players as each being expert in different areas of the game (playing as Egypt vs. Iroquois) and enabled players to run specific experiments (e.g., exploring China) as modes of participation.

- *Facilitating inquiry.* The most useful teaching activities encouraged community by compiling data across games and comparing emergent patterns.

Framing learning as play invites transgression, experimenting with rules, and taking on new social identities (whether it be Tony becoming friends with Dwayne, or Dwayne becoming invested in school). We are now reconsidering this mode of learning in schools, although it may be older than school itself.

If games *can* be used in schools for learning, what kinds of experiences *should* students have? What kinds of games *should* we build? To think more deeply about these questions, we return to studying the aesthetics of games, specifically why they are engaging for players and what kinds of experiences they make available. This means leaving schools (briefly) and going back into the digital wild, trying to understand how people learn with games.

CHAPTER 7

The Aesthetics of Play

In 2003 (right when I entered the job market), most educators were deeply skeptical about video games. Teachers saw games as contributing to the problem, not the solution, of their classroom management woes. A handful of colleagues such as Elliot Soloway embraced studying games, updating how John Bransford (Cognition and Technology Group at Vanderbilt, 1990), Roger Schank (1993), and their colleagues created problem-based learning environments and goal-based scenarios using laser discs and CD-ROMs. But those were the exceptions that proved the rule.

Then I met James Paul Gee. He asked me, "Designing games is fine, but do you have any interest in studying games *on their own terms?* What about studying game *cultures* for insights on how to *change* schools?"

I paused. "Umm. Yes?" I answered. "In fact, I was just playing *Animal Crossing*. It's the perfect family game. It's like a massively multiplayer asynchronous game. It's reshaping how families play together."

Jim's smile got bigger. We started talking about *Animal Crossing*, *Pokémon*, *Deus Ex* . . . Jim wasn't concerned about shoehorning games into schools. He wanted to ask how digital media might *change* schools.

Gee's approach is based in literacy. He asks not just how we can use new media to reach old educational goals, but how media such as books, film, or games can *transform* how we learn and what we value as a society. Chapter 4 opened this discussion, and this chapter explores it in depth, asking:

- How might games *change* content-area instruction, and what is worth teaching in a digital, participatory age?
- How do contemporary games function aesthetically? What does this mean for learning?
- How are gaming communities organized, and are they models for designing game-based learning organizations?

The bulk of the chapter is driven by two studies: an analysis of *Viewtiful Joe*, a contemporary action-adventure game, and an ethnography of Apolyton University, an online community of *Civilization* players. Implicitly, the chapter argues for crossing back and forth between basic and applied research and between studying games "in the wild" and designing educational ones so as to stay relevant in a fast-changing field.

GAMES, LEARNING, SOCIETY: BUILDING A PROGRAM

Jim said I should study games and gaming cultures, but as an untenured faculty member in education, I was skeptical. Educational technology journals were largely interested in issues around "scalability" and "scientific research on learning" and seemed unlikely to publish analyses of video games or gaming cultures. Game studies had a fledgling community (Digital Games Research Association) with one annual conference (DiGRA) and a journal (*Game Studies*). This interdisciplinary group was largely based in the humanities. Would studying video games be the end of my career, as some colleagues hinted?

Luckily, Jim's book, *What Video Games Have to Teach Us About Literacy and Learning* (Gee, 2003), offered a singular, coherent vision for how and why games were important and opened doors for me and others to walk through. Overnight, conference organizers, book and journal editors, and professional groups started looking for research on games. Everyone from librarians to teachers wanted to know what games were about.

We imagined an integrated initiative, which we called Games + Learning + Society (GLS), that would research what games mean for learning, how to design game-based learning environments, and how organizations need to change in the digital age. We became a university research and development group, rather than an academic department, so as to stay interdisciplinary and cross-institutional. Technology research is tough to do if you are sequestered in your office, and access to educators, media developers, and policy makers is critical to staying current. Understanding games requires knowledge in visual art, computer science, cognitive psychology, architecture, and animation, to name a few areas.

We started, though, by simply gaming together. Game players, scholars, and designers (particularly from Raven Studios) came from all over Madison to our little arcade tucked away in the school of education. When *WoW* launched, we, like many gamers, took those gaming nights online.

THE AESTHETICS OF GAME-BASED LEARNING

Informal conversations can lead to more formalized research studies. Dan Norton (who has since cofounded his own games company, Filament Games) and I discussed how few educational games actually required a player to *master* something in order for him or her to claim to be *good* at the game.

Dan had become interested in amusing failure states—design elements such as explosions or humor which serve to increase motivation—and how that idea could be applied to educational games.[1] In *Playing to Win*, game designer and theorist David Sirlin (2000) writes about these skill-based games as competitive games, meaning that they can support robust competition among players. If the key to educational games is making *game play* and the *learning goals* one and the same, then we had to understand how game *play* produces learning. So-called mindless fighting games are a great place to look for deep gaming mastery.

Ninja Gaiden and *Viewtiful Joe*, like all hardcore games (see In Defense of the Hardcore sidebar) reward learning in not so subtle ways. Jim Gee was lionizing *Ninja Gaiden* to anyone who would listen, particularly how the boss levels (i.e., the climactic confrontations with the powerful enemies that guard each level's end) functioned as "tests" for the players, requiring them to master key moves (see Gee, 2007). *Viewtiful Joe* (see Figure 7.1), an action-fighting game released in 2003 for the GameCube, was similarly difficult, and I wanted to analyze how it was designed for mastery.

So I committed many days and nights to mastering *Viewtiful Joe*. The first striking thing was the primacy on *doing* as opposed to *telling*. Getting good at the game involves exploring, trying, and practicing, but not much text or verbalizing. In contrast, schools value very little of exploring or doing, but emphasize learning a lot of decontextualized words. It doesn't matter whether you have a declarative knowledge of *Viewtiful Joe*'s 14 moves or their strategic significance. What matters is that you *use* them appropriately. We learn through increasingly complex cycles of trial and error. *Viewtiful Joe* doesn't start with complex explanations of the game's controls; it starts by describing two commands (A = jump; Y= punch), and then it lets players figure out their meaning. You learn the reach of a kick or its strength by *doing* it rather than by reading complex descriptions. This model of knowing

---

1. Will Wright's games do this well. He knows that making failure fun motivates players to persevere. Whether it's an enormous explosion, a cinematic cut scene, or humorous deathbed dialogue, "after-death" events punctuate action and encourage trying again. This is a great example of an idea educators can "steal" from game designers even if the teacher never makes a game.

is a *functional*, or *pragmatic*, way of knowing, because we make meaning through interacting directly with the world and observing our actions' consequences.

For fun, I mapped out the combinations of moves and tactics for confronting one boss, Hulk Davidson, a cross between the Incredible Hulk and a biker-looking dude (for an abbreviated character analysis, see Table 7.1). There isn't anything unusual about Hulk. He has 7 moves he can make against Joe (you), and Joe has 14 moves (which are gradually unlocked as the game unfolds) he can use to defeat Hulk.

It sounds easy enough. Hulk is big and slow, so you might imagine attacking him as a bumble bee would attack a bigger foe: "Get a few hits in then run away." Rinse, then repeat.

This strategy is completely wrong. But first, to make an obvious observation, button mashing gets you nowhere. Push random stuff and you die fast. This is why *Viewtiful Joe*, as a hardcore game, may not have sold 2 billion copies, but is great for learning. It asks more of the player. You need to study Hulk's every move to understand what he's doing and how it interacts with your capacities.

Successful players see patterns in the movements, which can be thought of as game states (Hulk is charging, swinging his ax, and so on). Comparing the odds of success across these states, a pattern emerges: Fighting Hulk up close works best. This seems counterintuitive because he has a very big ax that you instinctively want to avoid. However, when you stand far away, Hulk throws the ax at you, causing it to fly off screen unpredictably. Not knowing where the ax is means losing control of the action, losing the ability to anticipate and direct the flow of events. Joe *controls* the flow when he's close.

**Figure 7.1.
Viewtiful Joe and
Hulk Davidson, from
*Viewtiful Joe***

In Defense of the Hardcore

So-called hardcore game mechanics are currently out of vogue. *WoW* succeeded commercially in part because it removed "hardcore" features from the genre. If you die, you lose a little time, but not much else. Players don't risk losing items like Nate, Eric, and I did in Avatar (see Chapter 3).

Yet our goal in education is facilitating learning and creating meaningful experiences for players to take with them. In fact, hardcore mechanics, which require deep time commitments, specialized knowledge, and sacrifice among players, all support learning.

We might even say that education has always been a game with "hardcore mechanics." In fact, the rules of school are often so hardcore that even the most brutal video game is docile in comparison. You have one and only one chance at taking a test. School has "permadeath." If your school identity is tarnished or trashed, there are few paths to recovery.

Educational game designers shouldn't attempt to recreate the hardcore mechanics of school. However, certainly we can embrace some of the mechanics that are employed so wonderfully in MUDs or earlier games that have been cast aside in the name of "broadening markets."

Table 7.1. *Viewtiful Joe* **States**

Situation	Heuristic	Salient
Hulk is off screen	Get closer to Hulk.	You have few ways to attack, and Hulk can throw his ax, which is hard to see. Hulk can also shoot white rockets, which initiates fire. Fighting closely, you can dodge attacks without breaking Hulk's shield.
3 seconds without action or signs of Hulk Davidson	Enter slow motion.	Hulk rarely goes more than 3 seconds without performing a move, and the distance moves (i.e., ax throwing) usually take 3–4 seconds to arrive. Entering slow motion has little cost and allows dodging.
When Hulk charges	Jump to platform to dodge; jump down, use Hot 100.	Hulk is stunned and takes damage; works reliably and is repeatable (leads back to ax swing/jump sequence). Thus, the player wants to be in situations where Hulk is likely to charge.

The game mechanics, which *force you to scrap like a real hero*, reflect the aesthetic genius of *Viewtiful Joe*. I loathed fighting Hulk like this, particularly in my tiny little body (I prefer to play ranged characters), but the game forced me to master complex moves. *Viewtiful Joe* employs similar techniques throughout the game. For example, a previous boss involves fighting your twin, who has all the same moves that you have, forcing you to look in the mirror and reflect your own strengths and weaknesses as an opponent. It's brilliant design.

The next logical move is to beat on Hulk's ax. Try this and you learn that Hulk's ax can be destroyed. This seems good! However, once his ax is destroyed, the sky rains fire. Hulk starts running around and stomping crazily, which sends you also running around in circles trying to avoid him and the fire. Trust me, you'd rather have Hulk keep his ax. Each boss monster tests players. The basic monsters teach players basic skills. Mini-bosses require combining those skills, and then the main bosses (such as Hulk) ensure mastery by requiring players to *apply* those skills in unique situations (such as fighting up close). Subsequent levels use the "normal" levels as practice problems, with the bosses functioning as tests.

AESTHETICS OF BEING *VIEWTIFUL JOE*

The aesthetics of *Viewtiful Joe* hold critical lessons for understanding games as art or for education. As I struggled through difficult or repetitive levels, I found myself asking, "Why do I want to do this?" For us as educators, there may be no more crtitical question that we can ask: how might we inspire students to commit to learning *academic content* with the same sort of vigor?

Entrainment[2]

Part of the joy of *Viewtiful Joe* is in the activity of playing. There is a rhythmic quality to how *Viewtiful Joe* works when you are in the flow—the careful timing of moves, the beat and rhythm to the fight. This is partly why we think of video games as being inherently pleasurable (much like playing catch or knitting). Indeed, almost every action game has a rhythm. Try playing a shooter like *Quake* and juxtaposing different soundtracks behind it to see how different rhythms capture

---

2. This is an extension of a concept explored by Brian Moriarty in his visual essay, "Entrainment" (1998)."

different games. These rhythms capture different moods, a concept explored more fully in polyrhythm (see Polyrhythm sidebar). Indeed, rhythm-action games from *Guitar Hero* to *Rock Band* are all about this rhythm-based play (see feature essay at the end of this chapter).

Polyrhythm

In *Arcadia*, developed by GameLab (led by designer/theorist Eric Zimmerman), players tackle four games at once, each game based on classic Atari-style games. Each game is a random selection of four mini-games played simultaneously in one fourth of the screen. Each game has the core elements of its ancestor, but strips play down to a single mouse click. Mixing and matching games like *Pong* and *Mario Brothers* creates an entirely new game experience, particularly when they are stitched together to maximize flow.

The most instructive aspect of *Arcadia* may be its play with rhythm. Each mini-game has its own rhythm, and as each new game is added, layer upon layer of rhythm is added until the game becomes truly polyrhythmic. In music, a polyrhythm is different rhythms played simultaneously. In polyrhythm, underlying rhythms are relatively prime to each other; if picked apart, their basic beats and patterns do not match up. *Arcadia* teaches us that in addition to story and character, games are deeply rhythmic experiences.

In action games, there is a secondary benefit to such rhythmic play: We become *entrained* to the *timing* of the game system. Moves take specific time durations to complete, characters move at particular speeds, spaces (i.e., rooms) take fixed durations of time to explore. Games are balanced with each of these variables in relation to one another. In a game like *WoW* this explains a function of grinding (killing monsters over and over). Through grinding, players become entrained with the rhythms and timing of the game system. For example, in *WoW*, grinding helps the timing of the *cooldowns*, the period of time after using a skill or spell in which the player must wait before using it again (which varies from .5 seconds to 6 seconds for most skills). After hours of grinding, the timing of these moves becomes instinctual. In chaotic situations in which the player must *improvise*, the player can respond *instinctively*, reaching for the right move at just the right time without having to worry about whether the cooldown is up.

The Fantasy of Being Expert

I also wanted to be the first in our group to beat *Viewtiful Joe*. A great pleasure of gaming is becoming an *expert*, developing dozens of commands to have at your disposal, and being recognized as such socially. Each term, I poll my class about what games they have gotten good at and why, and invariably everyone describes games that they play socially. Games are like sports in this way: We practice for hours and hours and bust them out for the "big game." When everything falls into place—the problem is just beyond our skills, but we reach for that special move and pull something off that we maybe didn't even know was possible—we have a memorable moment.

To illustrate, one of my most memorable gaming moments in *WoW* didn't directly involve me at all but my friend Trevor Owens. Trevor, a druid, was healing in Molten Core. There was an amazing moment in which the tank character whom Trevor was healing was about to die. Trevor spontaneously, and against every rule of raiding, swapped out weapons and popped into his "bear" form, becoming the tank. He "grabbed" aggro from the old tank (i.e., he taunted the boss to hit *him* instead of the old tank). Over the next few minutes, chaos ensued. What on Earth was he doing? Trevor quietly reassured us that it was alright, and he proceeded to tank the boss and save the raid. Trevor's completely unorthodox move made him the hero.

But even in the single-player scenario there is a deep pleasure in the experience of *being* expert. It's rewarding to develop and use skills, and for video gamers, oftentimes this involves reading and manipulating complex information flows (like the moment-to-moment moves of Hulk Davidson). We seek out more and more challenging experiences with every game.

Flow

Mihaly Csikszentmihalyi's theory of flow (1990) describes this trajectory of expertise well. Csikszentmihalyi argues that humans engage in a pleasing state of "flow" when their abilities are perfectly matched with challenges. When challenges are too easy, we are bored. When they are too difficult, we are frustrated. Game designers have a variety of techniques to keep players in "flow" states. One such technique is leveling out skill levels through purchasing equipment. In *Viewtiful Joe*, every time the player beats a monster, he or she gains currencies to purchase power-ups. A weaker player might struggle for the first few levels but then gain more currency to purchase power-ups so that the levels become easier. This simple technique autobalances the game and provides incentive to try again after failing (because of the increased power).

Csikszentmihalyi describes three conditions for flow: having a balance between challenge and skills, constantly having a goal, and receiving immediate feedback on that goal. Good games sequence levels to create a contract with the player that helps induce this flow. Goals are always apparent. The game always provides feedback on where players are in relation to those goals. Challenges never go beyond the players' skills. The game might demand that players *stretch* skills, which, as Gee (2003) noted, provides a sense of being "difficult but fair." In a good game, the action is difficult, but players feel that they know what they did wrong or right (sufficient feedback) and that they have the tools to do better next time.

Flow describes how and why we choose various difficulty levels in games. Sometimes, we want to experience *control*, so we look for comforting games beneath our skill level. Solitaire is the classic example of this. We all know how solitaire games end, but solitaire is great for giving our hands and mind something to do while we think about other things. Grinding in MMOs (massively multiplayer onlines) functions similarly, although there's also a pleasure in revisiting skills we've mastered.

Amplification of Input

A central idea of good game design (explored by Stephen Poole in *Trigger Happy*, 2000) is that the player's actions should be *amplified*. Players do a small thing, and they see big effects. This amplification need not always be violent. Not to knock explosions (after all, they are kinda cool), but there are many ways to achieve similar effects, and it's often the amplification of input and sensory experience we crave. Take *Okami*, for example, a game in which the player is a wolf helping characters save the world. One of *Okami*'s key moves is healing cherry blossom trees. When a level is sufficiently healed, explosions of pink cherry blossoms fill the screen. Who knew that planting trees and flowers could be made as exciting as blowing stuff up? Jenova Chen's *Flower* operates similarly, as players guide flower petals through fields, bringing life to dreary lands.

Orchestrating small actions on screen that have large consequences is particularly compelling. Players love setting up situations to create big impact. Simulated world games illustrate this. In games like *Thief, Deus Ex, Bioshock*, or *Splinter Cell: Chaos Theory*, the experience isn't so much about being told a story as it is about being enabled to tell one's *own* story (a concept Doug Church, 2000, called *abdicating authorship*). Clint Hocking (a UbiSoft developer) explained how this works in a 2009 Game Developer's Conference presentation. Hocking showed a player-created video from *Splinter Cell: Chaos Theory*, a Tom Clancy espionage game. The sequence begins with a government agent boasting to the player, "Who does this guy think he's dealing with? Amateurs?" before charging toward the player. The agent kicks down a door, but an explosion is set off, causing the agent to fall down an elevator shaft to his death. The player used his knowledge of nine game mechanics and 36 interconnected relationships between those mechanics. The player had to understand the underlying artificial intelligence of the guard in order to trigger the guard to taunt the player and kick down the door. The player also had to understand the game's physics so as to know how to catapult the guard down the shaft. Plus, he had to set up the cameras to "film" the whole thing.

This example is fun because there's little in the actual game that would have predicted it. The game play on screen is an interaction between the game system as a narrative engine and the player's goals. The player isn't simply replaying a designed narrative, but using the narrative elements to play the game. Remove any one of these capacities (especially the arrogant agent), and it cannot happen. But overlapping systems with potential narrative moments enables the player to play creatively. This sort of interaction (as simple as it is) is a goal of interactive narrative within game design. How do we create the *educational* contexts so that players create their own interesting experiences in academic domains?

Narrative and Satisfying Experiences

This returns us to *narrative* in games. Narrative works in many ways in games, although sometimes games' quest for legitimacy may lead us to compare them with more traditional media such as literature and film, rather than to focus on the games' uniqueness. For example, games are really good at producing feelings of guilt. In the opening of *Deus Ex*, the player is handed a Taser and a "real" gun and told to rescue hostages being held in the Statue of Liberty. The player is instructed to avoid killing anyone if possible. Upon entering the statue, the player learns that the captors may have been the "good guys" after all. On the way back down the stairs, the player passes by the bodies he or she killed through carelessness. Because *you the player* were actually *responsible* for what happened, there's a deep feeling of guilt in games like this that is hard to produce in other media. Pride and accomplishment are other emotions produced better through games than other media.

Games employ narrative techniques to produce these emotions. In *Viewtiful Joe*, for example, narrative devices poke fun at the player when he or she loses, creating *amusing failure states* to remind the player that it is just a game. Next, the encouraging narrative intercedes to remind the player that "Joe must go on." Throughout *Viewtiful Joe*, the player is encouraged to *become* Viewtiful Joe, a character *who will not quit* despite any odds. With every battle, the dialogue is constructed to reinforce that identity.

What commits players to learning *5, 10,* or *20* hours into a game? Drew Davidson took on this question in a series of articles analyzing *Prince of Persia* (2008) and *World of Goo* (n.d.). Davidson describes the process as transitioning from player *immersion* to *investment*. *World of Goo*, for example, uses stories to help guide players through portions of game play in which the skill curve flattens. An interest in resolving a plot line or identifying with characters motivates us to complete the game.

Layering Davidson's framework of *why* we play on top of a trajectory of how video game expertise develops, we can better understand *how* and *why* players are motivated to reach each new phase of gaming. Players are frequently drawn into games through curiosity about the subject matter or because their peers are playing the game, but they must become *involved* to develop mastery over its lexicon. Involvement is produced by many different factors, ranging from the social (participation in a group) to an interest in exploring the game's system. As the case study of *Civ* players in Chapter 6 suggests, one game might appeal to five different players for different reasons, and involvement is inherently a coupling between the player's goals and interests and the game's capacities. Investment is when we are committed to seeing through an experience to its conclusion (promoted by narrative completion, or the completion of long-term goals). The most advanced stages of game expertise are profoundly social and are explored more fully in the next section.

APOLYTON UNIVERSITY: TRAJECTORIES OF PARTICIPATION

If many games are about the aesthetics of being an expert and having an impact on the world, then do game communities function similarly? How do gaming cultures promote expertise?

Let's consider Apolyton University, an online "university" of gamers. To understand how I enrolled in Apolyton University, we need to go back to the spring of 2004. I was discussing my dissertation research with Soren Johnson, lead designer of *Civ4*. I was arguing for the changes I'd make, ranging from clearer feedback to a greater emphasis on peaceful win states. "Don't cut things out," I told them. "Make the game smoother, more learnable."

Soren jumped in. "Well, that's what we're doing," he said, and explained how the *Civ* developers were going with a "global" theme and playing the game on a sphere, rather than flat map.[3] I couldn't believe it. It was like talking with Mick Jagger and Keith Richards between *Sticky Fingers* and *Exile on Main Street*.

---

3. As you might imagine, this led to robust arguments about map projections within *Civ* communities.

"Have you looked into Apolyton.net?" Soren asked. Indeed I had. I built on their scenarios in my dissertation. "Great. It's one of the most sophisticated gaming communities I've seen."

> I would like to propose a new group effort. We should do experiments, like Aeson's iceberg, Arrian's UP™, Sir Ralph's effort to create WWIII, etc. I also think it will be useful to start developing a more advanced lexicon for strategies, tactics, and exploits. We've been doing that informally, but it will make life a lot easier for new players. (Theseus)

With this comment posted on Apolyton.net, Theseus launched Apolyton University, an online school of strategy where students sharpen their *Civ3* skills and share their experiences in a series of thematic games. I'm pretty good at *Civ*, but I wouldn't even be a B student at Apolyton. Hundreds of players were designing custom games, holding tournaments, and writing *courses*.

Theseus was motivated by a desire to learn. He was already good at *Civ* (expertise), but he wanted to get sharper, because learning is enjoyable (interest-driven learning). Theseus emphasized that the school would produce *new* knowledge, such as a war academy, in addition to enculturating newcomers in a boot camp. Theseus's two metaphors, "boot camp" and "war college" are instructive (if you can live with their military roots) in that learning requires both occasions for creating common, shared understandings as well as a context for developing and testing new understandings. This second function—producing *new* knowledge— is something that we do too infrequently in educational games or in classrooms.

I showed Apolyton University to Levi Giovanetto, a graduate student who had played *Civ* with his dad since he was 6 years old. We enrolled, played its games, took its courses, and studied its participants (for the full study, see Squire & Giovanetto, 2008). The first thing we experienced is that learning online can be *deeply* personal. It was unnerving to put our knowledge on display so publicly. The school itself was open—inviting, even. Theseus posited a set of values for the school:

> When playing an Apolyton University game, gaining and sharing knowledge is more important than getting a high score, or even winning the game. Participants are encouraged to share their strategy after the game, and even to try several attempts.

It was exciting participating in a culture in which we were *supposed* to admit what we didn't know, ask questions, and keep trying until we got it right. This ethos builds on natural gaming practices such as debriefing, but is different from gaming cultures that privilege elitist, or "1337," discourse that is openly hostile to newcomers.[4] The point of Apolyton was learning, plain and simple. How many *schools* can even claim to live by this principle?

Courses soon formed, ranging from Give Peace a Chance, designed to teach players the diplomatic system, to The One City Challenge, challenging players to win with only one city (see Table 7.2). Each course features a downloadable game. Students play, take notes, and post them as "During Action Reports." At the time of our analysis, Apolyton University consisted of 19,302 posts by 74 registered members with perhaps another 100 lurkers (estimated through analyses of the number of "reads" per post). Participants monitor the forums fairly closely; the median response time for feedback was between 2 and 5 hours.

As courses piled up, the university formed a curriculum committee. The committee reviewed course submissions, identified subjects lacking coverage, and researched best practices. They also became responsible for the official "best of the best" game mod, which was the most well-balanced version of the game they could make. Building an official mod encouraged synthesis and oriented the school toward a common form of knowledge production.

How does this content creation system contrast to those in schools? In school students and faculty rarely gather to *make* anything. When we do (e.g., to a school parade float), it's rarely tied to academic learning. Curricular decision making is centralized and is being pushed farther away from teachers (let alone students!) and toward the federal government. In Apolyton, curricular decision making is *entirely* open, both in terms of *who* can participate and in *how* the curriculum is determined. Students are *encouraged* to post new courses, ideas for future courses, criticisms on existing courses, and suggestions to the canon. If you want to know why a course isn't in the canon, look it up or, better yet, make your own. It isn't that *expertise* is devalued; rather, expertise is recognized through *accomplishment*.

DURING-ACTION REPORTS:
COGNITIVE ARTIFACTS THAT ORGANIZE PRACTICE

During Action Reports (DARs) became a central community practice. A DAR begins with a *recap* to help the reader understand the player's goals, motivations, and thinking. Next, the player crafts *narrative*, interweaving actions, goals, and interpretations

---

4. 1337, or "elite" speak is a style of written communication that originated in bulletin board systems in the 1980s and filtered into online gaming discourse as a way to convey status.

Table 7.2. Sampling of Apolyton University Courses

Course Number	Course Title	Author
AU 101	Crowding and War	Theseus
AU 102	All We're Sayin' Is Give Peace a Chance	Alexman
AU 302	OCC (One City Challenge)	Dominae
AU 502	Celtic Power—Swords and Ploughshares	Ducki

of the game's underlying model. The post ends with descriptive statistics about his or her civilization, which other players use as raw data for comparisons. Discussing DARs puts participants simultaneously in the role of student, teacher, and researcher.

These DARs function as *cognitive artifacts* to coordinate game play across time and place. I might be playing in Madison, Wisconsin, in January 2005, whereas another player may be playing in Greece in the fall of 2007. Through DARs, we can play together. Studying multiple games can give *me* insights, such as that I build my cities too far apart. The following post by Aqualung sums it up: "Wow! I think I'm finally starting to learn this game!"

Later, Aqualung analyzed another colleague's game and provided in-depth feedback. This feedback was similar to mini-lectures I gave *Civ* players at MATCH, but because Apolyton players all shared the *same* game, everyone had an intimate knowledge of the problem space and the resulting feedback was more specific. A post by Aqualung illustrates:

> With a granary, Delhi can spit out a Settler every 4 turns or a Worker every 2. I'd also suggest a few Warriors, which may prevent that AI Persian Warrior from declaring war on a Civ with 4 cities and not a single military unit! I see you've got another Settler heading out to capture the dyes. Next town should probably be near the flood plains to keep growth moving along, which helps with commerce.

It's tough to understand what he's talking about if you aren't playing that specific scenario. Playing the same game is powerful because players receive context-specific expert feedback. Alan Collins and others (1989) call this *cognitive apprenticeship*, which is a powerful arrangement for learning because players gain access to experts' reflection-on-action. *Learning* and *thinking* become the object of activity. Through DARs, participants' game play—and the thinking that goes into it—became visible.

Soon, the community identified effective strategies, such as "rapid expansion" (shortened to "REXing"), which means creating many cities early on at the expense of everything else. Rapid expansion encompasses smaller concepts such as "settler pumps" (cities that pump out new settlers and hence, new cities). These ideas started through narratives in DARs, were codified into particular terminology (REXing, settler pumps), and then were employed to analyze games. Knowledge in this way was a tool for understanding.

Watching people generate new knowledge was exciting, and I realized how infrequently I (either as a teacher or researcher) had seen students create *new* knowledge. At Apolyton, it happened routinely, through new vocabulary, courses, and mods. Rapidly generating knowledge created an original, even cryptic lexicon. See if you can make heads or tales out of this post:

> Unlike everyone else I didn't road the silks . . . but game/forest to the north, as my playstyle usually means researching hard and prioritising trade roads early on. I wouldn't need the silk just yet, but I wanted the income ASAP, and obviously wanted to work the game tile. Nor did I start with barracks and warriors, but with a warrior-warrior-settler, planning on a Ralph-style archer rush from 4 cities.

Anyone who could "read" this post understands *Civ* from the perspective of this community. Simply parsing a post required background knowledge of *Civ*'s mechanics, the community's history, and what they value as important. Some concepts like the Eternal China Syndrome are unique to how this group thinks about the game, but others, like culture flipping (engaging in cultural warfare so that a civilization's people identify with a new culture more than the one that is currently in power) are more transparent.[5] One real-world example of culture flipping is the United States' strategy to win the "hearts and minds" of Iraqis so that they embrace American democratic politics, free trade capitalism, and liberal social policies.

If you find Apolyton posts hard to read, you see the problem with textbooks, particularly with how they fail to help us understand *why* something is important. Knowledge is created in action, and as we attempt to transport it to others, it becomes cryptic. Even more important, we lose an appreciation for why that

---

5. Eternal China Syndrome refers to how *Civ* models every civilization as if it were an "Eternal China," one unified civilization starting in 4000 BC and continuing for 6,000 years. The community was dissatisfied with this, and some members attempted to create mods to rectify it, but the general problem as outlined by the developers remained: It's hard to create easily understandable and workable game mechanics with splintering civilizations.

knowledge is even worth knowing. As a result, most students just accept that they are supposed to memorize and regurgitate it for a test.

In response to this growing, changing body of knowledge, the Apolyton community developed a handbook. One participant, Lemmy, saw that posts were becoming impenetrable and that there was a need for a compendium of terms and strategies—a dictionary of sorts. Before long, they nominated an official "dean" to accommodate the growing number of courses, students, and materials. Apolyton was becoming institutionalized.

Notice that Apolyton didn't create a list of important terms and concepts as a prerequisite for enrollment. Instead they honor a principle that James Paul Gee (2007) calls "performance before mastery": It's difficult to comprehend specialized texts until you've been immersed in situations where they are useful. First start playing the game. Then post your game. Then start reading. When you are in the middle of a game, these posts make total sense. But before you've ever played it, it's not worth trying to understand. Gee notes that a problem in secondary schools is that we give people the book before they are ever allowed to play the game.

DESIGN THINKING

So what did our *Civ* participants learn? After studying posts, interviewing players, and reflecting on our learning, Levi and I developed the trajectory of game expertise introduced in Chapter 2 (see Figure 2.3). The process began with newcomers' entering the community as *competent* players. A novice player knew *Civ*'s terminology and understood their meaning as a result of playing for hours, meaning that they had mastered the controls and had basic knowledge of the game's vocabulary. Most were highly skilled, *invested* players looking for more.

The Apolyton community pushed players to *systemic thinking* as they explored new game *systems*, similar to how I directed the MATCH school students (although Apolyton's games were played at a higher difficulty-level setting). Most players depended on particular strategies (military, science, or diplomatic victory), and the community pushed them to explore new game systems (identifying and transcending exploits). In order to enforce this strategic thinking, the community identified and fixed broken rules in their best-of-the-best mod. Creating a best-of-the-best mod involved changing rules, the next step along the trajectory of expertise.

The next phase of understanding could be described as *design* thinking. The "best of the best" mod was crucial for encouraging tinkering among players. Interestingly, this mod also required some semblance of staying true enough to history, which required players to think in more broad *design* terms.[6] In advanced courses, players create unique mods that illuminate relationships, which gets at designing *rule systems*. As players tinkered with and created rules for participation, they engaged in the design of social systems, creating the social context of play. This form of play is similar to how Janet Kretschmer and the McGuffey students designed levels, areas, and experiences in the MUD environment (described in Chapter 3).

We interviewed players to see how this design thinking might transfer elsewhere. The following excerpt with Steve, a 20-year-old American male and a typical participant, suggests how *Civ3* mediates players' thinking:

Interviewer: Do you ever draw comparisons between current events and *Civ*?
Steve: Yes. In *Civ3*, stronger cultures make it harder to occupy other countries. We already saw the golden age of America—that's behind us now. There is a *Civ3* term: Golden Age.

Steve immediately uses *Civ*'s concept of culture to think about contemporary military occupations. Steve believes that the United States was in a golden age (an age in which its actions correspond with its values and strengths) but no longer is. He returned to current events, particularly the Iraq War (interview conducted in 2004):

The situation in Iraq might flip back to the Baath Party, flip back to its original owner. But in some ways our culture is very strong. Go to Europe and see our commercial products. Capitalism—that's the American culture—that mindset. In *Civ3* terms, the American mindset is influencing so much of the world that basically we've won a cultural victory already. You know how in the *Civ3* city screen, they still retain their identity of being Iraqi, but they're a part of our culture? We want to give them an American mindset, an American ideology. Like a cultural outpost, you're building all the cultural buildings.

---

6. How they think about this balance is interesting. The primacy in Apolyton to some extent is game balance. However, some adherence to historical rules is required; you don't see people adding implausible features. There may be a belief that history itself is a well-balanced game, and what *Civ* players do is interpret it.

Steve's comments illustrate how the "meanings" of *Civ itself* are fluid. *Civ* (and its encompassing community) provides a set of representations (like food and production, but also culture flipping) that Steve uses for his analysis. Much as Dan didn't blindly accept *Civ*'s model of colonialism, Steve doesn't simply adopt the game's model, or even an interpretation gleaned from a community. Rather, he draws upon it as a flexible resource to analyze history. *Civ* gave Steve a symbol system and interconnected set of rules to analyze historic questions.[7]

"I actually learned a lot more history and geography through *Civ3*. I will probably learn more through scenario design and *Civ3* than I will in this class because it's so basic to me." Steve had recently built a historical Rome scenario, and was sharing it with his professor. Steve enjoyed playing through content pertaining to his academic work. Maybe it's good that a fully customizable version of *Civ* wasn't available when I was in college; I may not have graduated.

By having such flexibility in their rule sets, games give players substantial degrees of freedom in interpretation—particularly as players become accustomed to modifying the underlying rules to meet their fancy. To a player like Steve, *Civ* is a *game* to play, a *framework* to think with, and a *toolset* to author with. *Civ* is most compelling educationally not for its accuracy as much as its allure for players who explore and revisit it over time.

Once players begin modding, the ways that *Civ* promotes and constrains certain ways of thinking become even more complex. A player creating a mod might use *Civ*'s underlying rules to model new phenomena, such as the rise and fall of Rome. They must consider how to take the game's systems and repurpose them. *Civ3* can't be used to simulate *everything*; it could never be used to simulate the interworking of the Roman Senate. A designer could model most prevailing theories, including the Sassanid (Iranian) threat, plague, crop failures, improper growth (causing political instability), and good, old-fashioned invasions. Yet Joseph Tainter's "diminishing returns on investments in social complexity" theory sounds tough to simulate with *Civ*, inasmuch as I even understand it. So a designer is ultimately locked into *Civ*'s grammar when using it as a model to think with, although it still can be used flexibly.[8]

---

7. Incidentally, Steve supported the war in Iraq, but not its execution. Within *Civ* communities, there was no dominant view toward the war in Iraq, nor was there any dominant political ideology.

8. I'm not suggesting that other media aren't interpreted differently. People read films and books differently, and sometimes authors or directors aren't sure how a story should be interpreted. But there is something profoundly different about games that create ways for players to experiment, draw conclusions, and make modifications to promote their own arguments.

Games function differently from other media in this regard (and perhaps are closer to fiction than to nonfiction). Books typically tell stories or make arguments. Films typically tell a story from the point(s) of view of a character or characters. Games, in contrast set up *relationships among rules* that players *design* within. There is no one *Civ* game. Players play *Civ* multiple times at multiple time scales with multiple rule sets.

But could Apolyton really teach you to become a designer? Surely there's a difference between sitting in your living room arguing about the One City Challenge with random strangers on the Internet and *really* designing a game, right?

As it turns out, not really. Midway through a course, Apolyton was discussing the game's artificial intelligence. Out of nowhere, the AI programmer on *Civ3*, Soren Johnson, popped in to clarify a misconception. He then thread-jacked the discussion by challenging participants to decipher the algorithm behind barbarian uprisings (meant to simulate occurrences like the Mongolian horde).

As you might imagine, the place went nuts. About 75 posts followed in the next week. Players ran in-game experiments. Side topics spun off, including debates about the origin of the word *barbarian*. Finally, Soren declared DeepO, a German PhD student and AI programmer, the victor, as he had most closely deciphered the pattern (see Designing the Past sidebar).

Designing the Past

All *Civ* players love to hate barbarians, the bane of early civilization existence. The algorithmic trigger for barbarian uprisings was, as Johnson explains, "the second time a civ entered a new age (once for the Middle Ages, once for the Industrial Age, once for the Modern Age). The intention was to basically simulate the barbarian hordes that knocked out Rome and (to a lesser degree) the Mongols. This made a little more sense back when barbarians were more destructive, but having half your civ knocked out for seemingly random reasons was deemed not much fun. Instead, we flipped the concept around and gave a temporal bonus (the Golden Age) instead of a temporal penalty." This is an illuminating example of how designers wrestle with historical modeling (how to create barbarian uprisings) and entertainment (no one enjoys random penalties) in a manner that yields a reasonably realistic, yet satisfying, play experience. See playthepast.org for a lively community of educators who are exploring these issues.

DESIGNING *CIV4*

The claim that "to participate in Apolyton is to become a designer" soon became very real. As we were completing the study, Apolyton University was dying but we couldn't figure out why. One day, Levi rushed into my office with the following data point from a veteran participant:

Interviewer: Do you think Apolyton University will jump to *Civ4*?
Jacko: Yes, certainly, but as so many veteran members of AU are on the beta test team, maybe we won't have to do much modding. I will definitely help to test the mod, although I doubt I will be able to help with the modding.

What was that, "So many veteran members of AU are on the beta test team"? Soren Johnson, instigator of that AI experiment, had been promoted to lead developer on *Civ4*. One of his first moves was to recruit Apolyton's leaders to participate in a "closed beta test program." Johnson wanted Apolyton and *Civ*fanatics players to test *Civ4* before the game came out so that it would be as tight as possible.

Luckily, our research team discovered this early enough to get in on the action. We spent the next summer playing *Civ4*, scouring it for loopholes, imbalances, and weak points. Over 100 gamer-testers were included in the credits of *Civ4*. Three modders were hired by Firaxis as full-time designers.

By treating players as designers, Firaxis recognized that communities such as Apolyton know infinitely more than a handful of designers. This relationship between knowledge and communities suggests a formal realization of Pierre Levy's (1997) notion of *collective intelligence*. Collective intelligence is the idea that in modern society knowledge is distributed among collectives, rather than in individual heads. Intelligent things are produced by collectives that apply their problem solving toward things of collective interest. The production of *Civilization 4* embodies this thinking. How do you most efficiently play-test a game with nearly infinite possibilities? Call in the collective.

As was explored in Chapter 3, online communities pose a challenge and an opportunity to education. Right now, a young kid interested in game design has access to game communities that are so robust that lead game developers themselves use them as a compass. Yet we design our classrooms as if all learning should flow through one teacher.

Apolyton University is unique in terms of its organization and professionalism, but it is indicative of how game communities work more broadly. Designer Raph

Koster has long noted how "official" MMO designers are a step behind the player communities in knowing the details of their game. Fan sites typically become the design bible. In *WoW*, the network of quasi-professionals is so robust that cottage industries have formed around them (e.g., sites like Thotbott collect data from players' games, aggregate it, and publish it for gamers to use when researching).

Such communities are a training ground for game design. In fact, it is common for amateurs to be hired by game companies. Famously, Warren Spector declared that he looks for new hires among the modding communities rather than in the stacks of résumés on his desk. Valve has hired, funded, and brought in high-profile modders (see McKenzie, in press). The online shooter *Counterstrike* was developed as an amateur mod, and, more recently, *Portal*, a *Half Life* mod, became a top-selling game. In MMOs, vocal, articulate fans are often hired as designers. Scott Jennings, who ran the blog *Rantings of Lumthemad*, was hired by Mythic Entertainment. Jeffrey Kaplan, a lead game designer at Blizzard, was hired based on his reputation as Tigole, a raid leader in *EverQuest*. Amateur *EverQuest* player Curt Schilling founded his game company, Green Monster Studios, to fulfill his vision for next-generation massively multiplayer games. However, that's a bit unusual, as he was more famous for being a Hall of Fame–caliber pitcher.[9]

This is why when former Electronic Arts exec Bing Gordon was asked, "How would you design a game for education?" he said, "To get an A in my class, you have to make something that people would actually use." We usually think of games as "separate" from reality, but studying game communities shows us that to play is to design, and social structures can guide people from being newbie designers to becoming experts. That's exactly the kind of trajectory that we want to promote in schools.

TOWARD AN AESTHETICS OF GAME-BASED LEARNING

Learning, game play, expertise, and social context are all intertwined. Games like *Viewtiful Joe* sell players the fantasy of becoming powerful superheroes who change the world. Communities like Apolyton thrive by letting people become experts and knowledge producers. They don't survive by selling players the fantasy of being incompetent, powerless, forced to follow arbitrary rules, and impotent in the world.

---

9. I do think that Schilling deserves to be in the Hall. In addition to his stellar World Series performances, the fact that he was never on steroids (we can be pretty sure) changes his numbers. Either way, he was one of the most memorable performers of his generation who came through in the clutch.

We need a discussion about the aesthetics of learning *in schools*. We too quickly devolve into debates about conservative versus liberal education, presented in the media as a choice between pandering to the whims of children and fulfilling their innate desires. In fact, aesthetics can be built into materials and experiences of all kinds. In Montessori, as discussed in Chapter 3, the simple pleasure of a well-built wooden toy is central to the system. Framing these questions as the aesthetics of experience encourages us to ask, What are the experiences everyone ought to have? What are the pleasures of learning in particular domains? How can we create meaningful intersections among students' learning goals, socially valued content, and social structures?

The aesthetics of games reminds us that learning—experiencing new ways of doing and being—is inherently engaging. Learning may even be most rewarding when it provides increased power within the world. Just as MMOs feel more consequential because we participate in real groups of real people, games that offer a powerful fantasy of *actually getting better at something that has social value* could lead to new experiences that blend learning and entertainment. What if games sold us the dream of actually making a difference in the world?

THEORY AND PRACTICE

This chapter began by asking, "How do games function?"

- *Video games give players experiences through which they explore having a dramatic impact on a world.* Video games provide well-crafted experiences through which players explore learning, being expert, and changing the world. It's ironic that video games sell youth themes of mastery, expertise, and knowledge and most school systems don't. As a simple test, how often do students have the opportunity to teach their teachers something? If students encounter more and more experiences of mastery and expertise outside school, they could become further alienated by schools.
- *Game communities can enable the experience of developing knowledge and even participate in legitimate activities that span across other social organizations and have real-world impact.* Participants at Apolyton developed, not just design knowledge, but also opportunities to engage in the practice of design. This design work eventually bled over into the design of the *Civilization* game itself. A key feature of educational games should be providing opportunities for players to rub elbows with experts in the context of doing complex, authentic activities. Participants might design *artifacts* such as *Civ* mods with experts,

but they also might design the social systems themselves (e.g., Apolyton University). Participatory communities expand students' *professional networks* way beyond what schools can do. Apolyton University enabled DeepO, despite living in Germany, to connect with Soren and the *Civ* team in Maryland.

- *If this blurring of lines between professional and amateur (pro-am) communities is indicative of broader trends (see Chapter 3), then educators face serious challenges to integrate such communities along with opportunities to break down classroom walls.* In almost *every* field, a novice can participate in communities of practice that lead toward authentic participation in complex activities. "Professionals" and "amateurs" work side by side, enabling enculturation into communities of practice (such as game design) and producing new knowledge.

- *Learning should blur distinctions between play and work.* Apolyton blurred play and work. People were able to take their life's love and turn it into their job. This same process is happening more and more often in participatory cultures (see Chapter 4). Whether it's Mike Pegram leaving his job to run a website about Indiana basketball or Lumthemad turning his passion for MMOs into a job designing them, this seems to be a predominant feature of the participatory age.

- *Learning, even in complex content areas, can be playful.* Thus far, we've avoided strictly defining *play*, as it is an ambiguous term.[10] There is something, however, about how these participants are following their passions that needs to be preserved or we'll lose what makes games special. There is something life enhancing and transformative about meaningful game play, and there is something playful about people's participation in such online communities. There is a playfulness about "fixing" one of the best video games ever developed, and there's something playful about "starting an online university to make people better video game players." There's something playful in the lead programmer's derailing the entire "university" by throwing down a challenge, and there's something playful about his later hiring these same people to work with him.

Apolyton has so many nifty features like During Action Reports that it's easy to

---

10. In the classic *The Ambiguity of Play*, Brian Sutton-Smith (2001) argues for the centrality of play in human experience, contending that play can be thought of in several ways. There are the ancient four, (a) fate, (b) power, (c) communal identity, and (d) frivolity, and the modern discourses of (e) progress, (f) imaginary, and (g) the self. The concept of "play" is often subsumed by the theoretical framework from which it originates. So, a Piagetian thinks about play as working through cognitively challenging and developmentally appropriate puzzles. A Vygotskian might emphasize how role-play prepares us for participation in social life.

lose sight of this playful spirit (or ludic stance). This same playfulness can be found in the McGuffey kids deciding to rewrite their school as a MUD or my dissertation participants adopting a logic of colonial imperialism to justify Native American expansion. Even if we never build a decent educational game, maybe we can interject this playfulness back into our conversations about education. Today's discussion has become so mired in the particulars of schooling (e.g., scalability, test scores, and teacher accountability) that the ethical dimensions of designing experiences for students seem to have been hopelessly lost. Games provide a playful new way forward.

As educators, we have fewer and fewer excuses for denying students opportunities to participate in professional or quasi-professional learning communities. This move toward participatory learning can happen via any number of digital media communities; recall that participatory learning occurs everywhere from sports to politics. In fact, Beck and Wade (2004) surveyed thousands of young workers and showed that gamers were more likely to prefer self-directed learning, experimentation and failure, and searching out experts on a topic. The following chapters explore our attempts to teach based on these ideas.

I LOVE ROCK 'N' ROLL

by Henry Jenkins and Kurt Squire

Ripping a power chord on a Les Paul through a Marshall stack can be transcendent, or at least the folks at Harmonix seem to think so. The high concept in Harmonix games is that "every person should have the experience of making music" and video game players have the basic skills (rhythm, timing, fine-motor skills, ability to rapidly process visual information) to be musicians.

The first trick is letting players achieve immediate successes. Adhering to the adage that players should experience new successes after 5 minutes, 15 minutes, and an hour seems to pay off. But it's not enough to just "feel" successful; it helps if you're *actually* learning. Fans of music games will notice that *they* added fourth and fifth buttons to the guitar controller in *Guitar Hero*. This enables the difficulty to progress. Medium difficulty introduces the fourth button (which requires you to use the pinky). Next comes the fifth button, which requires you to "shift" your hand into a second position.

Watch anyone play *Guitar Hero* and you notice the *performative* aspect game play. Cleverly, the game requires you to physically tilt the angle of the guitar, posing like a rock star in order to unlock bonus points. Part of the pleasure is impressing friends by nailing a tricky passage and stylistically posing with the guitar to unlock "star power."

Fine. You're getting better at clicking buttons at the right time, you're posing like Nigel Tufnel, but what makes this *musical*? Nonmusicians claim that the game teaches them to *listen*. By matching visual patterns to controller actions— and by requiring movements to *make* sounds—they isolate the guitar track from the rest of the song and tease out what the "real" guitar player is doing.

Other design features reinforce the musicality of the experience. The game rewards correctly playing "phrases" of notes, and players must learn *passages*, including the space between the notes. You're not playing "I Love Rock 'n' Roll" unless you can nail down the huge intro guitar riff.

Does *Guitar Hero* turn you into a real guitar player? No. But it may help people overcome a fear of making music and lead them toward picking up a real guitar. This is what games can do as art. They open new experiences to us that can provide trajectories into new ways of being in the world.

CHAPTER 8

Design Literacy: Productive Play

Even *I* was getting burnt out on *Civ*, but I was curious: Could an after-school *Civ* Club engender the design thinking showcased in Apolyton University? Levi and I soon recruited two more graduate students, Shree Durga and Ben DeVane, to build an Apolyton for kids struggling in school. These weren't "expert" players, but 5th and 6th graders, many of whom were African Americans from lower socioeconomic backgrounds. Our questions were

- Can we build educational environments based on participatory learning principles?
- What learning occurs through participating in them?

The impossible reality of trying to turn a dozen 8- to 14-year-olds into designers quickly smacked us in the face. In the entrance interview, I asked Morgan, "Would you like to learn game design?"

"No, it's too hard," he said. Marcus added, "No, that's not something I could do." These responses floored me. I'd worked with a lot of kids, but had never met a game player who didn't want to design games.

These were not the ruthlessly tech-savvy kids we hear about in the media. None could navigate a Windows file structure. In fact, the *most* technologically savvy student in the group once took a *Civ* CD-ROM home and couldn't figure out why his game wasn't saved on it. (Answer: because it saves on the computer hard drive.)

I asked Josh, one of the more academically inclined students, "Do you like school?"

He said, "I don't really like school, unless there's something fun going on. That's the only time there's actually something to do. You just sit there going . . ." (puts hand on head as if to sleep).

"How do you feel about social studies?" I asked. This answer was even better.

He said, "Social studies can be fun depending on what you're doing. Last year we made a mountain out of graham crackers and made it stick together out of frosting, and in the end we got to eat it." I sighed inside when I heard that, imagining the teacher struggling to inspire these kids. When we did pre-tests, not surprisingly, few could locate ancient civilizations or modern countries on a map.

We had a *long* way to go, but they took to *Civ* right away. Levi created a new mod based on the ancient Middle East to eliminate the issues that frustrated the new players we met in Chapter 6. His mod provided 1:1 mapping to 6th-grade social studies standards such as "Understand the placement of ancient civilizations, important ancient technologies, and the relationship between geography and the formation of cities." Players could be the Egyptians, Sumerians, Babylonians, Phoenicians, Hittites, or Medes. The biggest change was shortening the game to encourage experimentation and recursive play. Just as with Apolyton, we wanted to throw students in over their heads with sophisticated terminology and teach them to swim.

We were short on computers, so we paired them up, which worked brilliantly. I recommend pairing up students when games are played in class because it (1) prompts players to reflect in action as they discuss moves; (2) requires students to vocalize their intentions, providing insight into what they think; and (3) gives students someone to share struggles with. We saw far less frustration than in our earlier study, covered in Chapter 6. Sharing struggles and triumphs produced relationships that lasted throughout the summer.

For every player, g*ame play was fundamentally social*. By week 3, every game was multiplayer in some way. Nowhere was this more evident than with the girls. Two pairs of girls actually traded games midstream to fix one another's games. Soon, more joined. Each girl developed a special skill (such as city building or diplomacy) and became a specialist who was called in to help during certain situations. Spontaneously, girls were "jigsawing" to share expertise. Their entire gaming experience, even when playing single-player games, was cooperative and collaborative. Many boys wanted to play a competitive multiplayer game, so we teamed them with facilitators to avoid out-of-control competition.

Competitive multiplayer was a massive hit. We feared rampant fighting, but they wanted to beat the *facilitators* more than anything. A competitive culture emerged in which negotiating, bragging, and haggling were the *core* game play. Players formed alliances, had epic battles, and talked trash. They started coming to class earlier and staying later to concoct plans.

DEVELOPING GAME EXPERTISE

A subset of 6 to 7 players (half boys, half girls) were becoming experts, such that their trajectory roughly matched that of Apolyton players. This expertise arose at the intersection of their specific historical interests, gaming strategies, and role within the group. For example, Sami, who was 8, played as Rome. Playing as Rome gave him strategic advantages (e.g., the natural barriers of the Mediterranean and Alps) and strong defenses in the form of legionaries (whom he called "legendaries"). He avoided direct conflict with the older kids, although he often "accidentally" attacked others.

A reporter called to learn more about the program. We gave the phone to Sami.

"How do you like to win?" the reporter asked. Sami was pretty shy, but he slowly responded: "Building wonders. Like the Colossus, the Statue of Zeus, Temple of Artemis, Hanging Gardens, and Pyramids." Sami couldn't sit in a chair because his feet didn't reach the floor, but he carved out an identity as the world wonder builder.

Josh, in contrast, played as the Scandinavians and re-created Viking attacks. He liked being away from the ruckus of the Mediterranean and swooping down with galleys to attack with berserkers (the Viking's special unit). He explained his strategy:

"I put berserkers on the galleys and attack cities close to the shore. I can use them to attack whoever is in the city."

We asked Josh about his berserker strategy, curious if he made any connections between it and the Viking marauders. Josh commented on its realism:

"Actually it is realistic because the berserkers would take this stuff which they made called wolf-bane . . . like with Ivan the Boneless, which is my name in the game."

Levi interrupted him. "Umm, where did you learn this?" (Neither wolf-bane nor Ivan the Boneless were terms used in *Civ*.)

"It's from a book I'm reading," Josh explained. "It's a fantasy, but all the land and stuff is just like real Europe. They have Iceland on the map, and the longships."

We wondered if this were something he did in school or for pleasure, so Levi asked, "Have you read about this at school at all?"

"No." It was something Josh just read for fun. Josh, like all seven regular players often brought in books from the library and watched History Channel programs pertaining to his game.

Each participant showed increases in school performance, as evidenced by an increase in grades for these participants. We obtained grades for Josh, Morgan, and Rebecca, all of whom earned As in social studies that year, having received mostly Bs and Cs the previous year.[1]

---

1. We were not able to obtain grades for the other participants and cannot make claims about their in-school achievement. Sami was too young to get grades in social studies.

DEVELOPING GAME FLUENCY

With Levi's encouragement, the kids used the editor to modify scenarios and create custom games. Josh was building a Scandinavian scenario, as he explained in an interview: "Well, I am Scandinavia, and I have the island that I really wanted—or that I had to get to if I wanted to win the game—because it has every resource. Every island has horses and iron and the basic stuff." Josh initially used the editor to give himself access to iron and horses. These two resources were key to the Middle Age scenarios, and obtaining them always involved Central Europe. Josh figured, "Why not build a scenario that happened to include plentiful iron and horses across Scandinavia?"

Josh mostly learned to use the editor on his own, with some help. One Friday night, for example, I was in Orlando at a conference, and my cell phone rang. It was Josh, who had tracked down my number from an Institutional Review Board (IRB) form. He wanted help with the save-file system. For about a year, these calls became a semi-regular occurrence (I'd never had research subjects track *me* down for follow-up questions before).

We queried Josh on the historical accuracy of this hypothetical scenario. His fluency with the time period surprised even us:

> Well, the Vikings were up in the Netherlands, but they also controlled Iceland and the northern tip of the United Kingdom. They were kind of isolated. If you saw them in battle or if they came to your town, you were very unlucky because—well you were kind of lucky and kind of unlucky because they don't really attack a lot. If they are sailing, they go to different islands, and if there are no people there, they will leave guys there to start building up cities. Then they'll just have more people come to the city. They'll just keep on taking over the land. If there is a village in their way, they will destroy the village.

This passage was remarkably accurate in terms of the Viking age. Josh's understanding is an amalgamation of information and experiences culled across several sources but driven by his interest in *Civilization*. It arose through both his game play strategy and his role in the group, meaning that his learning of Scandinavian history was profoundly social in origin. And this performance stands in stark contrast to his attitude at the beginning of the camp, when he was uninterested in game design and largely disaffiliated from school.

Within the year, Josh, Morgan, and a few others regularly created their own game scenarios. They experimented with different starting points for civilizations, how to speed up or slow down the game, and how to allocate resources to give themselves advantages. For these kids, the desire to modify games was not an abstract goal, but rather a natural outgrowth of their desire to entertain friends, express themselves, and achieve status.

Multiplayer games—even competitive ones—transformed the lab into a *collaborative* game space, which accelerated learning. Although there's no way to directly compare this with a "control" situation, we observed that sophisticated gaming practices formed and spread quickly when participants played together. Forming alliances, negotiating treaties, trading technologies, and sharing resources required them to reflect on their games and develop a language for discussing the game world. Game events themselves became the object of shared analysis as players planned, discussed, and analyzed strategies.

GAMES AS OCCASIONS OF THEORY BUILDING AND TESTING

Teachers playing games with the kids similarly transformed the play space. Levi, again, was the biggest proponent of this approach. One day he asked me, "If you were playing golf, wouldn't you want Tiger Woods to play with you?"

"What, are you the Tiger Woods of *Civilization*?" I snapped back. No, he said, but he was better than Josh, Morgan, or me. Playing alongside experts was critical to Apolyton, so we tried it. Playing with them enabled us to model good gaming practices and intervene in squabbles. Multiplayer *Civ* games can get intense, as this following exchange illustrates. Morgan had just threatened his little brother Sami.

"What? Why are you killing me?" Morgan asked.

"Because you said you would attack me," Sami responded, defensively. "You shouldn't do that. I'm teaching you a lesson." Emboldened now, Sami declared, "*Everybody: Hunt down Morgan!*" Morgan appealed to Levi and then to the group to intervene. No one rushed to Morgan's defense, so eventually, Morgan fought back.

"That's it. I'm coming over. Sami, you're done right now," said Morgan. The reality of a massive war fell across the room, and it became quiet. Levi tried to lighten the mood and turn the attention back to scenario design (Morgan had built this scenario).

"So have you learned something about building a scenario?" Levi asked.

"Yup," Morgan said confidently. He explained how he learned about the importance of proximity between civilizations. A well-balanced game requires that civilizations be close enough for contact, but not so close as to be constantly colliding (recall the lessons from my dissertation).[2]

---

2. Indeed, this seems to be a big lesson of *Civ*. In one discussion of historical scenarios, Theseus commented, "It seems that some parts of the world are destined for armed conflict." War will inevitably break out in the Middle East as civilizations bump up against one another.

Sami grumbled off in the background, criticizing Morgan's scenario. Given that Sami was only 8 years old and struggled with advanced strategies like preparing for counterattacks, everyone knew how this would end.

Shew, shew shew. The familiar sound of archers' arrows broke the silence.

"Ha ha! I captured your city. Thank you, Sami!" Morgan stood on his chair. He recapitulated how he beat Sami in glorious detail. Students eagerly "reflect" on a learning event in a game when bragging or saving face.

Levi reassured me that it was OK, and he secretly traded with Sami to keep him alive. The facilitators (especially Levi) were like big brothers in that they guided interactions, enforced rules, and sometimes imposed justice. Like the older kids in my neighborhood growing up, Levi steered the game in ways so that it's rewarding for everyone. As organized activities like sports or music lessons fill more of children's lives, video games are one space in which kids can learn the conflict resolution skills that my generation learned at the playground.

In the midst of the chaos, Levi used geographical terms like *the West*, which created an implicit motivation for learning academic vocabulary. We tried to make it *smart* and *cool* to use academic language. If a player wanted to steal hints, you had to know geography to do it.

Multiplayer games create a context for analyzing events, interpreting actions, making arguments about the game world, and predicting outcomes. In short, they *externalize* the "observe, predict, and act" cycle that is so core to game play.

Student learning increased when we went multiplayer. We experience a shared virtual world that we have co-inhabited and co-created. The *collectiveness* of this virtual experience can also be found in squad-based games, or MMOs, but *Civ* is unique in that we *create* the world. *Civ* starts with a blank slate. The cities, roads, army units, and alliances are all created by players. Other apropos metaphors are creating a communal fish tank or ant colony, or perhaps a "game" of Legos.

COMPETITION AND LEARNING

Educators usually think of such competition as bad for learning, but in *Civ*Camp the opposite was true. Oftentimes, competition led directly to learning. In this example, I was playing with the group. Daniel saw my warrior in his territory and asked what I was doing.

"I'm just trying to find the Sumerians!" I explained.

Daniel bought my explanation, but Kira did not.

"Leave me alone! What are you doing!?" She called out. "Traitor!" Kira, who was the Sumerians, decided that I was acting aggressively, and she wanted to attack first. Kira's reaction was over the top, considering my actions (sending out a lone warrior to explore). Kira wasn't just boasting; she was picking fights. She turned to Matt, another facilitator.

"Don't touch my settler," she warned. "I don't know what Matt is doing, but I want to *go up there and take his city.*"

"I'm waitin' for ya," Matt interjected, with a nonchalance that further tweaked Kira.

"I'm *tryin'* to get all my men and start killin'," she taunted back. This struck me as gruesome. Did Kira have to be so vivid? Later, Kira explained that her favorite games were fighting games. She enjoyed playing and talking trash with her brothers. We were struck by how Kira (a very sweet girl, actually) and her friends confounded stereotypes about gender and games (see Gender and Games sidebar).

The boys, in contrast, treated games like other pursuits such as sports or hunting. Many gamed with their brothers, fathers, and uncles. Almost every house with men played Madden regularly. Play is deeply tied to gender identity, culture, and social norms, and embracing play requires an awareness of these dynamics.

Twenty minutes later, Ben looked at the clock and noted the day was ending.

"All right, 2 more minutes!"

"Why can't we just keep playing? Just one more turn." Someone literally said, "Just one more turn."

"We've got to go soon," Ben reminded everybody.

"Uh oh . . . I was *so close* to taking over his city," Kira said with frustration. Kira and Matt's battling escalated until, in a move of unprecedented braggadocio, Matt offered to buy an *entire* pizza for anyone who could capture one of his cities. Kira responded with a singular mind toward crushing him, but no one succeeded.

In the debriefing, Ben probed what they learned. We used debriefing to synthesize and apply learning toward future games (knowledge as preparing for action).

"Who built a swordsman?" Ben asked.

Kira immediately volunteered, "I built a swordsman." We were pleased that Kira, still a newcomer, was participating.

"All right. How did you do it?"

Kira spoke up. "You've got to have ironworking, and a road between it and your city." This simple explanation may not seem remarkable, but the students at MATCH—who were much older—struggled with this same idea. Several design decisions—starting students in pairs, refining our scenarios, and embracing multiplayer games—had improved the program.

Kira learned to make swordsmen because she had a very specific goal: taking Matt's city. This goal arose from (mostly friendly) direct, head-to-head competition. She learned through a variety of means (peers, teachers, and direct observation) how to attack cities. She learned how to make workers, how to identify and exploit resources, and which resources she needed.

Gender and Games

Many girls reveled in confrontational play at *Civ*Club. *Civ*Club was a socially acceptable space for identity play. Brenda Laurel (2002) has argued that girls do often play competitively, but often prefer complex activities with layers of friendships, competition, and ways to participate.

These girls bucked many stereotypes about girls and technology. They were confident, bold, and astute, and they embraced direct competition with the boys. They loved fighting games and complained that their brothers wouldn't share controllers. They reported frustration that boys owned the consoles and kept them in their room. So although every child had access to a console at home, the girls often had to go through their brothers. This finding is important because advanced activities like modding require substantial access to technology.

When we discuss gender and gaming, it's critical to consider social norms, cultural values, and age. Through studying girls from many different backgrounds (middle class, working class, White, African American, Puerto Rican, Mexican, Haitian, European American, Asian American), it is shown that attitudes toward gaming are influenced by many variables, including cultural notions of womanhood. If a "cute boy" was playing one day, more girls showed up and reported an interest in gaming. Once these same girls became teenagers, they started working jobs, helping raise siblings, and going to school, and they increasingly described gaming as a waste of time (although they also spent a lot of time on MySpace and Black Planet; see also Lenhart, Rainie, & Lewis, 2010).

ORGANIZING BY COMPETITIONS

We soon embraced competition as a way to organize learning (see Competition and Learning sidebar). As a class, we held special "summer games" that lasted several days. The trial games, in which players tried many different strategies, were separated from the high-stakes games, in which the best players competed. Holding a special event in which everyone agrees that they are deploying their best strategies is a good way to conceptualize summative assessment in a gaming context, which normally encourages learning through failure.

Unbeknownst to us, several boys held a sleepover to plot a secret attack against the adults. They were going to forego the "official" competition and turn it into one big attempt to defeat Levi. As Josh explained later,

> We (Korea and Japan) saw how close Greece was and figured that Australia had to be closer. So we got out maps. I have this big map (at home), and we built a galley with settlers and were going to create a civilization and research how to sail to Greece to make a secret attack on Levi.

Josh, who previously described his social studies experience in terms of graham crackers, was now hosting sleepovers that involved clandestine map study. I can imagine them huddled under blankets with flashlights calculating distances between East Asia and Australia.

If you have played *Civ*, you know that their plan isn't going to work. Reaching Australia requires seafaring technologies. Seafaring technologies arrive so late in the game that you will never build an empire from Australia to compete with the old world. Regardless, this entire exercise was educational and, most important, *fun* (what Papert, 2002, calls *hard fun*).

We held similar culminating events once per season to sustain participation and assess learning. These kinds of structures (not grades, curriculum, or mandated texts) could be a way to design future educational systems. They promote reflection—both on the front end, as students research strategies and afterward as they reflect on what happened.

We also used them to introduce complex practices (such as scenario design). One spring, for example, we held a "*Civ* Olympics" with three competitions: best scenario design, highest single-player game score, and winner of the multiplayer game. For the multiplayer game competition, we set up a scenario around the Hundred Years War. In addition to being historically important, it was ripe with conflict, and they knew virtually nothing about it, enabling us to compare pre- and post-tests on their understandings.

Not surprisingly, they could correctly identify the historical actors and facts about the time period in post-tests. They did especially well with military history, naming important military units and so on. Again, students showed no real confusion between "real" history and the game. Most could identify that the conflict was centered around France and England in the 14th and 15th centuries. Most correctly identified the "surface" causes (typical territorial disputes and claims to land).

But the Olympics excelled at driving students toward modding. Four students entered the modding competition, and Morgan narrowly beat out Josh in a presentation in front of a panel of judges. Morgan decided to model the war in Iraq. He reported spending about 25 hours on the mod, mostly at home before and after school. (Morgan, like several participants, obtained a computer specifically to play *Civ*.)[3]

Morgan struggled with many issues typical to simulation design. What map should he use? What scale was useful? What would he include, and what would he leave out, given that *Civ* let him allocate only 12 civilizations? (He settled on combining many European countries into one civilization.) How could he best model Al Qaeda, which isn't a nation-state at all? And, one of my favorites, who was the president of Mongolia, what is its political system, and what was its stance toward the United States' invasion of Iraq? I had no idea. The books in the room were of no use. Thankfully, Wikipedia had an extensive entry on Mongolia, and Morgan returned to it frequently as a reference.

Figure 8.1. Morgan's Iraq War Mod

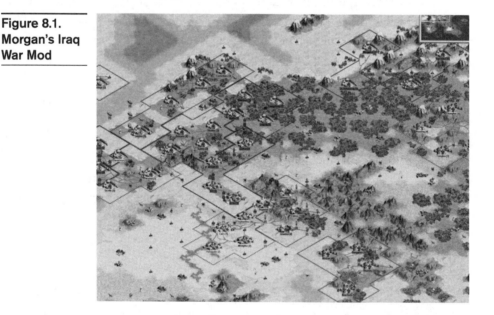

3. When I started with *Civ3*, it was a new game that required the latest computer. Only 5 years later, it was a bargain bin game and played on a $50 computer. Most of our students had access to a hand-me-down Pentium II era computer. Jason refurbished his own computer, built out of spare parts, including a graphics card purchased from Ben.

Competition and Learning

Direct competition as a force for driving learning struck us as particularly interesting because the research literature suggests that direct competition creates anxiety and reduces enjoyment in learning. Indeed, "zero-sum, high-stakes game structures" such as normed tests (i.e., grading on a curve), class rankings, teachers' favor, and competitions for limited access to "advanced courses" can have bad consequences. These competitions turn learning into a game with few winners and lots of "losers." Even worse, the "losers" start to think that school isn't for people like them, rather than that they could study differently or try harder. So competition as it is generally implemented in schools (grade point averages, access to limited resources) does seem to have deleterious effects.

But maybe this is just poor game design. Having only one way to win is not enjoyable if you lose, and so maybe it's not surprising that many kids opt out in favor of their own value systems (such as being a rebel or being the class clown). Likewise, a game that is always high stakes and gives only one shot to "get it right" is going to lead to players' internalizing feelings about their competence. Where is the chance to experiment and learn through failure?

Indeed, if you look beyond schools, the idea that competition can drive learning seems obvious. In sports, competition drives players to stay up at night studying videos of their moves. In games, competition (friendly or direct) drives us to practice moves or study strategies. The Brown County firefighters playing *Biohazard* craved competition. At MIT, there are competitions for almost everything, from robotics to game design. The trick is in how to create good competition that is engaging, fair, and equitable. In that spirit, we need to not only critique competition in games, but also critique competition in schools just as carefully.

Morgan's mod (see Figure 8.1) was about potential alliances in the Middle East. He wrestled with how to give Iraq any sort of viable strategy. What it lacked in professional polish, it made up for in scope, given that it was the first mod he had ever created and that he dug into the particulars of modeling nongovernment groups such as Al Qaeda. When he found out he won the competition, a tear literally came to his eye. He said that he had never worked on something so hard in his life.

Morgan's practices represent just the kind of *design literacy* the New London Group (2000) describes as valuable in the 21st-century world. Morgan wrestles with what message he wants to convey through the mod and how to work within the modding tool's constraints, and then reflects back on how it will be received by players. All this is within the challenge of managing a 20- to 30-hour project with a hard deadline. Morgan researched across multiple media sources and weighed the value of established sources (such as encyclopedias) versus online resources (such as Wikipedia).

Morgan's interest in historical modding extended beyond the camp, suggesting a form of transfer. The next month, we found a paper with Morgan's name on it saying, "10 things I want to learn next year in social studies." All 10 things were *Civ* related. They included "How would you show religion in *Civilization*?" and "Can *Civilization* model revolutions?" Morgan's teacher wanted to know what he wanted to learn next year, and Morgan explained that this was it. He started building an American Revolutionary War mod for his social studies class. He put another 30 to 40 hours into his Revolutionary War mod before abandoning it when *CivIV* was released with a Revolutionary War scenario that surpassed his.

TRAJECTORIES OF PARTICIPATION

One day that following summer, in the middle of an otherwise ordinary game, Morgan looked up and said, "This whole game has changed my life. Yep."

Levi paused briefly, then asked, "My Rome scenario or *Civ*?"

"I mean like the game, ever since I played it . . . Most of the other videos games are boring, but this isn't." Thank goodness the tapes were rolling. "Yeah, and my family plays it," he added.

Sami, always the cantankerous one, called out, "No they don't." This was ironic coming from Sami, who begged to be let into *Civ*Camp so that he could play with his brother.

Morgan corrected him. "Mom and Dad want to. My mom does." In fact, his sister did, too (she had come to camp). We asked about this later, and on many occasions, Morgan's mom took an interest in his *Civ* play and played alongside him.

Later that day, while engaged in some deep trade with another civilization, Morgan blurted out (again, good thing the cameras were rolling), "I want to become a senator some day."

Levi asked him to clarify (in an admittedly leading way): "Is that from playing this game?"

"Pretty much." Of course, we wouldn't claim that playing *Civilization* directly caused him to aspire to public office. However, playing the game fed into a desire to learn more about history and politics. He also watched television shows, checked out books, and eventually volunteered on the Obama campaign. Undoubtedly his parents, friends, or other mentors contributed to his motivations, as well. However, this example suggests the kinds of identity transformations that games can provide, particularly when they extend interests into new areas.

CENTERS OF EXPERTISE

Gaming may be most effective as a *leading activity* for academic practices. Playing *Civilization* in after-school settings led students to develop an affiliation for history that fueled game play, and each became expert in overlapping areas of *game play* and in *history*. Josh was the master "game player" and most interested in the game as a system. Morgan developed a unique style of historical game play and would often bring history books and "replay" specific events. Likewise, Sami was the builder. This increased their interest in social studies and in turn steered them into more academically valued practices such as reading books or watching documentaries.

The term *centers of expertise* captures how games like *Civ* can motivate, develop, and sustain multiple, overlapping forms of expertise. The expectation in *Civ*Camp was that each participant *should* develop unique expertise. Schools, in comparison, provide surprisingly *few* opportunities for original expertise to emerge and, unfortunately, appear to be embracing standardization through No Child Left Behind and calls for "scientific research" that values only the skills measured by standardized tests. We showed how learning, knowing, and being an expert are deeply pleasurable for these players, yet they considered school "boring."

*Civ*Camp was a bridging space for participants, creating a recreational space that connected their out-of-school and in-school lives—a crucial, but difficult, achievement for underserved and underprivileged youth. Morgan, Josh, or Kira didn't have to give up their interests or identities to participate in *Civ*Camp; rather, it extended them in new ways. *Civ* isn't alone as being a good candidate for driving this kind of change. In history, *Europa Universalis*, *Patrician*, Sid Meier's *Pirates!*, *Railroad Tycoon*, *Colonization*, and the *Rome Total War* series all have similar potential, and many have been used by teachers to support learning (Egenfeldt-Nielsen, 2005; McCall, 2011; Squire, 2005).

WHAT LEARNING OCCURRED? A COMMUNITY WELL PLAYED

Fast-forward one year after *Civ*Camp ended. We decided to get the old gang together and do "one more game of *Civ*."

Morgan and Josh were now both over 6 feet tall and in varsity sports. Both had a keen interest in history, politics, and social issues as a direct result of their participation in *Civ*Clubs. I asked if Morgan was still interested in being a senator. "Oh, yeah. I want to go into politics or criminal justice," he responded.

"What do you think about Obama?" It was December 2008; we had to ask.

Morgan replied enthusiastically. "I like him, and I think he's going to bring real change."

"I like him too," chimed in Josh. "You know, Obama has already brought change by signing executive orders such as closing down Guantánamo and stopping torture." The contrast between Josh's initial attitude toward history and his present attention to current events was striking.

We asked what they were studying in school, reviving the practice of playing games based on their interests.

"Right now, we're studying Mongolia," Josh volunteered. Without skipping a beat, Josh asked about the relationship between Genghis and Kublai Khan, which no one could recall. Josh consulted Wikipedia for the answer: Kublai is Genghis's grandson. The discussion turned to how one would "play" as Mongolia if they could turn back the clock.

"Well, Mongolia is sandwiched between Russia and China," added Morgan, who often played as Russia. Ben observed that Mongolia didn't have much arable land. Josh and Morgan both nodded as if Mongolia's low rate of precipitation was common knowledge for a 14-year-old.

Josh said that if he were Mongolian, he'd attack Russia or China to access farmland. We next discussed the expansion of the Mongolian Empire and its historical impact on Asia. Both Josh and Morgan already knew a good deal about the Mongols from other sources (recall Morgan's looking up Mongolia for his *Civ* mod); I was a bit more rusty.

Notice how Josh and Morgan both immediately thought about Mongolia from their geohistorical position, identifying potential goals (finding arable land) and analyzing how their historical position would affect their future. And notice how casual it is for both Josh and Morgan to be hanging out and talking about Mongolia, looking it up on the Internet and speculating about hypothetical historical scenarios. They had become, in this context, the kind of person who asked questions about history and marshals resources to answer questions.

This exchange typifies the consequences of becoming an expert player-designer with *Civilization*. There is a disposition toward putting yourself inside a system, looking for its leverage points, and devising strategies to make your goals. Josh and Morgan engaged in this sort of historical thinking *constantly*.

We settled a North African–Mediterranean World War II mod, and the metagame started. Who had to be the Germans? Eventually, I was stuck being Germany because Josh and Morgan wanted to gang up on me in a morally justified manner. Plus, my family is German. This led to a discussion of everyone's ancestry, which included Scottish, Irish, Cameroonian, German, English, and Tamel—pretty multicultural for six people.

Negotiation

"Kurt's in the lead over there. How many cities do you have?" Ben asked. I led on the "point system" (a rough indicator of each civilization's strength), and the jockeying to interpret the system began. Ben used the occasion to focus attention on me.

"Oh, not many," I lied. I actually had more cities than anyone, and they were totally unguarded. If Josh learned my strategy, I would be toast. I sent archers to distract him. Nestled between Josh and me were mountains of gems and iron, as well as two barbarian camps. I needed a foothold in those hills to chase the barbarians toward Josh. Whether Josh or I controlled this region would dictate the winner.

Each game exists in a *personal* history. Josh and I were continuing a theory of how to play with one another. Josh built the dominant ancient capital—a large city that was full of workers, buildings, and wonders—but had *zero* military. I never would have predicted this, and Josh knew I'd never attack him, so he exploited that.

Back on the other continent, Ben and Morgan's games also co-evolved. Ben was stuck in a jungle, and he grumbled about this repeatedly, playing the "woe is me" card. Ben's score crept along in last place, so we bought his narrative of events, that is, until the game announced, "Hinduism has been founded by the Indians," namely, Ben, which was a major event. All eyes turned to him. "Oh really, now?" Morgan asked. What was he up to?

Again, negotiation dominated play. Players analyzed maps, compared relative strengths, and settled into relationships. Players "spun" narratives to suit their goals, downplaying or playing up strengths as the situation required. Every event—from the sight of a galley to the discovery of a religion—was subject to interpretation.

The Aesthetics of Multiplayer Gaming

This table talk occurs "on top" of building cities and infrastructure, scouting for resources, fighting barbarians, and so on. Recall Nitsche's (2008) five planes of gaming. The first level is the game encoded in the box; the second is the game on screen; the third is the game we imagine in our head (e.g., how we pretend *The Sims* is our own family); the fourth plane is the action in real space (the mouse clicks in *Civ* or dancing in *Dance, Dance, Revolution* and so on); and the fifth plane is our discussions, the social plane in which the players interact. To an observer, this *Civ* game would look *very* social.

The "real" game play is the intersection across them, and part of what makes a *Civ* game compelling is when these five elements work in concert, with the player developing a robust mental model (level 3) of the game system, which is being responded to by feedback occurring on screen (level 2), and then negotiated through social interaction (level 5), and so on. Good games also have this deeply rhythmic quality to the clicking (level 4), too.

THEORY AND PRACTICE

Imagine if learning could be so pleasurable in school. Could we create learning environments that drew on these pleasures for the purposes of learning? The next chapter explores early attempts to do so. Returning to our guiding questions, we find

- *A program based on Apolyton succeeded when it was driven by competitions, events, and strategic leveraging of social relationships.* Competition was central to learning, both at the microlevel as we competed to spin narratives of game play and at the macrolevel as we organized competitions around modding or multiplayer games.
- Formalized practices such as DARs were difficult to implement, but *playing collaboratively promoted reflection-on-action and cognitive apprenticeships.* However, *Civ*Camp looks and feels much more like a gaming community than school, and may be best suited for informal educational environments.
- *Players learned to become designers*, developing along a trajectory similar to that in Apolyton in which players developed basic knowledge, systemic understandings, advanced strategies, and design thinking skills. Discussions a year after the camp concluded showed how players (in this context) internalized question-asking, problem-posing, and information-gathering practices introduced at the camp. They thought through historical questions by entering the game space and thinking like a *Civ* leader. We saw evidence of the use of these experiences outside *Civ*Club, including increased academic performance, applying ideas and practices from *Civ* toward academic work

(e.g., the *Revolution* mod), and embarking on life trajectories (game design, politics) based on these interests. Although we saw compelling evidence of *Civ* play affecting school performance for these participants, even more interesting was how it generated new interests that tied to their life goals outside school. In other words, game play sparked their interest in domains pertinent to life inside and outside school (such as attending law school).

Oftentimes, we ask, "Does game play transfer to school work?" as if increasing school performance was somehow the goal of education. If we consider, instead, that the point of education is to enhance life out of school, then game communities like *Civ*Camp or Apolyton pose challenges to educators. In an age in which we can access games that inspire new interests and pursue those interests within affinity spaces, what is it that we want to do with formalized schooling? One answer might be addressing equity gaps; not every student has equal access, supports, or preparation for participation in a community such as Apolyton. Josh and Morgan both said that game design was too hard, and they would have struggled with the relatively sophisticated language used at Apolyton. Youth with parents (or older mentors) who identify, nurture, and extend these interests will accelerate. Schools that do not face the threat of being closed under No Child Left Behind (or the similar programs that follow it) will likely experiment with these pedagogies after school (and eventually in school). There may also be a particular role for educators to expand horizons, to raise new interests in areas that students may not self-select.

The next chapter examines attempts to scale game-based curricula in schools. We tackle the constraints of schools as they are today (such as compulsory attendance and age-graded classrooms) head on.

CHAPTER 9

Games Go to School: Situated Learning, Adaptable Curricula

Ivan Vasily is dead. Police claimed that he drowned while fishing by the south shore of Lake Mendota. Between January and the time of his death, Ivan put on 25 pounds and started drinking heavily. His health condition deteriorated considerably.

As one of his friends, your task is to investigate the case with two of your best friends. It is your duty to present the causes and effects to the public.

"I bet that Ivan died of poisoning," Dr. James speculated. "The baby was feeling bad too, and so is the mother" (implying that the whole family was poisoned). "Neither of them is overweight," he added.

Agent Stevens, a government official who was responsible for understanding the legal case, noted an inconsistency. "But he never saw Santiago!" Santiago worked with Ivan and was also ill. A coincidence? He didn't think so.

"Remember that he showed the same symptoms as his wife and son," noted Dr. James, who had seen their medical charts (only doctors can gain access to patient records) and saw too many similarities within Ivan's family to ignore the possibility of food poisoning.

"See . . . both of them [Ivan and his wife] are overweight, but Ivan was the only drinker, so it could have been alcohol [interacting with the toxin]." Dr. James hadn't definitively diagnosed the problem, but perhaps alcohol played a role, too.

Agent Andy Stevens didn't buy this theory, but it was worth thinking through. "OK, let's see: Poisoning. But is it like *food* poisoning or is it *poison*?"

"I think it's fish poison . . . because there is tons of mercury in the lake." None of the records mentioned mercury, but Dr. James knew of mercury in fish caught from Lake Mendota. Ivan liked fishing; perhaps they had ingested it from fish?

Agent Stevens nodded in agreement, "I know."

Dr. James continued this line of thinking. "I don't think it would have been *intentional* poisoning, Andy." Doctor James didn't see anyone wanting to *murder* Ivan.

"Well, we don't actually know any motivations yet," Agent Stevens reminded them. Stevens didn't want to jump conclusions prematurely. Dr. James steered the conversation back to medical facts.

"Remember, the wife and child were showing signs of being overweight, and so was the dad. The wife and child . . . who are not drinkers . ." Dr. James puzzled through the data. "It could have been the alcohol" (mixing with the toxin), Dr. James concluded.

"Yeah," agreed Agent Stevens. This sounded reasonable.

Dr. James continued, "And if they were all eating fish—that's the only thing we know they are consuming." It looked more and more like fish interacting with alcohol. This would explain how Santiago, the mom, and the baby all got sick, but only Ivan died.

"Right," Stevens said. He was coming to the same conclusion—and without indulging in wild speculation.

They still needed to rule out other factors. They returned to the docks. Was the water deep enough for Ivan to have drowned?

Willy Loman, a fast-talking insurance representative, stopped them.

"Let me tell you the truth. Ivan's death was an insurance fraud. This man could not live without a full-time job, and he had problems finding one. The alcohol made him sick, and he simply lost the will to live. He was a good husband, but he could not afford to raise his family. What would you do if you were Ivan? He set everything up to make it look like an accident so that his wife could get insurance compensation from his death. I know that it is hard to swallow, but is there evidence to suggest otherwise?"

Dr. James wouldn't stand for it. This *wasn't* suicide.

"He is wrong. I think obviously it is runoff from . . . well, *something* put mercury in the lake. The catfish ate . . . consumed the plankton and absorbed the mercury. And then Ivan ate the catfish and brought some home for his wife.

"That's why his wife and kid are sick. And he is sick. And the wife transferred it to the baby through breast milk but not substantially. And the kid is suffering from nervous disability, so honestly he must have died of mercury or something else."

* * *

The preceding vignette wasn't an episode from *Law and Order*, but an exchange between two students playing *Mad City Mystery* (see Figure 9.1), an augmented

**Figure 9.1.
Students
Playing *Mad
City Mystery***

reality (AR) game designed by Mingfong Jan (the transcript is cleaned up for read-ability; for the full study, see Squire & Jan, 2007). In *Mad City Mystery*, each student plays a different role. In addition to the medical doctor and government agent, a third player is the environmental scientist. Each role has unique capacities. The doctor can take vital signs, the government official has access to secret documents, and the environmental scientist can sample for toxins. Each role is required to de-velop a full picture of the case. Virtual characters like Willy Loman were designed to provoke their thinking and encourage reflection.

This jigsaw design seeks to support engagement and learning. First, it im-merses each player in a role with unique abilities, which we hope increases role identification. Second, differentiated roles require players to synthesize what they read. Third, it creates *responsibility*, as players are accountable to their group for un-derstanding their information. Finally, it creates a cooperative, distributed puzzle-solving game, which provides a pleasurable context for meaningful interactions with content.

To give away the ending, there is no one right answer, but Ivan's death was probably caused by exposure to TCEs or PCBs. Our doctor was on the right path, but he was incorrect in several ways. Mercury poisoning (which probably caused the baby's low birth weight) won't kill you overnight. It can cause a variety of neu-rological disorders, most acutely in young children. Yet, whatever affected Ivan was sudden. One day, he was fine (albeit overweight and drinking too much), and the next day he was sick enough to drown, suggesting direct, recent exposure to a contaminant. He and his colleagues all experienced dizziness and shortness of breath. The documents reveal that there had been a TCE spill in Ivan's factory. A case could also be made for him ingesting PCBs.

This chapter uses games like *Mad City Mystery* to investigate the following:

- How do we create game-based curricula that are tied to academic standards, playable within classroom constraints, and yet retain game-based learning features (e.g., piquing interest, systems thinking, engaging students as designers)?
- How can we experiment and innovate within schools in order to build the capacity to transform educational institutions as digital media becomes more widely adopted?

This chapter follows the story of my research team's attempts to put these ideas into practice and turn a prototype into a curriculum that works with 20 or 30 teachers. Ideally, I hope it provides an example of how to do educational game design in schools today. At the very least, maybe it will inspire an interest in game-like learning.

PLACE-BASED GAMING

Mad City Mystery pilots convinced us that the *unique* benefit of augmented reality (AR) games was turning your world into a game board (see Figure 9.1). *Mad City Mystery* players saw their neighborhood through the lens of science, and this was *fun*. They viewed everything from architecture to sewer pipes as data sources. They connected observations with what they knew and asked new questions. Recall how the medical doctor brought his knowledge of mercury *into* the game. Another player then projected it outward and asked, "I wonder if mercury comes out of the downtown coal plant." This caused the group to ask more questions. One player eventually asked, "What is with that coal plant in downtown Madison? Isn't that dangerous?"

Jim Mathews, a local teacher and graduate student, had his students play *Mad City Mystery* and was inspired. Jim believed that a game that was even more rooted in the students' physical surrounding could be compelling. We introduced Jim to MIT's Augmented Reality Gaming platform and let him have at it.

Jim's game (or more accurately, situated documentary), *Dow Day*, pushed our thinking further. In *Dow Day*, players are journalists on October 12, 1967, who are covering student protests in Madison, against Dow Chemical Company. Dow manufactured Agent Orange, a chemical sprayed on millions of civilians (including half a million children) during the Vietnam War, and now the company was on campus interviewing for jobs. Some students believed that Dow should not have access to university facilities, and they planned a peaceful sit-in to protest.

Dow Day was a defining event in U.S. history in the 1960s, as detailed in David Maraniss's (2004) *They Marched into Sunlight* and the 1979 Academy Award–nominated film *The War at Home*. The riots that Dow Day ignited spread to Chicago, disrupting the 1968 Democratic National Convention. Many student protesters drove to Chicago for the event, and some gained local and regional prominence, perhaps most famously Paul Soglin, a former Madison mayor and long-time civic leader.

Jim wanted to use *Dow Day* to teach critical media skills and historical empathy. Most of Jim's students thought the Vietnam War was deeply immoral and couldn't imagine how any good American would support it. Jim wanted them to understand how working-class police officers might view the protesters differently. How would these officers feel about protecting a group of privileged kids who were interviewing for high-paying jobs from another group of privileged college kids? What if police saw themselves as defending the rights of students (some of whom might be their children) to pursue pharmaceutical careers to help people? In the wake of Iraq, revisiting this chapter in Madison's history was timely.

Jim used roles, primary documents, media, and location more deliberately. Every conversation in *Dow Day* is based on primary documents drawn from original newspapers, books, or film. For example, players are briefed by receiving two primary documents. The player then goes to Bascom Hill. Players meet protesters, interviewees, police officers, and university officials—all real people speaking in their own words. On their mobile media device, participants view archival footage of protesters marching up that same hill, right up to where the students are now standing, and watch skirmishes breaking out under the bell tower. The game directs their attention to aspects of the physical space that contributed to the escalation of events, such as the narrow hallways in the campus buildings that made escape difficult (see Figure 9.2).

Back in class, Jim also presented these same primary documents to players and asked them to write their story. They compared their stories with historical reports, each of which is biased in many ways. The "official" city papers fabricated details (such as reporting that one student brought a meat cleaver to the rally), and student papers vilified police officers as unthinking pigs.[1] Through Jim's game design, students are

---

1. The image of the student holding a giant meat cleaver is priceless. The absurdity is readily apparent: How could a student walk around a rally wielding a giant meat cleaver and not be noticed? Where did the student get it? How could it be concealed in such a crowd? And, if it was used, where is the bloodied police officer?

Figure 9.2.
Dow Day **Game Space and Objects**

encouraged to think beyond their own personal perspectives to see that *Dow Day* was an unfortunate tragedy caused by several interacting and complex forces, not just mindless malice from cops. As a reflection activity, Jim's students are asked to add a character not originally in the game and then to restructure the game to reflect their own historical interpretation. This approach eases players into designing games.

PLACE-BASED LEARNING

Teachers like Jim Mathews and Mark Wagler (see Figure 9.3) transformed our AR games from a technology into a *curriculum* by reimagining AR games as an educational method. After playing *Mad City Mystery*, Mark wanted his 4th- and 5th-grade class to *design* a game. Mark already taught with place-based inquiry methods; his science class investigated local issues (such as migratory birds) and published their results in a student-run journal. In social studies, they researched historical events in the local community (such as about Wisconsin's immigrant Hmong population) and turned them into cultural tours. Language arts, math, and even art were all connected as they painted, sculpted, and wrote pieces connected to place.

Mark thought his students could design a game about their neighborhood called *Greenbush*. Greenbush is a Madison community settled in the early 20th century by Italian and Jewish immigrants as well as African Americans migrating from the South. It was the one Madison community that accepted everyone regardless of color, culture, or religion. As a result, a vibrant, diverse community

**Figure 9.3.
Mark Wagler Working
with Middle School
Students**

Photo courtesy of Mingfong Jan

formed with many unique features, including gardens with roots in Sicily, Africa, Russia, and the American South; integrated dance halls that hosted a wide range of national performers, including Duke Ellington; and synagogues that became the Jewish center of Madison. The multiethnic gardens, a precursor to the urban gardening movement that is so hip with the kids these days, were especially fascinating. Greenbush, or "Bush," was gutted in the 1960s when a city-supported hospital complex broke up the community under the guise of "urban renewal". As neighbors and families were displaced across Madison, the social structures (churches, union groups, synagogues) that tied life together were lost.

LEARNING THROUGH DESIGN,
OR HOW TO DESIGN AN EDUCATIONAL GAME

Mark, Mingfong, and another graduate student, John Martin, created a curriculum for students to design a game based on their neighborhood, Greenbush (see Squire et al., 2007). The first thing that kids asked was "What kind of a game would it be?" There were crimes in the history of Greenbush that cried out to become a mystery game like *Mad City Mystery*. But what would that say about Greenbush? Residents had been "policed" by the Ku Klux Klan for being perceived as un-American. Did the class want to reinforce stereotypes that already caused immense damage? Designing a game about other people's lives—representing who they are and how they live—is tricky.

Mark, a veteran community organizer, immediately enlisted several amateur and professional historians to guide the class. Joe "Buffo" Cerniglia became a class favorite. Buffo led neighborhood walks, shared stories about the Bush, and introduced students to residents. Buffo became a compass that the class used to gauge whether their ideas were true to the lives of Greenbush residents.

The project quickly ballooned out of control. Students collected thousands of primary documents, including photographs, diaries, and newspaper clippings. They created dozens of audio and video interviews with former and current residents. They even developed and administered a survey to 1,000 residents and analyzed the data. Not bad for 4th and 5th graders, but what to do next? They could spend their lives wading through all this stuff.

They first published their materials online through the Center for the Study of Upper Midwest Cultures. You can visit their website and see their work at csumc.wisc.edu/cmct/greenbush. Next, they organized a meeting for anyone interested in Greenbush. They wanted to celebrate what they found, involve more people from the community, and see how people responded to their interpretations. They created posters, invited speakers, and made their own presentations—all at the Italian Workmen's Club (see Figure 9.4). By now, the project was in its 2nd year. Mark's students kept it going, in part thanks to his mixed-age classroom. Every year, half the class returned so that the veterans could teach the newcomers the classroom standards (much as with Apolyton).

They decided to have players keep the same roles that they had while designing the game (historians, ethnographers, and community planners). What better way for players to learn than to replay their roles as researchers? We have since latched on to this concept as a design tool: The roles you take on while researching a game are often good player roles.

They had roles and resources, but they still needed a driving *challenge*. The story of 1960s Greenbush, a time of great conflict, was alluring and clearly contested. The city and university were buying land to "clean up" Greenbush, but its residents didn't see anything wrong with the Bush. They wanted to keep their homes, churches, community centers, and traditions. The story had a classic David-versus-Goliath theme. Bureaucratic city planners wanted to break up established neighborhoods because they were "unseemly"—and happened to sit on desirable land. This was ironic given that the Greenbush was poor specifically *because* it was the only place that would allow immigrants to settle.

Historically, this period reflects national trends. Sadly, most American cities have a similar story, and this game could be replicated across the country: Immigrants, African Americans, and rural poor poured into cities at the turn of the century. They stuck and were stuck together. From the late 1940s through 1970s, their communities were bulldozed in the name of renewal. Neighborhoods such as the Bush were soon robbed of the local ownership that gave them their vitality.[2] Today's Madison (like most cities) is dealing with the aftermath of such policies. Communities are fragmented, impoverished areas are still segregated, and there isn't substantial intermingling in schools or churches. As one Greenbush resident

---

2. The issues of contemporary schools are directly related to the consequences of these decisions. Many cities are trying to "undo" these design decisions (such as returning businesses to local ownership). Unfortunately, the dominant metaphors for understanding poverty-stricken areas (e.g., "decay" or "cancerous") persist and suggest that urban problems can be solved by "surgically removing" bad housing (or, even worse, the people living in them). Such tactics continue as if the structural racism and xenophobia that created these conditions are gone. Indeed, the "problem" with schools today goes back to these designs, because school attendance is determined geographically. Where students go to school is determined by where students live, which is determined by culture and class and the perpetuation of de facto segregation.

Figure 9.4. Wagler's Class at the Italian Workmen's Club

Photo courtesy of Mingfong Jan

commented, back in the day, if you moved up in social class at least you didn't have to leave the neighborhood. You could buy a home one block over. Now, because of real estate practices that subtly enforce segregation, if someone "makes it," they move and take their money out of the neighborhood. Such immigrant neighborhoods are common in many cities (from Brooklyn to Madison) and are far from perfect, but they have historically included features now considered cutting-edge in city planning, including multifamily dwellings, close neighborhood associations, and mixed-income properties.

The class wanted to share this insight through a game that helped players see traces of the old through the face of the new. Scratch beneath the surface and signs of the old Greenbush remain. Haberdasheries and Italian delis dot the main thoroughfare. The local pizza joint was built by Italian workers as a safety net and to improve living conditions. The largest Catholic churches and synagogues are still there, and many Orthodox Jews still live nearby. Understanding the history of the neighborhood unlocked a more nuanced understanding of it. *Greenbush* provided a key for opening conversations about the neighborhood's future.

Greenbush takes place in the present day. It starts with a city council meeting on a proposal that will shape its future. The university wants more land to feed its growth and is eyeing two areas: a swath of unattractive government housing built in the 1960s and the last tract of original Greenbush homes. Although there are no known plans for such a development, it's a plausible scenario that could actually happen within the next decade.

The game play involves traveling back in time to historical Greenbush. Players visit locations, meet residents, and choose which agenda to prioritize. It's tempting to just bulldoze the ugly government housing and homes to make "better use" of the land. However, the history of the Greenbush shows how these poor residents will probably be moved to the farthest, least desirable land, far away from their workplaces, health care facilities, and public transportation. In fact, in the 1960s, this is just what happened, causing the creation of Madison's "problem areas," commonly called Allied Drive.

The game's central idea is to invite players to "peel back the layers" to see not just the *structures* but also the historical *forces* causing this change. As players travel through time, they become immersed in the period by interacting with the massive number of resources Mark's students collected. Standing on a street corner, they see photos of the vibrant community that once occupied the space. They hear stories about the city's gardens, churches, and dance halls. The game also showcases hidden Greenbush gems, such as the Italian Workmen's building, the memorial to the old neighborhood, and a bocce ball field.

FROM GAME DESIGNER TO COMMUNITY ORGANIZER

It's easy to see how Mark's kids honed their reading, writing, analytic, mathematical, and social studies skills designing this game, but Mark valued how the game design encouraged students to *look at their own neighborhoods as constructed objects.* Game design forced students to think more deeply about how outsiders would experience their game versus how they would experience the students' articles, artwork, or websites. Being a game designer offered an integrated identity in which academic skills were mobilized toward redesigning the world.

After presenting their work to the Greenbush community, they drafted a resolution for the city council asking the council to honor and restore historic Greenbush values, to commit to "never doing this again," and to continue the tradition of Greenbush being a mixed-use, mixed-income, and mixed-ability community (see Figure 9.5). On June 6, 2006, the resolution was passed unanimously by Madison's city council. As of this writing, there have been two successful Greenbush Day festivals, each attracting hundreds of attendees.

What happened next was surprising. Mayor Dave Cieslewicz turned to the 5th graders to ask what they thought should be done about Allied Drive, the segregated, lower-income neighborhood on the outskirts of town created, in part, by the Greenbush "urban renewal" policy. Mark's class suggested that they start by "asking what the residents themselves think should be done," which apparently was unusual, but should sound familiar. As simple as it sounds, *listening* before offering solutions is the first step in the successful, thoughtful design of everything from neighborhoods to schools.

The students spoke of this learning experience as being deeply transformative. A few cried after the city council meeting. Their interview comments reflected this, as they said things like, "I never knew 25 5th graders could accomplish so much." Participants reported applying these insights to new situations. As one commented, "When I visit new places, I wonder what their past is, and if they ever had something happen like what happened in the Greenbush." Others wondered if their planning could increase the sense of community. It astounded me to see 5th graders make such an impact. Think of how much energy lies sitting idle in rows of classrooms. This design curriculum could marry inquiry- and project-based curricula, using games to engage kids in specific ways of thinking while opening up the learning experience for them to design (see Barron, 2002; Hmelo-Silver, 2004; Savery & Duffy, 1995).

Games aren't just a tool to teach the same old things in new ways, but a catalyst for mobilizing students' knowledge to encourage them to think systemically in their interactions with the world. Designing *Greenbush* drove the students' engagement in complex academic practices (from reading academic texts to designing and administering surveys). This work involved *authentic* participation in a project with real-world implications and legitimate social impact. Students designed a playable game, built a public website for its distribution, held a real conference, and helped author actual legislation. This sort of authenticity is *participatory authenticity* where students take part in goal-driven activities of real-life import (see Barab, Squire, & Dueber, 2000). Such education lessons develop

**Figure 9.5.
Student Presenting
Work to the Madison
Common Council**

naturally from games, but they also tie to older pedagogical movements. Mark's work is based largely in inquiry- and place-based learning, and there are echoes of Dewey in this idea that education isn't *preparation* for life but *participation* in life.

COMMUNITY ORGANIZING AS CURRICULUM

So how do we create integrated game-based curricula that is tied to standards and honors the values of game-based learning?

Games spark interest in new domains and inspire design. To elaborate from the examples of Mark's class and the *Civ*Camp experience, games:

1. *Spark interest-driven learning in students and teachers.* Games are really good at getting people excited about a topic—and not just in the content of the game itself. Playing *Mad City Mystery* ignited students' interest in their neighborhood and got them asking why things were the way they were. One reason *Greenbush* worked is that the content arose from *passion*—both in Mark and in his students. We can't overlook the importance of curriculum in engaging *teachers*. The more we teacher-proof materials, the more we lose this opportunity and drive away talented teachers. In contrast, when a class and teacher collaborate to pursue their mutual interests, transformative learning will follow.

2. *Create new interests.* In our examples, enjoyable learning led to new questions and interests, which drove further learning. These interests were highly personalized. Mark's students took away interests in topics ranging from Jewish and African American history to local politics, just like Morgan in *Civ*Camp took away an interest in history and Josh became a game designer.

3. *Lead to intrinsically motivated authoring.* Much like Morgan built Revolutionary War mods in *Civ* for fun, Mark's class went far beyond what was required in the assignment out of personal interest and a desire to make a difference in the world. Mark's students held meetings on evenings and weekends; one student even worked all summer to complete his own variant of the game (which was about the Jewish experience of Greenbush). Ultimately, games are a unifying framework that allow students to become legitimate media producers. Applying the *trajectories of participation* framework (from Chapter 2), in Mark's class the students shifted from novice players to expert players to game designers to community organizers and designers of social systems, which some have called "soft modding" (see Gee & Hayes, 2010).

Interest-driven learning is similar to learning inspired by games in purely entertainment venues (as *Civ* did for me). Games enlist our dreams and desires and activate our identities. They raise new questions and open new possibility spaces. When games teach us skills and give us tools, they often motivate us to act. Thus, there seems to be a nonintuitive, but natural, fit between games and participating in the world. It seems counterintuitive that games (i.e., fantasy) could enhance civic participation, but there are at least four reasons that they might.

First, games engender a "ludic spirit," a spirit of playfulness. The moment we invite kids to see the world in a playful way, it connects pleasurable emotions with learning. It's fun to see your world in new ways and to realize that you can make an impact. Local games ask players *to see their worlds differently* and to ask, "Why is this so?" and "Could it be different?" Fantasy breaks from the world and imagines other possibilities; when used creatively, this can be fundamental to learning.

Second, games are inherently participatory. There is no game without the player. As a gamer, there is a feeling of "shared hallucination" in the sense that we actively construct the game reality we are temporarily inhabiting. This is true of both single-player and multiplayer games, but the experience is most profound when it's shared.

Third, once a person has had profound learning experiences in a world that is noticeably "designed" (or "socially constructed"), there is a tendency to ask, "Why is our world designed the way that it is?" and "Could it be designed differently?"

Fourth, games engender expertise within simulated systems and encourage us to ask how these skills could pay off elsewhere. If I have led civilizations in a game simulation, maybe I start thinking of becoming a policy maker. If I lead a successful NFL franchise in *Madden*, maybe I could coach or manage another kind of group.[3] If I lead a guild of hundreds online, maybe I could become a successful leader in other communities.

This participatory gaming doesn't necessarily result in "community organizing" (particularly as it is practiced as a discipline), but it often requires organizing in a literal and metaphorical sense. Whether it's *Civ* players organizing Apolyton University or *World of Warcraft* players organizing raids, multiplayer gaming requires working with other people. It's an open question whether this tendency to go from *game player* toward *community organizer* is typical of games or unique to the

---

3. Bill Simmons (2007) writes, "Why wouldn't they [coaches] also have some slacker college student who has played 250,000 hours of *Madden* in the past 3 years and faced every conceivable football situation on hand to throw out advice like, 'Dude, let them score here; we can get the ball back down eight'?" *Madden* players are literate about even the most arcane football situations.

game-playing cultures we specifically fostered in our study. But games researchers like Dmitri Williams (2006) have found empirical evidence that gamers are more likely to be civically engaged than nongamers. This relationship requires profound gaming experiences (particularly in which players shape the world). It requires clear models of how to link gaming practices to practices outside the game in everyday life (e.g., how game design can relate to community design). These are the links we tried to build in our *Civ*Club. Can we scale them to an in-school program?

RAMPING UP

"Kurt, they're taking away my multiage classroom," Mark told me. I stared into my phone, unable to believe my ears.

"They're doing what?" I asked.

"Yep, my principal insists."

"Well, then, Mark, you'll have to work with us." What better person to lead technology workshops than a man raised as an Amish Mennonite?

Core Features of Local Games

Eric Klopfer (from MIT), Chris Dede (from Harvard), and I were awarded a Department of Education grant to explore games' potential for teaching reading comprehension, argumentation skills, and writing. We wanted to create tools and resources for teachers to create their *own* games tailored to their classroom constraints. We started with model games that teachers could adapt, each of which included the following core features:

1. All activity is situated within *roles*. The moment the unit starts, students are no longer "students" and are instead "professionals." This sets them up to be competent performers learning under a new value system.
2. Learning is driven by emotionally compelling *challenges*. You want kids to learn because it's relevant in the world, not for a test or because "it's good for you."
3. Players access *authentic tools and resources*. Learners should use complex, realistic tools of the sort they would encounter in authentic situations outside the classroom. Usually these resources are beyond their current skill level, and the game provides *motivation* and *context* to help students master them.
4. Game mechanics promote *collaboration*, such as *jigsawing*. In addition to being a sound instructional strategy, it promotes communication, a goal of education.

Critically, we didn't offer one curriculum for teachers to implement, but a framework for thinking about games and education. This approach is based on a *process* theory of change. We saw the materials not as the *solution*, but as a *catalyst* for creating conversation, reflection, and teaching. Too often, we treat educational materials as a change agent (or silver bullet), but doing so deprofessionalizes teachers. Teachers have their own values, goals, and knowledge. We shouldn't "teacher-proof" curricula so that it can be tested; instead, we should create compelling materials that address teachers' needs and inspire them to teach creatively and effectively.

This stance treats educational reform as a *process*, not a *product*. Systemic school reformers who have worked for decades to transform classrooms, schools, and districts toward more learning-centered practices conclude that the educational reform cannot be rooted in your pet solution (e.g., educational video games), but should engender conversation among stakeholders (students, teachers, parents, and community leaders) about the core purposes of education and how they are manifested in particular designs such as classrooms, grades, and so on (see Jenlink & Carr, 1996; Reigeluth & Garfinkle, 1994; Squire & Reigeluth, 2000). The moment one group "hands" another the solution, you have failed. Efforts that invest the time in developing consensus about underlying values can weather the setbacks that characterize all reform efforts. Not coincidentally, these are the same principles community organizers use. A community organizer can't go into a community and say, "Here's what you need to do!" The point is to empower people to take ownership.

Chris Dede wanted to require interdisciplinary teaching partnerships to catalyze creative reflection. We designed four games: *Sick at South Beach*, *Saving Lake Wingra*, *Riverside*, and *Hip Hop Tycoon*.

Integrating New Methods in the Curriculum

Before turning to the games that were widely adopted, we should briefly touch upon *Hip Hop Tycoon*, a game by Ben DeVane (now a professor at the University of Florida) and Chris Holden (now a professor at New Mexico). Ben noticed that many of our "*Civ* kids" were enthralled by hip-hop culture. Ben, a closeted hip-hop aficionado, wanted to use entrepreneurism, a core value of hip-hop culture, as a way to develop kids' financial literacy. Citing precedent in games such as *Railroad Tycoon*, Ben felt a game that blended hip-hop and finance could grip kids.

As Ben researched business loans, he noticed disturbing facts about subprime adjustable rate loans. "These things are crazy!" he shouted to anyone who would listen. "This whole sector is going to implode. We *need* to make a game about it." So Ben and Chris designed a game in which students play as business financiers, sales staff, and human-resource directors competing to run hip-hop stores. Running a store requires mathematics, reading, and financial skills for comparing loans and making budgets.

You would think that after the recent subprime mortgage meltdown, people would crave curricula that educated students about these issues, but that couldn't be farther from the truth. There is no natural fit for financial literacy in the curriculum. Math teachers feel tremendous pressure to cover content, and anything that strays from the textbook is a hard sell. Social studies teachers were more interested because their standards cover entrepreneurship (although it is rarely ever taught). Although we did use *Hip Hop Tycoon* in one school, we eventually abandoned it due to the uphill battles.[4] It's almost as if schools are structured to ensure that people don't learn useful things that make a difference in the world.

SITUATING LEARNING AT SOUTH BEACH

The most popular of the three games was *Sick at South Beach*, a modification of *Mad City Mystery* based on a real story. In *Sick at South Beach*, four girls who had gone swimming get sick from *E. coli* poisoning. You might think the girls contracted *E. coli* from the large sewage outflow nearby that dumps untreated water into Lake Michigan an average of five times a year or from a contaminant from the rusty well nearby, but it turns out that the *E. coli* was caused by the goose poop that piles up on the shore of Lake Michigan and gets washed into the water when it rains. It is common for *E. coli* to spread this way.

By focusing on a real issue, we could bring in concrete data. Rather than inventing plausible contestations of space, we simply researched data for that place. Jim Mathews, the lead designer, found news reports of sewage overflows, *E. coli* outbreaks, and community efforts to care for their beach. Watching footage of untreated water flowing from exactly where you are standing proved to be as compelling as watching protesters march during *Dow Day*. The Great Lakes Water Institute provided access to their decades of data, which included good graphics and charts.

---

4. When a Milwaukee paper wrote a nice story about the game experience, the right-wing blogosphere jumped on it as "pandering" to youth. Soon the story spread to talk radio, and we were under fire. It's no wonder that 30% of students drop out of school when we treat anything fun, however relevant, as "pandering." How ironic is it that the groups blaming "poor people for taking out bad loans" are the same ones blocking efforts to teach our children the skills to suss out such bad deals?

Teaching Teachers with Games

We worked with 30 teachers that first summer. First, we all played a game together and then discussed the game's gist and the concept of teaching with games. Next, we brainstormed how to adapt the game to local contexts. This invited teachers in as *designers*. Finally, we presented a model curriculum that teachers could adapt for their classrooms (see Table 9.1). Twenty-four teachers taught with *Sick at South Beach* that first year and we studied two classes in depth (for the full study, see Squire, 2010).

Table 9.1. Overview of the *Sick at South Beach* Curriculum

DAY	ACTIVITY
1	*Introduction and Roles.* Complete job applications.
2	*Employee Orientation.* Discuss roles and documentation.
	Data Log and Map. Discuss maps and data logs.
3	*Diseases.* Read and discuss diseases using reading strategies.
4	*Water Quality Web Quest.*
5	*Medical Records.* Build predictions based on medical forms.
6	*Game play:* Play *Sick at South Beach.*
7	*Group Debriefing.* Interpret test scores.
8	*Create Presentations.* Make final prognosis.
9–10	*Persuasive Writing.* Analyze persuasive writing samples and create presentation rubric.
11	*Presentations.* Present prognosis to community.

Supporting Role-Play

Our partner teachers modified the curriculum, which improved it vastly. For example, Lyndee Belanger had students *apply* for their roles. Seeing their job qualifications was not only cute, but also connected them to the game. Several teachers followed her lead, and we now often use the job application feature. Lyndee also had students wear lab coats and asked the school security guard to deliver information in confidential folders. The kids loved it. These ideas spread quickly to other classes.

Not every teacher used props like Lyndee, but they all role-played. Tina Kurtz, for example, used the students roles for classroom management. When a student acted up, she asked, "Would a scientist talk that way?" She also used role-playing to set expectations of quality. For example, here's how she introduced one day's activities:

> You are going to receive confidential copies of their medical records. In your group, keep in mind your job, who you are. You are speaking as that person.

You are looking for clues about these illnesses related to your job. But if you
see something really obvious not related to your job, point it out to the group.

Tina plays up the students' roles as *professionals* who are responsible to a team.
She divided students by professions and asked them to process information within
their disciplinary community. Then, they returned to their team for debriefing and
reporting (dual layers of jigsawing). The following exchange from a doctors' meeting exemplifies such interactions:

"It's cryptosporidiosis. That's what we think it is." The doctors had huddled
around their data for about 15 minutes and had finally reached a conclusion.

"Can you tell me why?" Tina challenged.

A second doctor in the group expanded on their conclusion. "Because they
had diarrhea, [reading now from a chart], weight loss, cramps, fever, nausea. If it
wasn't *that*, it would be *Campylobacter jejuni*, because this one had bloody diarrhea, but the first one didn't say anything about it being bloody. It also has fever,
nausea, and vomiting. And it is the most common cause of bacterial infection."
This back-and-forth was typical. It built on game play from *Mad City Mystery*,
but connected the experience across classroom activities—from discussions to
reading exercises—so as to produce deeper learning than in a tradition 1-day
experience.

Embedded Assessments

This exchange also illustrates how the game was designed to elicit misconceptions, a key step for using games for assessment. Through carefully placing
red herrings in the game, we were able to understand which sources of evidence
students used and which they did not, and to what extent they understood the
texts. The student arguing for cryptosporidiosis, or crypto, was partially correct;
judging solely by symptoms, it could have been crypto. But crypto is a parasitic
disease transmitted through fecal-oral contact (eww!), and they didn't have an
explanatory model for how it was contracted. Crypto enters the game because in
1993 there was a highly publicized outbreak in Milwaukee after crypto got into
the water supply, infecting 400,000 people, and over 100 people died. During
this outbreak the rusty well at South Beach was one of the few safe water sources
because it tapped into the underground aquifer. People flocked to it from miles
around, and we met old-timers who still go to the well for drinking water. At the
end of the unit, Tina had her class visit the well and fill milk jugs with its water to
see which kids would drink it.

Tina liked the game play because it wasn't about being right or wrong but about *arguing from evidence*. She explained, "In fact some of them made pretty strong cases for the wrong things. But they made a strong case and they talked to one another. They would argue who was right and who was wrong. It was exciting." For Tina, this argumentation was good because it engaged students as competent problem solvers. So she used it at the beginning of the year to set class expectations.

Supporting Customization

Our teachers came from diverse areas of Milwaukee, so they tied South Beach to different learning goals. Lyndee used the unit as part of a schoolwide reading-comprehension initiative. Tina coordinated reading across the curriculum, so she tied the game into her initiative for reading and writing across genres. As we learned about our participating teachers' contexts that first year, it solidified our view that "standardizing" one game across all contexts was boneheaded. No "one master intervention" would work for all. We could, however, provide compelling materials for teachers to adapt in various contexts.

Breaking Down Classroom Walls

We shouldn't minimize the difficulty of getting new curricula into schools. It took 15 months to go from first contact to getting permission to use materials that *teachers codesigned with us*. Curriculum coordinators told us that *they* decide what goes into classrooms, not teachers. They also wanted research evidence that the activities worked, and that was just the data we were trying to collect. In order to test the curriculum under our grants, it had to first be tested, creating a recursive loop nightmare (see Barriers to Technology Integration sidebar).

In addition, taking 75 kids to the beach to do science was scary. As difficult as it is to teach with technology, it's not nearly as difficult as organizing field trips. In profound ways, school is about putting kids in "safe" classrooms and cutting them off from the world. Managing layers of permissions, contact with teachers, and scheduling buses became Mark's full-time job. This struggle to simply let kids walk out the front door of their building doesn't bode well for technologies such as the Internet, which promise to "break down classroom walls." Schools, in many respects, are designed to keep the world *out*.

When we took the kids outside, the results were shocking. First, across each of our 50-plus implementations, students said that *going outside* was the highlight of the project. Kids pleaded not to cancel trips even when the wind chill approached zero.

Barriers to Technology Integration

When we introduced handheld computers into Milwaukee classes, the first issue the schools' lawyers raised was, "Can kids use these to get online?" Recalling attempts in the 1990s to wire every school, I chuckled. The next question was "Can kids use microphones to pass audio notes?"

I looked to Jim Mathews, who was fuming. "No, they cannot," Jim assured them. "But they can still talk with each other and write messages on paper."

The lawyers looked at one another as if to say, "Any way we can tie them down and mute them so that they can't communicate at all? That would be safer."

While school lawyers debate whether it is OK for kids to talk, students are getting wireless-enabled iPods, Nintendos, and cell phones. Soon, nearly every student will bring his or her own broadband multimedia device to school. This is a major technological challenge to the social order of schooling. There's no way that one teacher can compete with 30 kids who have broadband multimedia machines in their pockets. Already, there are stories of kids sharing pictures of exams or sending thousands of text messages in a month.

I don't think it can be stopped, any more than the Church could stop people from reading in the 15th and 16th centuries.

Many of the Milwaukee students were visiting Lake Michigan for the first time and were confused to find that they lived so close to the "ocean." One asked if the beach rocks were "real or fake." Research reports that many kids from poor areas rarely travel more than a few blocks from their home (something depicted in HBO's *The Wire*, based on true stories; see also Ludwig, 2008). I asked Lyndee about these results.

"Oh, yeah . . . Well, remember, most of them can't find Milwaukee on a national map." I also didn't believe that, so I took her up on it. The next day, we asked them to show us where they lived, and the majority thought they lived near Seattle. This was surprising to me, as I grew up on Lake Michigan, too, and it profoundly shaped my understanding of the world. To this day, I orient myself in new spaces in terms of Lake Michigan.[5] Yet the rhetoric coming out of Washington, D.C. (i.e., more federal control, curricula controlled by textbook companies)

---

5. I recently saw this mentioned on Facebook as "You know you're from Northwest Indiana when you still orient toward Lake Michigan at all times." Do people raised near other bodies of water navigate this way? If anyone knows, please let me know.

is about *reducing* students' opportunities to experience their local environment. The "one size fits all" style of education in vogue precludes learning about the world around you.

Situated Understandings

Once students visited the beach, their orientation toward the unit shifted dramatically. Students became emotionally engaged in the problem and identified more strongly with their roles—something constructivists call "taking ownership." Note, for example, the following heated discussion.

"It says right here, '*contaminated water*,'" Alice reported. "What does that mean?" She paused on the word *contaminated*, which was new. Words like *contaminated* aren't in kids' everyday vocabularies, and yet they aren't technical jargon, either (such as *eutrophic* or *hegemonic*, see Beck, McKeown, & Kucan, 2002). They are "bridging" words, words that appear relatively often, are used in specific ways, and connect common and specialized languages. Not knowing such vocabulary is a barrier for at-risk students because reading academic texts requires understanding them. *Sick at South Beach* was good at introducing these words, getting kids to identify what they didn't understand, and then providing experiences that contextualized their meaning. A primary power of games may be introducing such terms by showing how and why such knowledge is used.

Jessica interjected with a hypothesis. "I think it's crypto. And I'm not changing my mind!" Perhaps she was reflecting her "professional" conclusion as a doctor; perhaps she's just authoritative. Regardless, she was invested.

"It's the food," Susan declared, equally confident.

Jessica turned to Alice and shouted, "Burned!" Alice whispered back, "The teacher is right there!"

Tina chided them softly, "You mean yelling, 'Burned!' to solve your argument? I'm trying to find you making your case." Tina used the game's fiction to enforce classroom rules. Using the game to set high expectations was an unexpected benefit of the unit.

Alice, who was reviewing symptoms, noticed something. "Wait, you guys. It's not giardiasis." Susan agreed. "It's not hepatitis A either. It says here that it appears 1 to 2 weeks *after* exposure."

Jessica asked the teacher, "Can we look at our interviews again?" Notice how Jessica asks permission to review previous work; she feared that reviewing texts might be cheating (see Cheating and Teaching to Tests sidebar). "Yes, they are all in there," Tina said with a smile. At the point at which students asked for permission to reread complex academic texts, Tina knew she had won. The group turned to the chart.

Alice reiterated her position. "Listen, it can't be this one [pointing to giardiasis and crossing it off], because it appears 1 to 2 weeks after exposure." Alice organized their thinking by crossing off unlikely culprits. This exchange was typical for how groups debated explanations, each member vying to be the one who cracked the case.

Learning Through Interaction

In each class, representations like the chart shaped their thinking, particularly ones constructed to make sense of data. Students constructed many representations (see Figure 9.6), and their choice of representation (e.g., concept maps versus charts) affected their findings. Groups that made concept maps had the most accurate prognoses, as it encouraged synthesizing across data sources, whereas bar charts or graphs focused on single variables.

Class talk was decentralized, driven by the problem rather than the teacher. In his study of science classrooms, Jay Lemke (1990) characterizes most of the talk as being "teacher centered," meaning that teachers ask questions like, "Why did the kids get sick?" with students then vying for correct answers. If you map the conversation patterns, it looks like a bicycle wheel with the teacher in the center and kids at the edges. The teacher directs the interaction, and there is little if any extended student discussion.

Cheating and Teaching to Tests

What does it do to students' innate desire to learn when we teach to the test? What does it teach about how "professionals" learn?

For example, in Montessori schools tests are a foreign concept. When my class of 5th graders transited to "normal" schools, we started giving tests on Fridays to introduce the concept of testing. Once, a child left his seat to look up the answer in a book.

"What're you doing?" I asked. "Finding the answer," he dutifully responded. He said that he knew the answer but couldn't think of it offhand. I tried my best to explain that you can't do such things in tests. "But it's right there!" he said, pointing to the book on the shelf. I explained, "You can't get up and just look it up. In fact, you can't get up out of your seat without asking permission."

"Well, how do *you* get any work done?" another asked. I replied, "The trick is to keep from getting bored and stay out of trouble. The first thing you do is find someone who had the same class before you. Get the homework assignment. You can do it while your teacher is lecturing. If you're clever, you can ask questions about the assignment in class. Otherwise . . . well, you learn to space out a lot." Silence fell over the room.

In contrast, *Sick at South Beach* is problem centered and looks like a spider web of interactions among peers with the teacher being one of several hubs. Discussions were driven by the problem (solving the case). Kids argued with one another, brought in resources, and raised follow-up questions. From a learning perspective, this arrangement is desirable because kids are *thinking* and active problem solving is driving the activity.

Promoting Literacy Through Games

Some groups extended the curriculum beyond the formal framework, primarily through connecting literacy instruction to science. In language arts class, they edited their reports. Each group wrote a two- to three-page technical report on (1) the causes of the illnesses and (2) what they thought should be done. Getting students to *care* about writing was a perennial challenge for Brian, who said, "If I just have them write a letter for the sake of writing a letter, they don't get into it as much. Students revised much more in this assignment than usual." Brian attributed this extra revision to the fact that students perceived it as authentic. "They felt that they were valued; they were important. It wasn't just a school task, but a real-life situation that needed to be taken care of."

Teachers graded the reports by a rubric, and all of them received 3s and 4s on a 4-point scale, with roughly one half receiving 3.5 or higher. One third of the students

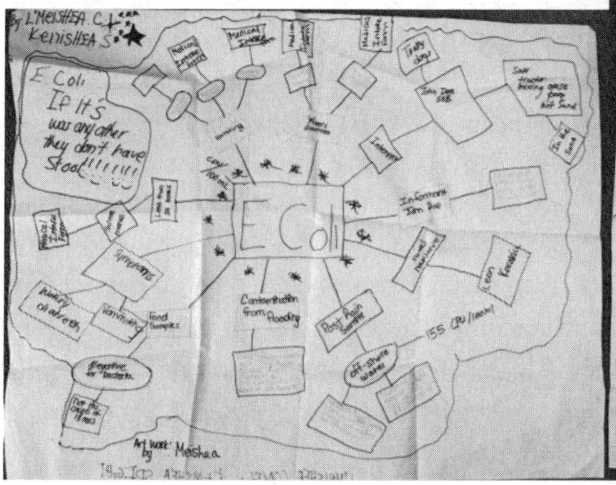

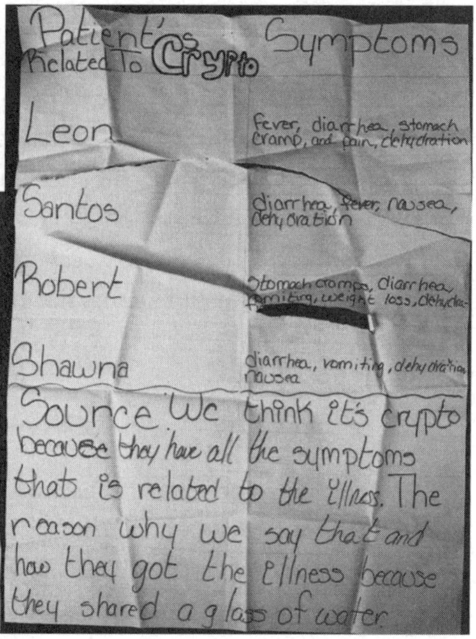

Figure 9.6.
Examples of Students' Representations of Data in *Sick at South Beach*

solved the problem successfully (attributing the illnesses to *E. coli*) and had a sound argument to justify their conclusion, incorporating the necessary and relevant facts and ruling out other diseases. Another third arrived at the right answer but with a weaker argument. The last third argued for crypto, based exclusively on patient symptoms.

Designing Games for Science

Sick at South Beach confirmed the hypothesis posited by MIT Games-to-Teach (2003) that it is worth pursuing teaching and learning science through forensic games. Kids compete to solve complicated problems. They learn academic language. They read about gross stuff such as "fecal-oral contact" (which middle schoolers love). The game play is challenging; it requires reading above their grade level, learning new vocabulary, learning concepts such as the water cycle, and reasoning from evidence—all of which map directly to academic standards. But the biggest educational benefit may be the holistic experience of conducting an investigation. Students experience *being* a forensic investigator and that it can be cool to do science. In post-interviews, being professionals (not handheld computers) was the first thing that kids mentioned. Even the water chemist said, "Before the game I had no clue what a water chemist was, but I found out what they do." A wildlife ecologist jumped in: "Same thing with the wildlife ecologist. I thought that they played with animals." Imagine if instead of reading little sidebars in textbooks about what scientists do, kids actually got to *play* as scientists.

Game Mechanics

We identified a few "portable" design features that succeeded in engaging students. The aforementioned job applications were one example, as was connecting videos to place. For another example, Jim used budget mechanics to force students to prioritize information. Different tests (e.g., *E. coli* vs. crypto) cost money, so kids had to carefully choose which data they wanted. The effect was for students to synthesize information across the entire game as they prioritized tests.

Sustainability

Our next major challenge was how to sustain the project beyond the grant. We could imagine teachers checking out machines and coordinating field trips, but in Milwaukee the average teacher lasts *1 year* before moving to the suburbs or quitting. (I hope you find this shocking). The curricular knowledge could not reside with the *teacher* if we wanted it to continue.

We started working with community organizations to increase sustainability. Such organizations play many roles: They guide the game direction, provide real data, and ultimately, "own" the game after funding ends. Plus, they invite participation after the game as a *real* citizen scientist, journalists, or volunteer. They provide trajectories for participation in more advanced design activities beyond the game.

SCIENTIFIC CITIZENSHIP

These ideas came together in *Saving Lake Wingra*, the final game of our study, which was built with help from *The Friends of Lake Wingra* (a similar game that was developed by the Urban Ecology Center in Milwaukee). The game opens with news of a "secret" plan to transform Lake Wingra, a quiet lake in Madison, Wisconsin, into a hub of recreation and commerce. *Saving Lake Wingra* explicitly asks students to debate the future of the lake. Ecologically, the lake is threatened by urban development. Storm water runoff clogs natural springs, ruining the lake for anglers, boaters, joggers, and aquatic species. And Lake Wingra's shores are among the most ethnically diverse gathering places in Madison. Hmong, Mexican, African American, and European Americans all use the lake and its surrounding land for bicycling, sustenance fishing, and recreation. It's the perfectly contested place (see Saving Lake Wingra sidebar)

Saving Lake Wingra increased competition by having players represent stakeholders with competing agendas. Environmentalists want to remove invasive species. Recreational users want increased lake access. Developers want condominiums (at least before 2006 they did). Learning how humans use natural resources represents a number of social studies standards. Native Americans began altering the lake thousands of years ago, and the lake's current shoreline was designed as a park in the early 1900s (concurrent with the development of Frederick Law Olmstead's parks).

In fact, the game's twist is that there is potential for a consensus plan to remove invasive species and maximize the lake's benefits. There is no "natural" state for Lake Wingra, or for inland lakes of its size; there are only dominant patterns of interaction. A Lake Wingra filled with sediment or overrun by carp serves *no one*— not fishers, not business and landowners, not environmentalists. Our goal was to get students to see through the divisive rhetoric dominating public discourse and to identify areas of mutual interest upon which they could build common ground.

Thus, the game's hook is "environmentalist vs. recreational users," but the *real* lesson is in finding common values to improve our futures. From a game perspective, the knee-jerk political responses made great red herrings, but once you understand the issues, the solutions became quite clear. We hoped that through playing the game students might ask, "Why aren't we doing anything about this?" and become compelled to act.

Saving Lake Wingra—a Student Reflection

I think that we should combine all four plans to clean up Lake Wingra. We should use the revenue from the condo plan and the marina plan to finance the storm water and invasive species [plans]. Not only would this clean up the lake but potentially create new jobs. The city of Madison could hire people with little or no education and pay them minimum wage or slightly above to take out invasive species. We could also sell condos for top dollar so maybe we could build a water treatment plant. If we do this, it will clean up the lake, create new jobs and homes, and make the lake more enjoyable. More people would use the lake and it would be clean. As for the condos and the marina, we would use only green materials and we would have to put signs that say "No Littering" and have monthly cleanups of the beaches. I would also like to limit the lake to nonmotor boats until the lake is cleaner. For the storm water plant, if we build the water treatment plant, we can clean up the water and then put it into the lake. We'd also have to build rain gardens all along the shores. For the invasive species plan, as I said before, we can hire people to take out the invasive species. This plan will make everybody happy.

Over the next 2 years we ran *Saving Lake Wingra* with 20 to 30 classes, including many different iterations and flavors. The vast majority of students chose to remove invasive species and prevent storm water runoff. In pre- and post-tests, students showed deeper understandings of water systems and scientific argumentation, as well as more sophisticated thinking about the lake, although we did not see statistically significant gains when compared with our control groups (more on this next). These results were good, but students didn't grasp key ideas of new urbanism, such as why condos on the lake could be *good* for the environment by reducing urban sprawl.

Students engaged in complex forms of argumentation, as they had in past iterations, but the most important feature of the game was how it positioned players as actors designing their own futures. One Hmong boy, for example, met a Hmong family that was fishing, and he shouted, "That's me! *I'm* Hmong!" He was hooked.

As one student described in a post-test interview from January 2009, "I feel I am higher ranked than I should be. Usually, I am a kid. I just work, copy it down, and write some questions or answer the questions."

Another player, Caleb, described how the game was validating:

Teacher is always ruling over you. Instead of [saying] the teacher's word is law, and that's the end of it, in this project, there was a lot more room for your opinion and stuff. Some teachers will say, "My opinion is right," so nobody can challenge it. And so then you have to learn this no matter what's your viewpoint.

School, for Caleb, is largely recapitulating what the teacher wants. Crystal agreed with Caleb and interrupted him to say, "Like, they were this [opening his arms to show the teacher's status] and we were this [closing his arms to show his status], and now we are both this [using arms to indicate the gap was shorter]." Our partner teachers generally *agreed* with students' critiques of school. They *wanted* to engage kids in authentic inquiry and focus on learning rather than control. Our project succeeded when it gave teachers compelling materials that inspired good teaching and enabled them to organize their schools around powerful ideas.

The most compelling evidence for learning arrived on my doorstep Christmas Eve, 2007. A few months after we ran our curriculum with Spring Harbor Middle School, the *Capital Times* ran a feature about the health of Madison's lakes. One student, Sulvan, who had played the game, read the story, and decided to write a letter advocating more funding for field trips to the lakes. the *Capital Times* included the following letter to the editor:

Let Students Lead Charge for Saving the Lakes
by Sulvan Gu, student, Spring Harbor Middle School

Dear Editor:

I personally think that we wouldn't have to give any money exactly to the lakes, but that we could give the money to schools.

Why? you ask. It's pretty straightforward. Schools could use the money to afford trips to the lakes so we could learn more about the disaster of the lakes.

Now you may be asking, "How could teaching children help save the lakes?" Doing this could do many great things.

A child might be astonished by the news and become inspired to volunteer saving the lakes.

Even though this is less likely, there is a very high chance that the child will spread the news. This could lead on to the people who received the news spreading it! The more people that heard the news the better we can save our lakes.

We can't say that we *caused* Sulvan to write this letter; who knows, maybe he wrote letters to the editor all the time, and he probably had supportive parents. But I love Sulvan's implicit model of change. You've got all of these kids sitting around in school all day. Let's put 'em to work doing social good!

SCALING

The question of how to help interventions grow beyond research communities is complex. It's framed as "scaling" in most communities. The metaphor of scaling is so ingrained that we often forget that it's a metaphor. There are many metaphors that one could use (viral spread of ideas, grassroots growth, and so on), and we often forget that scaling is rooted in designing mechanistic systems. The logic is simple: Build a small model (like a model car), get it working right, and then make it bigger. Some reformers see education similarly. Design a curriculum, get it working with a few teachers, train teachers to use it the way you intend (which is called implementation fidelity), and then roll it out to large numbers of teachers.

Implicit in this approach is the idea that educational specialists should be telling hundreds of thousands of teachers, many of whom they have never met, the best way to teach. Maybe this sounds fine in theory—if you believe that the educational experts know what works in local contexts. Mark Wagler's class fell victim to this logic. An administrator wanted everyone doing the same thing at the same time, and Mark's multiage classroom violated that. So his school lost one of its most highly regarded teachers. It's no wonder that good teachers are quitting in droves. Thus, the dominant scaling metaphor deprofessionalizes teachers and moves control further away from students.

Our change model is a process-oriented approach unconcerned with whether the interventions can be scaled up. We are more concerned with spreading reflective teaching practices that engage kids in advanced design thinking about themselves and their communities. We may not know how any one teacher should do his or her job, but we can provide that teacher with the resources to transform individual teaching practices as he or she sees fit.

I'd like to think that our project succeeded because collaborating teachers took away principles that applied to their teaching. Many teachers started conversations with their students about video games. One teacher enthusiastically reported how discussing *Grand Theft Auto* in class enabled her to connect with disaffected boys. In fact, this interest in games and youth culture was the idea that spread most easily and virally.

The most transformative learning occurred for those teachers who designed their *own* games. The best example came from Tina Kurz. Inspired by *Sick at South Beach*, Tina partnered with another teacher to create a semester-long technology course in which students designed, developed, and play-tested a game about their city, Oconomowoc. Borrowing our handheld computers was too constraining, so they wrote a grant to purchase their own. Tina's *students* actually made the pitch to the school board. They presented the rationale, the unit plan, and their findings from *Sick at South Beach*. They even used situated learning theory to explain why this was good education. In the end, they used the game to design and plant a new rain garden to protect a local stream.

This, to me, is the most powerful scaling you can get. Tina and her colleagues took on the ideas underlying the unit and creatively applied them to her own context. That is the goal of scaling—not getting 10,000 teachers to all do the same thing at the same time. In fact, if 10,000 teachers were all doing the same thing, our intervention would have failed. We *wanted* students and teachers to design games about their unique local communities.

THEORY AND PRACTICE

This chapter proposes a model for game-based learning that is interest driven and seeks to propel students into learning new domains by engaging in design activities. How can we promote change in schools? The answer to that question lies in building community partnerships.

- *One promising strategy to transform schools is to partner with community groups (recreational clubs, scouts, church groups, or volunteer groups like Friends of Lake Wingra).* Teachers, administrators, and researchers all come and go, but place-based community organizations such as Friends of Lake Wingra stay put. Our game design project connected youth to groups ranging from fishing clubs to environmental groups that steward local place and provide contexts for authentic participation.

- *Sustainability features are built into community groups because they are fundamentally interested in improving the quality of life for local community members.* They leverage on-the-ground social networks. They also provide third places—gathering places that are neither home nor school—so that kids can pursue their interests and identities free from who they "have to be" at home or school. They can meet mentors who can turn those interests into lifelong pursuits. Our *Civ*Club (working with the Wisconsin Youth Company) was this kind of third place. Gaming eventually led to other good school habits, many of which had academic value. Students developed identities as "experts" within the game, which, in turn, helped them feel comfortable being good at school.

- Thus, a productive avenue for games (as described in Chapter, 10) may be to *start growing innovations outside the formal structure of schools, which have a tendency to shoehorn innovations to meet the particular constraints of school* (45-minute time blocks, local standards). If we can provide deep learning experiences that compel teachers to bring innovation into their classrooms, perhaps we can empower more lasting change. This isn't to suggest turning our backs on teachers, and indeed our group continues to work with many teachers. However, we believe that to facilitate real transformative learning, we must be open to creating alternative structures to those provided by schools.

CHAPTER 10

The Future of Games for Learning

This book has explored how games function as a medium—how they can engage interest in learning and can lead to understandings of complex phenomena. We've explored game cultures, how they operate, and how they suggest participatory models of learning. We've presented the case for an emerging approach to education that builds on earlier traditions such as constructionism and progressive pedagogies. Still, there are tremendous challenges. Our educational system remains mired in an industrial model of "one size fits all" curriculum, and the history of education is replete with reform efforts that tried to tackle these systemic issues head-on but that were met with tremendous resistance (Collins & Halverson, 2009). This book has focused mostly on work from research communities, but a mature field of education and games needs to engage broader constituencies. This chapter asks:

- What might an integrated game-based learning paradigm for K–12 education look like?
- How can we get such games made?

CREATING EDUCATION MEDIA

Today, examples of quality educational media exist, from *Nova* to *Dora the Explorer*. Most successful properties share a common blueprint of academic-industry partnerships and longitudinal commitment. These properties (particularly *Sesame Street*) have "scaled up" not by adhering to a rigid formula, but by building on the successes of one another.

One of my favorite design principles of these early childhood programs is that powerful learning occurs when adults engage with children during viewing. The adult observes the child's interests, discusses the program, and extends those interests into new areas. These shows (such as *Jack's Big Music Show*) actively engage the parent through inside jokes. The success of this body of work as a whole shows what can be accomplished when there is significant investment over time.

But games aren't television programs. Broadcast media models may not help with questions like "How do we teach novices to become expert designers?" To explore what partnerships for a digital age might look like, let's reexamine the development, distribution, and publishing environment of games.

INDEPENDENT GAMES

With their cutting-edge technologies and huge economic impact (particularly sales, subscriptions, and profit margins), it's easy to focus on the high-end commercial entertainment gaming market. But a substantial independent games movement has thrived in the 2000s by producing niche games at a fraction of the cost, occasionally bringing their developers great profits, particularly on emerging platforms.

Game maker 2D Boy's *World of Goo* is a great example. *World of Goo* is a physics-based puzzle game in which the player controls "goo balls" that they channel across landscapes and into pipes, leading them to "the Goo Corporation." 2D Boy is a company of two developers who struck off from the behemoth Electronic Arts. The game's conceit is a metaphor for the games industry itself, with players channeling goo balls (i.e., workers) to feed the corporate machine.

Its puzzle solving is all about physics. As Drew Davidson (2008) describes, the lesson of the game is that "physics is your friend." As players build bridges and structures, they wrestle with concepts such as "center of gravity" and the material properties of the goos. During play-testing, the team realized that using physics enabled them to create more sophisticated levels in a fair manner (as opposed to using random "gimmicks"). Any game that makes "physics your friend" captures the playful spirit of academic content in a way that good educational games should.

World of Goo also suggests where the market for educational games might be. Not only is *World of Goo* a cute game, but it has received smashing critical success (90% scores across the board and many "game of the year" awards). And it's making gobs of money. Developed for about $96,000 (according to developer estimates), it brought in $496,000 in the first few weeks of release for the Nintendo Wii (see video game sales charts: http://news.vgchartz.com/news.php?id=2478). Combine that with the sales for the PC release, Steam direct downloads, Mac purchases, and so on, and you have millions in profit.

Few would say that *World of Goo* is educational, but it's instructive (as is another engineering game, *Pontifex*). You could use its underlying game play to teach engineering principles such as triangulation. One could imagine building educational materials around *World of Goo*, using it as the basis of giving kids' firsthand experiences with challenges requiring knowledge of physics. An educational version could point out these principles to users; if you don't already have an idea of "triangulation" it's hard to infer those concepts from the game in any articulated way.

World of Goo is but one example in an emerging independent games movement that is expanding contemporary models of gaming. *Braid, Flow, Fez, Diner Dash, Flower, Crayon Physics, Desktop Tower Defense,* and *Love* are all thriving games outside of the traditional marketplace (see *Flower* sidebar).

Production and distribution platforms such as Wiiware, Xbox Live, and online game aggregators such as Kongregate are paths for games to reach new audiences. It may not be this way forever, but there's an open window that educational games could exploit.

A key lesson for educational designers and developers, however, is the potential for leveraging the robust game development environment of software tools and engines. When we built *Supercharged!* simply importing 3-D models into a game engine took weeks if not months unless one spent tens of thousands of dollars on the Renderware tool suite. Now, this task is trivial and cheap (in the hundreds of dollars), with Unity's game development tools easily porting games to both computers and cell phones. *World of Goo* used Open Dynamics Engine, Simple DirectMedia Layer, PopCap Games Framework, TinyXML, Advanced Encryption Standard, irrKlang, and libcurl in its development. Other developers have made great headway with Flash and its many plug-ins. Likewise, the Torque Garage Games development community continues to gather steam, as does Unity. In an ideal world, educational game developers would expand upon these tools, creating their own software development niches. Nascent educational game companies like Filament or Fire Hose Games may become that community. Unfortunately, in the past, educational technologists haven't gone to the Game Developers Conference to learn game development patterns (such as the currently popular one-page design document; see Librande, 2010). Likewise, until very recently, game developers have avoided educational conferences.

These routes do not necessary translate to millions of sales, but millions in sales aren't required to be profitable. New pathways enable unique games to get made, and educators, if they are savvy, can use such games to find unique audiences. In many respects, this is a long-tail phenomenon of a large collective market for niche titles. Indie games are not attempting to compete with *World of Warcraft* (although recall that Nintendo sold 17 million copies of *Brain Age*, which is a pretty "lo-fi" game). Rather, they make use of new development models (oftentimes one or two people leveraging development tools), and they choose publishing deals that make the most sense for their title.

Flower

To simply describe the current wave of indie games as providing "alterna-tives" to the mainstream games industry sells short their aesthetic inno-vations. For example, in *Flower*, each level takes place "inside a flower's dream" as it sits in an apartment. The player flies a flower petal through fields and makes the fields come to life in an explosion of color.

Designer Jenova Chen described how "we just had this concept that every PlayStation is like a portal in your living room . . . that would allow you to be embraced by nature."

Critics may ask, "Why don't games just go outside, then?" It's a fair question. Most people I've shown the game to do in fact decide (however temporarily) to make experiencing nature more of a priority in their lives.

However, we wouldn't reject an Ansel Adams photograph because it "pulls people away from nature" or critique the sweeping outdoor shots in *Dr. Zhivago* because they keep film viewers indoors. *Flower* makes a statement about our blighted urban landscapes and the feelings of freedom that are lost when we lose open spaces.

Independent games like *Flower* show that games are capable of expressing a range of emotions, but developers may need to go around the mainstream industry to do it.

Educational developers could use similar channels for distributing games, par-ticularly in informal contexts. What's missing, however, is a mature game-*publish-ing* model. Educational developers need

- *Good research in educational markets* (including homes, large school districts, alternative schools, charter schools, after schools, and community organizations). Textbook publishers and educational service providers control school markets through a variety of means. Thus, channels other than schools may be the best place to start with game development and publishing.
- *Models of best practice for game development.* The commercial industry has mechanisms for sharing lessons learned, such as postmortems. No good mechanisms exist in the educational games community to critique one another's work and learn from successes and failures. Educational game publishers could help ensure quality by requiring best development practices.

Raising the resources to develop an educational game can be daunting, but often there are content providers, educational groups, or other stakeholders who can help. For example, *Building Homes of Our Own*, a game that has been used in industrial design classes, was sponsored by the National Association of Homebuilders. The future of games may require similar partnerships. Alex Chisholm and my colleagues at the Learning Games Network (see Learning Games Network sidebar) have begun pursuing this work, as has E-Line Ventures, a new educational game publisher.

All this discussion, however, takes place outside the traditional textbook publishing and adoption processes. Textbook publishing is a mess. In short, the textbook adoption process is dominated by the demands of large states (most notably Texas). To get approved, textbook companies acquiesce to state political pressures about what content goes into textbooks and what is left out. One (naively) assumes that disciplinary knowledge determines what goes into textbooks, but it's actually a political process.

The corporate publishers have locked up channels into schools. In fact, the move to "scientifically validated" materials may have been nothing more than an attempt to further control the school market. If you need very large studies proving that your materials "work," before you get into schools, innovation, particularly by smaller companies, is shut out. Imagine a small start-up trying to get their games into schools—even with a local teacher who is involved in its development—but it first has to show that their games work with thousands of students.

Learning Games Network

The Learning Games Network (LGN) is a nonprofit institution trying to spark innovation in the design and use of learning games through promoting collaboration among scholars, teachers, developers, producers, and so on. LGN develops model projects (such as iCue) to demonstrate how such partnerships could be done and builds general infrastructural capacity (such as an international group of teachers available for piloting and teaching with games across many contexts).

I'm the vice president of LGN and a founding member. Our hope with this initiative is that we can proactively shape the field by researching and disseminating best models of educational game design and development, helping to arrange partnerships between developers, content providers, and learning and media specialists and expanding the field. Games is an area in which one good proof of concept is often infinitely more persuasive than a research paper.

Selling directly to states or districts is difficult. As a graduate student, I worked with Sasha Barab consulting with Activeink, a Texas-based company producing on-line problem-based learning materials that was perfectly constructed for this problem but still struggled (see Squire, Makinster, Barnett, & Barab, 2003). A game-based company that had some success in 2000–2001 was LightSpan, which developed materials for Sony PlayStations. LightSpan thought that, as the PlayStation2 took off, the mil-lions of unused PlayStations would make good, cheap 3-D gaming machines. Their games were eventually adopted by thousands of schools in 43 states. Many schools dropped them after a few years and they were sold to PLATO Learning Inc. Recently, PLATO repackaged the same games for the Sony PSP and they've gained new life.

Indeed, the past decade has witnessed the rise and fall of many technology-enhanced learning companies. Whereas the Learning Company was bought for $2 billion then sold for pennies on the dollar, Riverdeep leveraged its market position to eventually buy Houghton Mifflin. The business activity of the period was typi-cal of the dot-com bubble and crash. Companies such as Activeink or Riverdeep saw wild fluctuations in value as people identified business opportunities in digital education media companies.

Yet almost every game designer sees the opportunity; the economics of text-book publishing, in which schools replace expensive textbooks every few years, is flawed. The company that can create an online system in which content is regularly updated, assessments are integrated into the curriculum, and reports generated that feedback into instruction (particularly providing assessment data to teachers and parents) will have enormous opportunities. Virtual schools are one good place to look for this innovation, as they are deeply tied to digital content and compete with traditional schools for students' tuition dollars.

The "educational games" that succeed in this era in all likelihood won't be typical games with traditional content, but learning systems that span home, school, and other interests (such as hobbyist pursuits). They will be assessment systems. These may be summative assessment systems used for credentialing (i.e., to pass a professional exam), and they also may be used to inform learning deci-sions. They will identify what the user does and does not understand and offer diagnostic guidance. Much as many games auto-adjust difficulty settings, they will present new levels and challenges based on previous performances. Just as a *WoW* player goes online to access videos to learn strategy, learners will have ac-cess to expert performance represented in a variety of ways.

An integrated game system can also suggest new games, levels, or experiences (off-line or on) for extending learning further. These systems need to function as our mentors did in our after-school *Civ*Clubs, allowing students to build on their interests and extend them into new domains. Many of these functions may be done by *people*, rather than machines. Teachers generally do better than machines with these tasks. In our work in *Civ*Club, this process was deeply social, driven by personal relationships and mutual respect.

Along with Constance Steinkuehler and Richard Halverson, I am currently exploring how to capture performance and represent it back to players for learning. The classic example of this is *Rise of Nations*. As Gee (2007) describes, gamers love to pore over charts and graphs to see how they can improve. You see the same thing in raids in *WoW* as players study damage charts to measure their performance, or in our *Civ*Camps as players analyzed games to improve future performance. There may be opportunities to adapt *new* assessment models, such as evidence-based design, into educational games.

A big challenge is how to combine good game play and meaningful data about learning. Good games mix open- and closed-ended game play. They often support creative and novel solutions. They include opportunities for transgression. They present deep problems that we return to over and over and can approach from different angles. Many designers creating games from an assessment perspective (such as evidence-centered design) put the assessment, rather than the game play, first. As a result, they generate games that are assessable, but may not really be worth assessing as games.

When approaching the question of assessing learning through game play, it's good to take it with a good slice of humble pie, as it's really hard work. Franziska Spring (2009) published a dissertation on dynamic feedback in the game *Hortus*, a construction game around growing plants. Her goal was to understand what type of feedback helps players and how to assess learning through game play. She found that it's really difficult to discern patterns in players' actions whenever there are meaningful choices (actually, it's tough in any situation). It still remains to be seen if we can construct snapshots of cognition based on mouse clicks of these sorts.

All this is promising, but it's also a *huge* departure from what's happening in schools. There are *potential* alliances between assessments and games, but the intrinsic values of games (personalized learning experiences, choice, access to expert communities, and permeable walls of the classroom) contradict the rhetoric of control dominating today's educational discourse. As a result, these innovations may flourish in informal learning environments such as libraries, community centers, or museums, and perhaps through supplementary services.

INFORMAL LEARNING CONTEXTS

Informal learning institutions have incentives to build relationships with new constituencies. If my local museum can track my interests, it gains valuable market research data that it can use. Right now, Facebook is the hub for such marketing and advertising. However, Facebook ultimately owns that data. It would be nice to have multiple affinity spaces that enable institutions to capture this data (as Ning aspires to), but people seem loathe to join 18 different groups and systems. However, if K–12 schools remain inclined to "lock down" their systems banning Facebook and so on, schools' relevance may fade further.

Once educators move into informal settings, the context changes entirely. Informal educators are largely free to pursue the goals they think are important (rather than those imposed by political bodies). If you're at a science museum, these goals might range from increasing ethnic diversity among scientists to fostering scientific citizenship in adults. Creating engaging materials and producing lasting interest in science is an almost universal concern. Stakeholders need to entice learners, and if you're a science museum and fail to attract repeat visitors, you go out of business.

If games do indeed capture attention, increase interest, and springboard to other educational activities, then they are the perfect fit for informal education contexts. In fact, in a recent study, Miller (2001) found that consumption of science media trailed only the completion of a college degree in predicting science literacy. This statistic is striking. If we really want to make a difference in areas like science, maybe we're best off targeting out-of-school experiences, creating compelling learning experiences that propel kids to investigate science, just as *Pirates!* and *Civ* propelled me to take an interest in social studies. The question for educators is how to connect those interests to communities and ensure equitable access. Indeed, the real reason that compelling educational materials don't get made, even when the field appears to be at the cusp of producing a wave of engaging, effective materials, is that such engaging materials require preexisting knowledge (and motivation), are expensive, and are best experienced with a capable mentor. Closing this impending participation gap could be a mission for schools.

Working in informal contexts enables educators to avoid the top-down requirement of uniform learning outcomes. In *Civ*Camp, differential learning goals and outcomes contributed to the distributed center of expertise. Thus, the historical "problem" of games supporting diverse learning goals becomes a "feature" in informal settings.

Imagine visiting the aquarium and picking up (or buying) a game on the way out. The game might feature "realistic" depictions of the aquarium and levels with actual habitats. It might alert participants to new programs. As the owner of a 100-gallon tank myself, I'd love to play with different setups and purchase new fish directly in game to be shipped to my house. That's the sort of fluid boundary crossing that informal science educators want, and the kind of funding model that might make it happen.

Perhaps the best way for games to have an impact on mainstream education isn't by marching through the front doors of schools and hoping that scores of teachers will embrace these principles (although surely some will). Perhaps the better route is to gather informal science educators, game developers, and content specialists to create compelling games, and then build networks of teachers who use them creatively in their teaching. My own next generation of research will explore whether we can partner with scientists doing cutting-edge work in areas such as nanotechnology, epigenetics, personalized medicine, or systems biology to create games that communicate the ideas in their fields to broader publics. There's a clear need for compelling materials in these areas, and games seem perfectly suited for it.

SCIENTIFIC CITIZENSHIP

Scientific citizenship is one potential leverage point for building educational games. Today's dominant social and scientific issues (such as climate change, gene therapy, pandemics, or personalized medicine) require an informed populace capable of understanding scientific advancements as they develop (as opposed to learning "all they need to know" in school). Yet scientific civic literacy rates in the United States struggle to reach 20% (Miller, Pardo, & Niwa, 1997). "Scientific civic literacy," according to Miller, requires

1. An understanding of critical scientific concepts and constructs, such as ecosystems, the molecule, or DNA;
2. An understanding of the nature and process of scientific inquiry;
3. A pattern of regular information consumption; and
4. A disposition toward taking action to make change in one's lifestyle as necessary (adapted from Miller, 1998).

This model of scientific civic literacy has some added benefits as a reasonable "goal" of science-based games. It builds on findings suggesting that role-playing as professionals can be engaging, and it creates a bridging identity much closer to where students are. Further, it avoids fetishizing professional science as a model of expert behavior and suggests ways for people to be engaged with their own communities. So often we base our interventions on getting "kids to think like scientists" when, in reality, we want them to be active participants in a democratic society. We *do* want people to understand how scientists think and to experience being a scientist, but relying on such an approach exclusively perpetuates the myth that only professionals can do science.

Scientific citizenship is a particularly useful framework for designing educational games because it suggests how we might mobilize a citizenry toward action around areas of pressing concern, from global warming to water issues. There are many additional strategic benefits: Materials in these areas don't exist, most of the scientific fields are deeply embedded in simulation as a way of knowing, visualization is key for understanding the phenomena, and games enable broad and cheap distribution via the web. Given the fast-paced nature of scientific discovery, informal science education is poised to play a crucial role in ensuring that our populace is prepared to meet tomorrow's challenges.

EXAMPLE: *CITIZEN SCIENCE*

As an example of what this might look like, let's examine *Citizen Science*, a game I'm developing with Filament Games with support from the National Science Foundation (see figures 10.1, 10.2). *Citizen Science* is the latest chapter in the game design sequence of *Environmental Detectives, Mad City Mystery, Sick at South Beach, Saving Lake Wingra*. The game is based around Lake Mendota in Madison, Wisconsin. Lake Mendota, in addition to being right outside my office, is also thought to be one of the most thoroughly researched lakes in the world. The University of Wisconsin–Madison's limnology department (as one might predict) sits on the lake, and researchers have been studying it for about 100 years.

However, like many of the world's aquatic systems, Lake Mendota is under stress. Agricultural runoff dumps tons of fertilizers and waste into the lake every year. This runoff adds phosphates and nitrates to the water, which causes algae blooms. These algae cloud the water, threatening to choke the lake by blocking oxygen and sunlight. This process, called *eutrophication*, is a common one and threatens many urban lakes and waterways. Even worse, the effects of these phosphates often aren't experienced until *years* after the dumping occurs. So whatever algae problems we experience right now in Lake Mendota are a result of what farmers did upstream 20 years ago. If we stopped the dumping right now, we would have to wait 20 years to see an effect on the lake.

Figure 10.1.
Citizen Science,
Developed by
Filament Games with
Matt Gaydos and Kurt
Squire

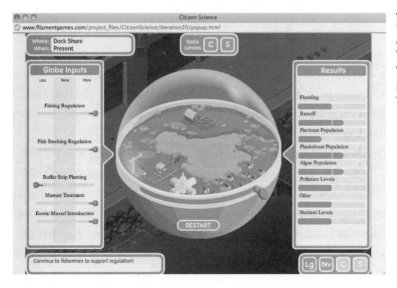

Figure 10.2.
An Embedded Model
That Players Use to
Test Theories About
Lake Mendota

Today, Lake Mendota isn't in great shape. It's a lot better than 40 years ago, back when they blatantly dumped waste into the lake. Still, Lake Mendota is nasty to swim in. When I first moved to Madison, this astounded me. Madison has this beautiful natural resource right on campus, blocks from downtown and the state capitol, and yet it is unswimmable.

Enter *Citizen Science*. One reason Madison hasn't done anything about Lake Mendota may be that people don't understand what's happening. Further, people haven't imagined Madison with swimmable lakes. One of the problems of any social design (whether it be schools or lakes) is that people get locked into mindsets of how things *are* and are unable to envision what they *could be* like. Could *Citizen Science* open up citizens' imagination by showing them what Lake Mendota *could* be like and then inspire people to action?

And wouldn't it be cool if game players had the experience of creating that change *themselves*? If you "saved Lake Mendota" in a game (much as you have saved plenty of worlds in role-playing games), might players develop similar dispositions in the real world? Such a game could have value beyond Madison or lake ecology. If you understand what's happening to Madison's lakes on a systemic level, then you have an intellectual toolkit to understand other key ideas in ecology.

MOBILE MEDIA

What is the next horizon for educational games research? Cell phones are one of the most quickly adopted technologies in history, although they have largely been overlooked by educators. The small screens and technological "thinness" of these devices make them easy to scoff at, but their educational potential is dramatic.

Already, over half of secondary students attend school with a mobile device in their pocket. For those who don't work with kids on a regular basis, this may be surprising, but cell phones are indispensable tools for coordinating busy schedules (Ito et al., 2008). This trend appears to cut across class lines. In 2009, the youth at *Civ*Camp all started showing up with iPod Touches (in addition to their mobile phones). They all know where the free WiFi is (i.e., in libraries, coffee shops, Culver's restaurants), just as the kids I taught 15 years ago knew how to get online at libraries with free broadband. Access is now ubiquitous. "Smartphones" (such as the BlackBerry, Palm Treo and Sidekick) were high-tech gadgets marketed to business professionals and technology geeks, but with the release of the iPhone (and, in response, Android and similar devices from their competitors), mobile media devices are penetrating the mainstream. It's a safe bet that mobile phones will be the first multimedia, networked computer technology to reach one-to-one penetration (Wellman, Smith, Wells, & Kennedy, 2008).

Skeptics might ask if youth will really access these devices in any broad fashion. My impression is an emphatic yes. Over the past year, our research team has begun studying this. We have interviewed kids with iPhones, we have bought iPhones for kids who didn't have them to see what happens, and we have experimented with teaching strategies in a classroom where *every student* had a broadband-enabled mobile media device.

The most obvious finding is that youth *love* their mobile devices. They love the ability to access personalized media in a mostly private environment. They love carrying their personal media libraries in their pockets, and they love being in touch with their friends anytime, anywhere. And they love games. The youth we studied with iPhones all download dozens of applications tied to their personal interest. Don't get me wrong, I love my computer, but I'm pushing 40. Today's youth see media differently. A mobile phone isn't a "weak computer" but rather a portable, indispensable media and communication device. Most often students have no control over their environment; mobile media devices give them tremendous power and control over their lives as they can pursue interests, participate in social networks, and consume and produce media wherever and however they want (see Squire & Dikkers, 2010).

Having an iPhone amplified these students' interest-driven learning. One of my favorite examples was a student named Tom, who, like many kids, was bright, but didn't do particularly well in school when he wasn't motivated. During a work period, I noticed him listening to something with his iPhone and futzing with it periodically while working on his project. I asked Tom what he was doing, and he showed me how he was listening to music on Pandora, looking up new artists that he likes online, using a guitar application to figure out chord progressions, and copying lyrics he liked into his notebook (or typing them into the notepad on his iPhone). Tom plays the guitar and is working on a band, and this was the "homework" he did in his spare time. He did all this while working on a neighborhood redesign project in Jim Mathew's class.

For Tom, the iPhone made it possible to pursue interests in a way that was unfathomable even 5 years ago. When I grew up you had to "know someone" to find out about new bands, which meant hanging out at record stores (if your town was lucky enough to have one) or finding the right 'zine. Five years ago, Internet-savvy people could do this at their computers, but broadband wasn't ubiquitous. Kids like Tom usually had to share family computers with parents and siblings. Today, Tom, with an iPhone, can pursue these interests while at the grocery store with his mom, on the way to soccer practice, or in between classes. In short, with mobile media devices we can pursue our interests throughout our day. This is profoundly important for youth who do not have the same unfettered access that many knowledge professionals—and parents—do.

In a very real way, these devices are reconfiguring our experience of place. Tom is simultaneously in his classroom, in his practice studio, and in contact with all of his friends. Many of the walls that have defined education (particularly to keep information or people *out*) are now removed.

Educators have only begun to pay attention to mobile devices, and mostly it's with the intent to ban them. Indeed, smartphones are incredibly disruptive to the dominant order of schooling. Every teacher competes for time with Tom's music, podcasts, film, and game collections, plus all Tom's friends and everyone he could potentially meet over the Internet. If a teacher says something Tom disagrees with, he can fact-check what the teacher said, perhaps without the teacher's even knowing it. Information (such as answers to test questions) can spread through a class or school in real time. In fact, there are already many stories of students taking pictures of tests with their phones and sending them around school. Texting answers is also reportedly on the rise, but most students I've interviewed report that if they cheated, it was easier to do it the old-fashioned way.

At the root of this disruption is a contradiction between the capacities of mobile media devices and the social order of schooling. The *private* nature of mobile media communication is key. A teacher has a hard enough time monitoring 30 kids when her back was turned. Now that they can communicate silently . . . good luck!

Cell phones won't dismantle the modern educational system on their own. In fact, every wave of technology going from radio, to film, to television, to the VCR, to computers, to the Internet has offered similar promise. However, personalized media devices should take a big chink out of the armor of the "teacher as lone authority-provider of information" model. *Kids are bringing them to school* whether educators like it or not.

Mobile media highlights how in every place but schools, learners are pursuing areas of personal interest with technology. The challenges mobile media present don't necessarily point to games as "the" solution. But games remain a good model to pursue given these conditions. Games excel at building and sustaining learners' interest in academically related areas. Games are models for teaching in which the goal isn't memorizing information, but *using* information to solve problems. Games enable and promote personalized learning (as players delve into different aspects of a model), and learning is often collaborative. And games allow for models of how students go from consumers to producers of information.

Indeed, future games probably will not live on one device or another, but will span any number of devices. In some ways, fantasy football or baseball are good models, in this regard. Games might collect data based on what players do, and then enable them to interact with the data back at the computer. This is a particularly good model for museums or community groups tied to specific places that want to continue a relationship beyond that experience.

At GLS, we're envisioning a class of applications that *deepen* a students' experience of place (rather than removing them from it) that learners can take with them everywhere they go (similar to Four Square). In the summer of 2010, our team launched its first iPhone application, ARIS (arisgames.org), which enables anyone to build a game like *Dow Day* or *Saving Lake Wingra* for their neighborhood.

CREATING THE FUTURE OF EDUCATIONAL TECHNOLOGY

It's an exciting time to be in educational technology—or it should be. Ideas that we once struggled to enact, such as simulation games, game-authoring systems, or knowledge-building communities, are now thriving. Educational technology sits at the intersection of technology, learning theory, and design and offers a crucial perspective for understanding how to design compelling educational media, question how they might change what it means to know, and research their impact with learners. I want to end this book with an argument for educational technology as a *creative* endeavor. This vision is inspired by Seymour Papert's desire to go out and *create* the future of learning rather than to simply study it. It represents a hope and passion absent in much scholarship today, given the current pressures for scientific rigor. Of course, we need to understand what works and what doesn't, but to frame our *entire* enterprise in such terms is, again, to risk standing on the sidelines of our own game.

I see more gamer- and Internet-generation students entering educational technology, and they are asking these questions. Many technology and learning enthusiasts are avoiding the academic sphere altogether and starting their own companies. New platforms like the iPhone should accelerate this. Regardless, today's youth have been raised with games, the Internet, and even cell phones, and they orient to this media far differently from the way I do.

I look forward to learning from them and reading the stories they have to tell. I hope you've enjoyed mine. We're working together to make this revolution happen.

On Researching the Effectiveness of Educational Interventions

A question nagging at many people (researchers in particular) is "This all sounds great, but where is the evidence that gaming really works?" Hopefully, this book has provided evidence that game-based learning *can* work, when executed well by creative designers and teachers, and that good education is always an interaction among students, materials, and teachers. But some people want something more definitive, a once-and-for-all, large-scale quantitative study proving that games are better than "X." Our research team and partners struggled with this demand ourselves at the completion of the *Lake Wingra* project. We wanted to compare the effects of the game to other curricula, both because our grant demanded it and because it felt intellectually honest. The grant required us to use randomized controlled trials (a technique borrowed from the medical industry) in accordance with No Child Left Behind.

GOLD STANDARD RESEARCH

Randomized controlled trials, or "gold standard" research, requires uniform treatments (everyone *doing* the same thing), being measured by uniform learning outcomes (everyone *learning* the same thing). The idea is that one group (the experiment) receives a treatment, whereas the other (the control) does something different (usually business as usual). Researchers want to demonstrate that the experimental group outperforms the control (as measured on standardized tests) and that the difference is due to the treatment rather than random variables. Already, critical readers might question whether an outside program is going to beat business as usual on tests if business as usual is the curriculum planned and executed by good teachers. Further, the best curriculum in this situation could be test prep, or at least improving kids' ability to identify correct answers (which is different from *constructing* a good answer, as in writing an essay or designing a game).

228

Underlying these statistical procedures is an emphasis on *uniformity*. The bane of such methods is *variation*, the fact that some kids in each group are smarter, or try harder than others, meaning that they're going to do better than others *regardless* of the intervention. Stick Albert Einstein in the control condition—wait, bad example; he did poorly at school. Place a good student in the control condition, and he or she will do better than a poor student in the experimental condition, no matter what you do. If you don't properly control for these differences—and every known cause of variance—success will appear to be "random" rather than caused by your intervention.

We randomly assigned students to treatment and control classes at the beginning of the unit, with roughly 30 kids in each group. This met our need for random assignment. Because they had the same teachers, we could rule out teacher effect. However, our results were less generalizable toward broader populations. Researchers often gloss over this problem; rarely, if ever, are populations truly sampled randomly. Usually convenience samples of classes willing to participate are used.

We knew that 2-week curricula rarely create statistically significant results. As a rule of thumb, you need at least 8 *weeks* to find anything. If you want to get a truly innovative 8-week curriculum going, you need a few years to work up to it. We plowed ahead with a 2-week experimental and control curriculum, kept the content and learning goals the same, but tested core features (roles, driving challenge, visit to Lake Wingra), through the experimental condition. We wanted *more* difference between the curricula, but the teachers objected. They normally taught with collaborative work and projects, and argued that removing these methods would be bad for the kids. Even though both groups read the same documents, did the same final project, and worked collaboratively, there were enough differences between them that it seemed worth testing.

In the end, both control and experimental groups showed gains on pre- and post-measures of around 20%, but we didn't find significant differences between them. So we had a "no significant difference" study. This well-known phenomenon says basically that it's hard to find differences between experiments and controls on learning with technology in schools when you hold everything else constant. You're asking a few changes in a curriculum to outweigh every other variable—motivation, ability, preexisting knowledge, and so on. Again, to make matters worse, you're measuring along predefined, static measures (rather than looking to see if kids write letters to the editor and so on).

The emphasis on standardization also prevented us from studying teachers like Tina in more depth. When Tina, Mindy, and Brian learned about our need to "lock down" the curriculum with predefined learning objectives, eliminate student game design, and include a tight experiment-control, they went their own way. I can't say that I blame them. Even sadder, they said, "Our standardized test scores are fine. Scripted instruction might be right for Milwaukee but not Oconomowoc."

We're not alone in these struggles. Not surprisingly, educators have had a tough time finding *any* program that is effective in such comparisons. A recent study by the Department of Education examining eight of its "scientifically" based curricula found weak or no evidence that six of them "worked," despite many millions in funding over years of development. The problems, as suggested here, are massive. How do you recruit schools to participate? How do you ensure that teachers use your materials? If a teacher believes that that method won't work for that class, do you still force him or her to use it?

The kinds of instruction that can be tested with these methods are limited. Anything where the teachers rework materials is out, because the "treatments" have to be standardized and compared to controls along predefined objectives. Anything that involves differential learning outcomes is out, because you're testing for *sameness* in outcomes in groups. In short, most of what works best through games (interest-driven learning, differential expertise, learning by design) is thrown out, because it cannot be tested under these methods. If this continues, our research procedures will drive how and what we teach.

"SCIENCE" FETISH

"Gold standard" research procedures come from agriculture, medicine, and to a lesser extent economics, as reflected by the name of the research designs (such as split *plot* factor from agriculture or randomized trials from medicine). The logic behind these procedures was developed to test fertilizers, weed killers, and drugs, things that have little in common with children. Let's begin with agricultural research, which can assume that all plants have the same attributes. Plants all come from the same seeds, plants don't have personal goals driving their growth, and plants can't choose not to grow. Agricultural researchers don't care whether the plant enjoys being fertilized, and a plant can't drop out of a farm to protest a farmer's methods. Agricultural researchers also aren't responsible for the health of the people who eat the food, a nontrivial thing given today's obesity problems.

Indeed, the similarities in policies—and inherent challenges—among agriculture, medicine, and education aren't coincidental. They are rooted in the pursuit of standardization and efficiency at the expense of *health*. As detailed elsewhere, the U.S. food economy that coalesced after the passing of the 1971 farm bill is bad for human and environmental health (see Pollan, 2006). Our food economy maximizes the production of calories through cheap corn. The effects on human health have been drastic. My generation is the first to have lower life expectancy than that of our parents, in part because obesity and diabetes, both partly traceable to diet (also perhaps to a lack of health care, to poverty, or to both). These agribusiness methods are *harming* our health because we produce and eat too much corn. This is to say nothing of the environmental effects of monoculture.

Why should educators emulate agribusiness (top-down control, maximizing returns, uniformity in outcomes)? The agricultural system has achieved many gains (diet soda and potato chips are cheap), but there have been accompanying bad consequences (decline in health). When educators embrace these methods, we see progress (rising test scores), but also huge side effects (the 4th-grade slump, increasing numbers of high school dropouts).

No single element needs to be changed (such as removing corn subsidies or standardized tests), but we need to overhaul the *system*. We can't blame teachers for reading scores or dropouts, any more than we can blame farmers for diabetes. Unfortunately, recent reform efforts involve much more of the same, as if dumping more fertilizer on crops will somehow cure diabetes.

Advocates of randomized, controlled studies believe that the real problems are *technical*, such as "low fidelity of implementation" (a teacher's customizing the curriculum), not controlling enough variables, or "dosage" problems (not enough contact time, as we experienced). It's shocking that this "dosage" metaphor is used without irony. On some level, researchers believe that curricula is an all-powerful "pill" that can save falling-behind children. Teachers may notice the assumption that they are basically Pez dispensers of knowledge.

Testing technocrats control the direction of educational research—particularly funding—at the federal level. Dissatisfied with educators' inability to show satisfactory results, they have begun importing specialists from other fields. The logic is that if we only had "harder scientists," such as economists or psychologists working in educational research, everything would be solved. During the Bush administration, the government legitimized these external research methods while declaring others unscientific. Ironically, anyone espousing this definition of scientific research would fail any introductory research course; scientificity is never a property of a method, but the fit between research questions, theory, methodology, and conclusions. But in fact, even that isn't how research works. In medicine, there is a long line of basic research that goes into developing a drug before it hits randomized trials (see Shaffer & Squire, 2006). Anyway, so much for smaller government.

Faced with this identity crisis, many educational researchers turn toward economics for more robust statistical models, which is precious, given that *our economy is going through its worse period in 50 years.* One could say, "Look, you economists couldn't see this real estate meltdown coming or deal with the declining American middle class, so clearly your methods are flawed," but we do not judge economists based on the performance of the economy. Yet educational researchers not only accept being judged based on the quality of the educational system, but *embrace* this critique.

If educational researchers are to blame for current educational practices, then logically political science and law professors are to blame for American politics and political discourse. Imagine the absurdity of blaming Bill Clinton's professors for his conduct. Similarly, should we blame *economists* for George Bush's economic policies or *philosophers* for the popular belief that Saddam Hussein was involved in the September 11 attacks? We don't hold any other group of researchers (or even practitioners) responsible for the state of its field/industry.

HEALTH CARE ENVY

This fetishization of technical methods from other fields is exemplified by educators' current penchant for the randomized trials of pharmaceutical research. Mapping this model onto education (students = patients, curricula = drugs, textbook companies = drug companies) makes little sense. I like to think of my children not as inherently sick, but as active, inquisitive people whose curiosities and skills need to be cultivated.

However, the medical model permeates educational discourse. The logic is that researchers should identify achievement gaps (illnesses) and use scientific methods to engineer curricula (drugs) to cure these illnesses, measuring the outcomes through science (randomized controlled trials). Once effective curricula have been developed, the challenge is to take them to scale, much like drug companies bring drugs to market. What could go wrong?

For one, there are unintended consequences. For example, we know that drill-and-practice instruction boosts reading scores up until the 4th grade, but that this approach doesn't help students read content for meaning and usually kills interest in reading later. When kids hit the 4th grade and need to read for comprehension in areas such as science and math, their scores plummet (hence the 4th-grade slump). Test scores aside, any reading intervention that hurts interest in reading is a failure simply for its long-term effects.

The elephant in the room is the horrid state of U.S. health care. Its failures are well noted: Costs are spiraling out of control, large swaths of people have no access, and there is no underlying emphasis on fostering health. Indeed, on surface-level features alone, the health care system is nothing for educators to emulate: Governed by profit, it provides limited access because of affordability, and *by design* does not work for everyone. These values could not be more antithetical to the historic vision of public education, which aspires to provide equal opportunity through universal access and to foster citizens capable of participating in a democracy.

Our health and educational systems are actually quite similar, although comparatively our educational system is *better*. We are somewhere between 20th and 30th in the world along most health-related and education-related measures: We are 33rd in infant mortality and mortalities under the age of 5 (although these are tricky numbers to compare). The United States is also around 30th in life expectancy. When the World Health Organization made its last rankings (year 2000), the United States was 37th in quality, sitting between Costa Rica and Slovenia. The United States has the most expensive health care system in the world but is the least fair of all countries in terms of who pays. In the 1990s the World Health Organization rated the United States 42nd when costs are considered.

In contrast, according to most measures, the United States is about 10 places higher—somewhere in the top 20—in education on most measures (although comparing is difficult, especially given how bad the measurement instruments are). U.S. schoolchildren perform differently at different ages, as is true in all countries. However, looking at two of the best measurement instruments, the 1998 UNICEF ranks the United States at 18th, and the TIMMS date on both math and science put the United States at around 12th. Like our medical system, our K–12 educational system is the most expensive in the world, although to a less-substantial degree. In fact, both systems are deeply colored by inequity. A person rushed to the emergency room in suburban Chicago has some of the best health care the world has seen, and a child attending public school in suburban Chicago attends one of the best schools in the world. A few miles away, millions of people have no access to basic health care and sit in crowded hospital rooms, and children attend schools rife with problems.

Schools at least *try* to provide universal access. Further, whereas teachers promote children's growth, doctors rarely promote health, instead treating disease. So educators should stand proud.

So what methods should we use? This book argues for design research models that instantiate pedagogical ideas in interventions co-constructed with teachers. This design approach is rooted in the pragmatic philosophy of Dewey. We can judge the quality of educational programs by how they *work* in the world, and we can measure these through a variety of methods (including quantitative and qualitative measures). Education is unique in spanning philosophy, social science, and basic and applied research. Dewey's lab school—a model of instantiating theory in practice—is but one way to recapture education's rich intellectual tradition unapologetically.

The pressing questions aren't which measurements to use, but how to rethink assessment and evaluation procedures for a more participatory age. As an Apolyton student or *WoW* player, I can challenge any claim made about my performance. I can challenge what evidence is used in claims about my performance, and I can muster new evidence to support claims I want to make. People enjoy participating in these systems in part because they have a voice in shaping the rules that govern them. This is oppositional to the idea that testing bureaucrats somewhere set standards, goals, and measurements and then see how well others live up to them.

We can design learning and assessment systems along similar principles, which we might think of as an assessment bill of rights. As a student (and teacher), my goals are reflected in assessment. I have the right to challenge any claims with counterevidence. I am responsible for arguing what constitutes valid evidence for learning. I should make claims and present my own evidence to bolster them.

Imagine students, teachers, and parents discussing what evidence constitutes successful participation in science. Imagine performance not being reduced to a single score on a normed test, but rather being measured through a battery of assessments (including those from peers) indicating what the student has done, is good at, and needs to work on in areas from game design to verbal communication. This future, I believe, is coming (in some way, shape, or form) in- or outside schools, and for certain learners. The timing is ripe for educators to participate in these dialogues, design these systems, and ensure that the future of education is equitable. I believe that games will be a part of that future. Everyone can see how games capture the imaginations of our youth, and developers of these systems are turning their skills toward education.

References

Barab, S. A., Squire, K., & Dueber, B. (2000). Supporting authenticity through participatory learning. *Educational Technology Research and Development, 48*(2), 37–62.

Barnett, M., Squire, K., Higgenbotham, T., & Grant, J. (2004). Electromagnetism supercharged! In Y. Kafai, W. Sandoval, N. Enyedy, A. Dixon, & F. Herrera (Eds.), *Proceedings of the 2004 International Conference of the Learning Sciences* (pp. 513–520). Mahwah, NJ: Lawrence Erlbaum.

Barron, B. J. S. (2002). Achieving coordination in collaborative problem-solving groups. *Journal of the Learning Sciences, 9*, 403–437.

Bartle, R. (1996). Hearts, clubs, diamonds, spades: Players who suit MUDs. *Journal of Virtual Environments.* Retreived from www.brandeis.edu/pubs/jove/HTML/v1/bartle.html/

Bauerlein, M. (2009). *The dumbest generation: How the digital age stupefies young Americans and jeopardizes our future (or, don't trust anyone under 30).* New York: Tarcher.

Beck, I. L., McKeown M. C., & Kucan, L. (2002). *Bringing words to life: Robust vocabulary instruction.* New York: Guilford Press.

Beck, J., & Wade, M. 2004. *Got game: How the gamer generation is reshaping business forever.* Cambridge, MA: Harvard Business School Press.

Bitz, M. (2010). *When commas meet kryptonite.* New York: Teachers College Press.

Black, R. W. (2008). *Adolescents and online fan fiction.* New York: Peter Lang.

Bransford, J. D., Brown, A. L., & Cocking, R. R. (1999). *How people learn.* Washington, DC: National Research Council.

Bransford, J. D., & Schwartz, D. L. (1999). Rethinking transfer: A simple proposal with multiple implications. In A. Iran Nejad & P. D. Pearson (Eds.), *Review of research in education, 24*, 61–101. Washington, DC: American Educational Research Association.

Bronfenbrenner, U. (1979). *The ecology of human development: Experiments by nature and design.* Cambridge, MA: Harvard University Press.

Bruckman, A. (1993). Gender swapping on the Internet. *Proceedings of INET '93.* Reston, VA: The Internet Society. Retrieved from www.cc.gatech.edu/~asb/papers/gender-swapping.ps

Cassell, J., & Jenkins, H. (1998). *From Barbie to Mortal Kombat : Gender and computer games.* Cambridge, MA: MIT Press.

Chan, A. (2002). *Collaborative news networks: Distributed editing, collective action, and the construction of online news on Slashdot.org.* Unpublished master's thesis, MIT, Cambridge, MA.

Church, D. (2000, March). *Abdicating authorship.* Presentation made at the annual meeting of the Game Developer's Conference, San Jose, CA.

Church, D. (2005). Formal abstract design tools. In K. Salen & E. Zimmerman, (Eds.), *The game design reader: A rules of play anthology* (pp. 366–381). Cambridge, MA. MIT Press.

Cobb, P., Stephan, M., McClain, K., & Gravemeijer, K. (2001). Participating in classroom mathematical practices. *Journal of the Learning Sciences, 10*, 113–163.

Cognition and Technology Group at Vanderbilt. (1990). Anchored instruction and its relationship to situated cognition. *Educational Researcher, 19*(6), 2–10.

Collins, A., Brown, J. S., & Newman, S. E. (1989). Cognitive apprenticeship: Teaching the craft of reading, writing, and mathematics. In L. B. Resnick (Ed.), *Knowing, learning, and instruction: Essays in honor of Robert Glaser* (pp. 453–494). Hillsdale, NJ: Erlbaum.

Collins, A., & Halverson, R. (2009). *Rethinking education in the age of technology*. New York: Teachers College Press.

Cook, T. D., & Conner, R. F. (1976). The educational impact of "Sesame Street": A review of the existing evaluative research. *Journal of Communication, 26*, 155–164.

Crawford, C. (2003). *Chris Crawford on game design*. Indianapolis, IN: New Riders.

Crecente, B. (2009, March 29). Maria Montessori, the 138-year-old inspiration behind *Spore*. *Kotaku*. Retrieved from http://kotaku.com/5164248/maria-montessori-the-138+year+old-inspiration-behind-spore

Csikszentmihalyi, M. (1990). *Flow: The psychology of optical experience*. New York: Harper Perennial.

Cuban, L. (1986). *Teachers and machines: The classroom use of technology since 1920*. New York: Teachers College Press.

Daer, A. J., (2010). This is how we do it: A glimpse at GameLab's design process. *E-Learning and Digital Media, 7*(1), 108–119.

Davidson, D. (2008). Well played: Interpreting *Prince of Persia: Sands of Time*. *Games and Culture, 3*(3–4), 356–386.

Davidson, D. (n.d.). *Well played*. Pittsburgh, PA: Entertainment Technology Press. Retrieved from www.lulu.com/product/ebook/well-played-10-video-games-value-and-meaning/10978743

Dean, K. (2001). Gaming: Too cool for school? *Wired*. Retrieved from http://www.wired.com/culture/lifestyle/news/2001/01/40967

DeVane, B., Durga, S., & Squire, K. (2009). Competition as a driver for learning. *International Journal of Learning and Media, 1*(2). Retrieved from www.mitpressjournals.org/doi/abs/10.1162/ijlm.2009.0018

Diamond, J. (1999). *Guns, germs, and steel: The fates of human societies*. New York: Norton.

Diamond, J. (2004). *Collapse: How societies choose to fail or succeed*. New York: Viking.

DiSessa, A. (2000). *Changing minds: Computers, learning, and literacy*. Cambridge, MA: MIT Press.

Dori, Y. J., & Belcher, J. (2005). How does technology-enabled active learning affect undergraduate students' understanding of electromagnetism concepts? *The Journal of the Learning Sciences, 14*(2), 243–279.

Dunn, R. E. (2000). Constructing world history in the classroom? In P. N. Stearns, P. Seixas, & S. Wineburg (Eds.), *Knowing, teaching, and learning history*. New York: New York University Press.

Egenfeldt-Nielsen, S. (2005). *Beyond edutainment: Exploring the educational potential of computer games*. Unpublished doctoral dissertation. Copenhagen: IT-University Copenhagen.

Forbus, K. (1997, May/June). Using qualitative physics to create articulate educational software. *IEEE Expert, 12*(3) , 32–41.

Friedman, T. (1999). *Civilization* and its discontents: Simulation, subjectivity, and space. In G. Smith (Ed.), *Discovering discs: Transforming space and place on CD-ROM* (pp. 132–150). New York: New York University Press.

Games-to-Teach Team. (2003). Design principles of next-generation digital gaming for education. *Educational Technology, 43*(5), 17–33.

Gee, J. P. (2003). *What video games have to teach us about learning and literacy*. New York: Palgrave Macmillan.

Gee, J. P. (2005). *Why video games are good for your soul: Pleasure and learning*. Melbourne: Common Ground.

Gee, J. P. (2007). *Good video games and good learning: Collected essays on video games, learning, and literacy—New literacies and digital epistemologies*. New York: Peter Lang.

Gee, J. P. & Hayes, E. (2010). *Women and gaming: The Sims and 21st-century learning*. New York: Palgrave Macmillan.

Gibson, J. J. (1979). *The ecological approach to visual perception*. Boston: Houghton Mifflin.

Giordano, A. (2008). Global tanning: The anatomy of a media virus. *The Field*. Retrieved from http://narcosphere.narconews.com/thefield/global-tanning-anatomy-media-virus

Gladwell, M. (2008). *Outliers: The story of success*. Boston: Little, Brown.

Goodman, D. A., & Crouch, J. (1978). Effects of competition on learning. *Improving College and University Teaching, 26*(2), 130–133.

Gordon, B. (2009). Bing Gordon foresees games replacing textbooks at schools. Panel presentation at the Game Developers Conference, San Francisco, CA. Retrieved from http://games.venturebeat.com/2009/01/23/gamesbeat-09-preview-bing-gordon-foresees-games-replacing-textbooks-at-schools/

Gredler, M. E. (2004). Games and simulations and their relationship to learning. In D. H. Jonassen (Ed.), *Handbook of research on educational communications and technology* (2nd ed., pp. 571–582). Mahwah, NJ: Lawrence Erlbaum.

Heckendorn, B. (2005). *Hacking video game consoles: Turn your old video game systems into awesome new portables.* New York: Wiley.

Herz, J. C. (1995). *Surfing on the Internet.* Boston: Little, Brown.

Herz, J. C. (1997). *Joystick nation.* Boston: Little, Brown.

Hmelo-Silver, C. (2004). Problem-based learning: What and how do students learn? *Educational Psychology Review, 16*(3), 236–266.

Holland, W., Jenkins, H. & Squire, K. (2003). Theory by design. In B. Perron & M. Wolf (Eds.), *Video game theory.* London: Routledge.

Ito, M., Horst, H., Bittanti, M., Boyd, D., Herr-Stephenson, B., Lange, P. G., et al. (2008). *Living and learning with new media: Summary of findings from the Digital Youth Project.* Chicago: The MacArthur Foundation.

Jacobs, J. (1961). *The death and life of great American cities.* New York: Random House.

Jenkins, H. (2006). *Convergence culture.* New York: New York University Press.

Jenkins, H., Squire, K., & Tan, P. (2003). You can't bring that game to school!: Designing *Supercharged!* In B. Laurel (Ed.), *Design research* (pp. 244–252). Cambridge, MA: MIT Press.

Jenlink, P., & Carr, A. A. (1996, January–February). Conversation as a medium for change in education. *Educational Technology, 36*(1), 31–38.

Johnson, S. (2005). Your brain on video games: Could they actually be good for you? *Discover, 26*(7). Retrieved from http://discovermagazine.com/2005/jul/brain-on-video-games

Johnson, S. (in press). Theme and meaning. Reprinted in C. Steinkuehler, K. Squire, & S. Barab (Eds). *Games + learning + society.* Cambridge, UK: University of Cambridge Press.

Karras, A. L., & McNeill, J. R. (1992). *Atlantic American societies: From Columbus through abolition, 1492–1888.* New York: Routledge.

Kilpatrick, W. H. (1914). The Montessori system examined. Boston: Houghton-Mifflin.

Kirschner, P. A., Sweller, J., & Clark, R. E. (2006). Why minimal guidance during instruction does not work: An analysis of the failure of constructivist, discovery, problem-based, experiential, and inquiry-based teaching. *Educational Psychologist, 41*(2) 75–86.

Klopfer, E. (2008). *Augmented learning: Research and design of mobile educational games.* Cambridge, MA: MIT Press.

Klopfer, E., & Squire, K. (2007). Case study analysis of augmented reality simulations on handheld computers. *Journal of the Learning Sciences, 16*(3), 371–413.

Koster, R. (2004). *A theory of fun for game design* (1st ed.). Phoenix, AZ: Paraglyph.

Kozma, R. (2000). Reflections on the state of educational technology research and development. *Educational Technology Research and Development, 48*(1), 5–15.

Kretschmer, J. (n.d.). Darii, the godmother. Retrieved from *www.outland.org/infusions/imm_info/ imm_list.php?imm_id=5*

Laurel, B. (2002). *Utopian entrepreneur.* Cambridge, MA: MIT Press.

LeBon, L. B. (2003). Students petition against TEAL. *The Tech, 123*(14), 15. Retrieved from http://tech.mit.edu/V123/PDF/N14.pdf

Lemke, J. (1990). *Talking science: Language, learning, and values.* Norwood, NJ: Ablex.

Lenhart, A., Rainie, L., & Lewis, O. (2010, June). *Teenage life online: The rise of the instant-message generation.* Pew Internet & American Life Project. Retrieved from http://www.pewinternet.org

Levin, D., & Arafeh, S. (2002). *The digital disconnect: The widening gap between Internet-savvy students and their schools.* Pew Internet & American Life Project. Retrieved from http://www.pewinternet.org/PPF/r/67/report_display.asp

Levy, P. (1997). *Collective intelligence*. New York: Basic Books.

Librande, S. (2010). *The one page game design document*. Presentation made at the annual meeting of the Game Developers Conference, San Francisco, CA.

Loewen, J. W. (1995). *Lies my teacher told me: Everything your American history textbook got wrong*. New York: New Press.

Ludwig, J. (2008, Spring). Conversation: Don't shoot—Social Service Administration. Retrieved from www.ssa.uchicago.edu/publications/ssamag/conversationsSp08.shtml

Malaby, T. (2009). *Making virtual worlds:* Linden Lab *and* Second Life. Ithaca, NY: Cornell University Press.

Manning, P. (2003). *Navigating world history: Historians create a global past*. New York: Palgrave Macmillan.

Maraniss, D. (2004). *They marched into sunlight*. New York: Simon & Schuster.

Mathews, J., & Squire, K. D. (2009). Augmented reality gaming and game design as a new media literacy practice. In K. Tyner (Ed.), *New agendas for media literacy* (pp. 209-232). Oxford, UK: Taylor & Francis.

Mayer, R. E., & Johnson, C. I. (2010). Adding instructional features that promote learning in a game-like environment. *Journal of Educational Computing Research, 42,* 241–265.

McCall, J.B. (2011). *Gaming the past: Using video games to teach secondary history*. New York, NY: Routledge.

McKenzie, N. (in press). Nurturing lateral leaps in game design. In C. Steinkuehler, K. Squire, & S. Barab, (Eds.), *Games + learning + society*. New York: Cambridge University Press.

McNeil, W. H. (1998). World history and the rise and fall of the west," *Journal of World History, 9*(2), 215–236.

Miller, J. D. (1998). The measurement of civic scientific literacy. *Public Understanding of Science, 7(3),* 203–223.

Miller, J. D. (2001). The acquisition and retention of scientific information by American adults. In J. H. Falk (Ed.), *Free-choice science education: How we learn science outside of school* (pp. 93–114). New York: Teachers College Press.

Miller, J. D., Pardo, R., & Niwa, F. (1997). *Public perceptions of science and technology: A comparative study of the European Union, the United States, Japan, and Canada*. Madrid, Spain: BBV Foundation Press.

Mitchell, E. (1985). The dynamics of family interaction around home video games In Personal computers and the family [Special issue]. *Marriage and Family Review 8*(1–2), 121–135.

Montessori, M. (1936). *The secret of childhood*. Andhra Pradesh, India: Orient Longman Ltd.

Montessori, M. (1967). *The absorbent mind*. New York: Holt, Rinehart and Wintson.

Moriarty, B. (1998). *Entrainment*. Retrieved from http://ludix.com/moriarty/entrain.html

Moulitsas, M. Z. (2008). *Taking on the system: Rules for radical change in a digital era*. New York: Celebras.

Nash, G., Crabtree, C., & Dunn, R. (2000). *History on trial: Culture wars and the teaching of the past*. New York: Vintage.

National Academies of Science. (2003). *Planning for two transformations in education and learning technology: Report of a workshop*. Washington, DC: NAS Press.

National Endowment for the Arts (NEA). (2004). *Reading at risk: A survey of literary reading in America*. Retrieved from www.nea.gov/pub/ReadingAtRisk.pdf

New London Group. (2000). A pedagogy of multiliteracies: Designing social futures. In B. Cope & M. Kalantzis (Eds.), *Multiliteracies: Literacy learning and the design of social futures* (pp. 9–37). New York: Routledge.

Nitsche, M. (2008). *Video game spaces: Image, play, and structure in 3D worlds*. Cambridge, MA: MIT Press.

Norton, Dan. *A practical model for seperating games and simulations*. Games+Learning+Society [Conference]. Madison, WI. 10 July 2008.

Palincsar, A. S., & Brown, A. L. (1984). Reciprocal teaching of comprehension-fostering and comprehension-monitoring activities. *Cognition and Instruction, 1*(2), 117–175.

Papert, S. (1981). *Mindstorms: Children, computers, and powerful ideas*. New York: Basic Books.

Papert, S. (2002). Hard fun. *Bangor Daily News*. Retrieved from http://www.papert.org/

Pearce, C. (2001). *Sims*, battleBots, cellular automata, God and Go: A conversation with Will Wright. *Game Studies, 2*(1). Retrieved December 6, 2010, from www.gamestudies.org/0102/pearce/

Pollan, M. (2006). *The omnivore's dilemma: A natural history of four meals*. New York: Penguin.

Poole, S. (2000). *Trigger happy: Videogames and the entertainment revolution*. London: Fourth Estate.

Prensky, M. (2000). *Digital game-based learning*. New York: McGraw Hill.

Randel, J. M., Morris, B. A., Wetzel, C. D., & Whitehill, B. V. (1992). The effectiveness of games for educational purposes: A review of recent research. *Simulation and Gaming, 23*(3), 261–276.

Rathunde, K., & Csikszetnmihalyi, M. (2005). Middle school students' motivation and quality of experience: A comparison of Montessori and traditional school environments. *American Journal of Education, 111*(3), 341–371.

Reigeluth, C. M., & Garfinkle, R. J. (Eds.). (1994). *Systemic change in education*. Englewood Cliffs, NJ: Educational Technology.

Rejeski, D. (2002, September 23). *Gaming our way to a better future*. Washington, DC: Woodrow Wilson Foundation.

Rieber, L. P. (1996). Seriously considering play: Designing interactive learning environments based on the blending of microworlds, simulations, and games. *Educational Technology Research and Development, 44*(2), 43–58.

Rieber, L. P. (2005). Multimedia learning in games, simulations, and microworlds. In R. E. Mayer (Ed.), *The Cambridge handbook of multimedia learning* (pp. 549–567). New York: Cambridge University Press.

Savery, J. R., & Duffy, T. M. (1995). Problem-based learning: An instructional model and its constructivist framework. *Educational Technology, 35*(5), 31–37.

Schank, R., Fano, A., Bell, B., & Jona, M. (1993). The design of goal-based scenarios. *Journal of the Learning Sciences, 3*(4), 305–345.

Schut, K. (2007). Strategic simulations and our past: The bias of computer games in the presentation of history. *Games and Culture, 2*(3), 213–235.

Shaffer, D., & Squire, K. (2006). The pasteurization of education. In S. Tettegah & R. Hunter (Eds.), *Advances in Educational Administration* (pp. 43–55). New York: Emerald.

Silberman, L. (2009). *Double play: Athletes' use of sport video games to enhance athletic performance*. Master's thesis, MIT, Cambridge, MA.

Silver, M. (2004, December 13). Stepping out. *Sports Illustrated*. Retrieved from http://sportsillustrated.cnn.com/vault/article/magazine/MAG1114662/2/index.htm

Simmons, W. (2007, January 12). Time for a new corollary. *ESPN Page 2*. Retrieved from http://sports.espn.go.com/espn/page2/story?page=simmons/070112

Simmons, W. (2009). *The book of basketball*. Bristol, CT: ESPN.

Sirlin, D. (2000). *Playing to win*. Retrieved from www.lulu.com/sirlin/

Sizer, T. (2004). *Horace's compromise: The dilemma of the American high school*. Boston: Houghton Mifflin.

Spiegelman, A. (1986). *Maus I: A survivor's tale, My father bleeds history*. New York: Pantheon.

Spring, F. (2009). *Learning and play styles in open-ended games for learning*. Unpublished dissertation, University of Zurich.

Squire, K. (2005). Toward a theory of games literacy. *Telemedium, 52*(1–2), 9–15.

Squire, K. (2010). From information to experience: Place-based augmented reality games as a model for learning in a globally networked society. *Teachers College Record, 112*(10), 2565–2602. Retrieved from www.tcrecord.org/Content.asp?ContentId=15930/

Squire, K., & Dikkers, S. (2010). *Mobile learning: Amplifications*. Paper presented at the Annual Meeting of the American Educational Research Association, San Diego, CA.

Squire, K., & Giovanetto, L. (2008). The higher education of gaming. *E-Learning and Digital Media, 5*(1), 2–28. Retrieved from http://dx.doi.org/10.2304/elea.2008.5.1.2/

Squire, K., & Klopfer, E. (2007). Augmented reality simulations on handheld computers. *The Journal of the Learning Sciences, 16*(3), 371–413.

Squire, K. D., & Jan, M. (2007). *Mad City Mystery*: Developing scientific argumentation skills with a place-based augmented reality game on handheld computers. *Journal of Science Education and Technology, 16*(1), 5–29.

Squire, K. D., Jan, M., Matthews, J., Wagler, M., Martin, J., Devane, B., & Holden, C. (2007). Wherever you go, there you are: The design of local games for learning. In B. Sheldon & D. Wiley (Eds.), *The design and use of simulation computer games in education* (pp. 265–296). Rotterdam: Sense Publishing.

Squire, K. D., Makinster, J., Barnett, M., Barab, A. L., & Barab, S. A. (2003). Designed curriculum and local culture: Acknowledging the primacy of classroom culture. *Science Education, 87*(4), 468–489.

Squire, K. D., & Reigeluth, C. M. (2000). The many faces of systemic change. *Educational Horizons, 78*(3), 143–152.

Starr, P. (1994). Seductions of Sim. *The American Prospect, 5*(17). Retrieved from *www.prospect.org/print/V5/17/starr-p.html/*

Stearns, P. N., Seixas, P., & Wineburg, S. (2000). *Learning history: National and international perspectives.* New York: New York University Press.

Steinkuehler, C. A. (2006). Massively multiplayer online videogaming as participation in a discourse. *Mind, Culture, and Activity, 13*(1), 38–52.

Steinkuehler, C. A., & Chmiel, M. (2006, June). *Fostering scientific habits of mind in the context of online play.* Paper presented at the 7th International Conference of the Learning Sciences, Bloomington, Indiana.

Steinkuehler, C., Compton-Lilly, C., & King, E. (2010). Reading in the context of online games. In K. Gomez, L. Lyons, & J. Radinsky (Eds.), *Learning in the disciplines: Proceedings of the 9th International Conference of the Learning Sciences (ICLS 2010) Volume 1, Full Papers* (pp. 222–230). Chicago, IL: International Society of the Learning Sciences.

Steinkuehler, C., & Johnson, B. Z. (2009). Computational literacy in online games: The social life of a mod. *The International Journal of Gaming and Computer Mediated Simulations, 1*(1), 53–65.

Stevens, R., Satwicz, T., & McCarthy, L. (2008). In game, in room, in world: Reconnecting video game play to the rest of kids' lives. In K. Salen (Ed.), *Ecology of Play* (pp. 41–66). Cambridge, MA: MIT Press.

Sutton-Smith, B. (2001). *The ambiguity of play.* Cambridge, MA: Harvard University Press.

Turkle, S. (2003). From powerful ideas to PowerPoint. *Convergence: The Journal of Research into New Media Technologies, 9*(2), 19–28.

Wallace, M. (2006, September 6). Blizzard's Pardo on WoW's success. *Gamasutra.* Retrieved from *www.gamasutra.com/php-bin/news_index.php?story=10773/*

Wellman, B., Smith, A., Wells, A., & Kennedy, T. (2008). *Networked families.* Washington, DC: Pew Internet & American Life.

Wertsch, J. (2000). Can we teach knowledge and belief at the same time? In P. N. Stearns, P. Seixas, & S. Wineburg (Eds.), *Knowing teaching and learning history: National and international perspectives* (pp. 38–50). New York: New York University Press.

Wiley, D., & Edwards, E. K. (2002). Online self-organizing social systems: The decentralized future of online learning. *Quarterly Review of Distance Education, 3*(1), 33–46.

Williams, D. (2006). Groups and goblins: The social and civic impact of online gaming. *Journal of Broadcasting and Electronic Media, 50*(4), 651–670.

Wineburg, S. (2000). Making historical sense. In P. N. Stearns, P. Seixas, & S. Wineburg (Eds.), *Knowing teaching & learning history: National and international perspectives* (pp. 306–326). New York: New York University Press.

Wolfe, C. R. (1995). Homespun hypertext: Student-constructed hypertext as a tool for teaching critical thinking. *Teaching of Psychology, 22*(1), 29–33.

Wright, W. (2006). Dream machines. *Wired, 14*(04). Retrieved March 4, 2011 from www.wired.com/wired/archive/14.04/wright.html

Zimmerman, E., Squire, K., Steinkuehler, C. A., & Dikkers, S. (2009). Real-time research: An experiment in the design of scholarship. *E-Learning, 6*(1), 119–140.

Zuckerman, O., Arida, S., & Resnick, M. (2005). *Extending tangible interfaces for education: Digital Montessori-inspired manipulatives.* Proceedings of the SIGCHI conference on Human factors in computing systems, Portland, Oregon. (pp. 859–868). Retrieved from http://portal.acm.org/citation.cfm?id=1055093/

Index

f, n, or t following a page number refers to a figure, note, or table, respectively.

2D Boy Games, 214
"100-Acre-Wood," 44–45
1337 discourse, 152
2008 election, 70

"Abdicating authorship," 148
Activeink, 218
Adult gamers, 38
Advanced Encryption Standard, 215
Aesthetics of game-based learning, 160–161
Aesthetics of games, ix, 140–163
Affinity spaces, 64–68, 69, 75, 220
Agent Orange, 186
Agricultural research model, 230–231
Alpha Centauri, 23n
Amazon.com, 48
Ambiguity of Play, The, 162
Amplification of input, 148–149
Android, 224
Animal Crossing, 140
Apolyton.net. *See* Apolyton University
Apolyton University, 150–155, 153t, 158–163
Application for game roles, 199
Aqualung, 153
AR, 183–211
Arafeh, S., 15
Arcadia, 146
Arida, S., 53
ARIS, 227
Arizona State University, x
Art direction, 86–87, 93–94
Asheron's Call, 81
Assessment, 200–201, 205–206, 205f, 219
"Assessment bill of rights," 234
Assessment systems, 218
Atari, xi, 67, 146

Augmented reality gaming, 183–211
Authentic activities, 162, 193, 196, 209
Authenticity in games, 36, 87, 196, 205
Avatar, 40–43, 44–45, 144

Balanced systems, 35
Banks, Wabash, 18
Barab, A. L., 218
Barab, S. A., 193, 218
Barab, Sasha, 218
Barbican, 62
Barnett, M., 95, 218
Barnett, Mike, 95
Barriers to technology integration, 202
Barron, B. J. S., 193
Bartle, R., 61
Bascom Hill, 186
BASIC, 79
Bauerlein, M., 70
Beck, J., 163, 203
Beckmann, Patrician, 93
Belanger, Lyndee, 199
Belcher, John, 90, 92, 94, 95
Belcher, J., 95
Bell, B., 140
Bell Labs Science Films series, 79
Berger, Nate, 44–45, 46, 47, 59
Best-of-the-best game mod, 152, 155
Best practices for game development, 216
Betrus, Tony, 63
Bias in games
  Civilization III, 121–122
  Civilization model, 135–136
  general, 22–26
  Sims games, 32
Bias in social studies education, 110–112

Bill Nye the Science Guy, 85
Biohazard, 86–87, 88f
Bioshock, 148
Bittanti, M., 47, 224
Bitz, M., 78
Black, R. W., 14
Black and White, 61
BlackBerry, 224
Blizzard, 8, 35, 65, 83, 160. *See also under*
    World of Warcraft
Book of Basketball, The, 69
"Boot camp," 151
Boston College, 95
Boston Museum of Science, 39
Boyd, D., 47, 224
Braid, 215
Brain Age, 3, 82, 87, 215
Bransford, J., 140
Bransford, J. D., 98, 136
Briggs, Jeff, 22
Brin, Sergey, 48
Bronfenbrenner, U., 81
Brookline, Massachusetts, 112
Brown, A. L., 12, 98
Brown, J. S., 153
Bruckman, A., 61
Budget mechanics, 206
Building Homes of Our Own, 217
Bullen, Dawn, 51
Bunsella Films, 93

C#, 100
Cambridge, Massachusetts, 74
Capital Times, The, 209
Capra, Frank, 79
Carnegie Mellon University, 86, 87
Carr, A. A., 197
Cassell, J., 62
Cell phone, 215, 224
Center for the Study of Upper Midwest Cultures,
    189
Centers of expertise, 177
Cerniglia, Joe "Buffo," 189
Chan, A., 63
Chen, Jenova, 216
Chicago, Illinois, 186
Child, Julia, 48
Chisholm, Alex, 74, 217
Chmiel, M., 34
Church, D., 90, 148
Church, Doug, 8, 68

Citizen science. *See* Scientific citizenship
Citizen Science, 106t, 222–224, 223f
CivII. See Civilization II
CivIII. See Civilization III
CivIV. See Civilization IV
*Civ*Camp, 128–131, 170, 177, 180, 181, 194,
    220, 224
*Civ*Club, 165–180, 196, 212, 219
Civilization
    balance, 156, 156n
    and bias, 22–26
    Civ Olympics, 173–176
    and competition, 172–176
    critiques, 133–136
    early popularity, 19–20
    editor, 130
    and educational value, 21–30, 34, 35, 36
    fluency development, 168–169
    "gameness" of, 29
    as geographical model, 26–28
    as ideological world, 29–30, 36
    lexicon, 165
    map, 130
    multiplayer, 169–170
    play aesthetics, 140–164
    and realism, 29
    as sandbox genre game, 106
    social factors, 10
    trajectory of experience, 34
    (*See also* Apolyton University; *Civ*Camp;
        *Civ*Club; *Civilization II; Civilization III;
        Civilization IV*)
Civilization II, 22, 29
Civilization III, 22, 109, 112, 113–136, 137,
    151, 156
Civilization IV, 22, 23, 15
Clark, R. E., 56
Class interactions, 204–205
Classroom game testing, 94–99
Classroom management, 113–115, 199
Class talk, 204–205
Cleslewicz, Mayor Dave, 192
Cobb, P., 119
Cocking, R. R., 98
Cognition and Technology Group at Vanderbilt,
    140
Cognitive apprenticeship, 153, 180
Cognitive artifacts, 153
Collaboration in gaming, 38–39, 105, 169, 184,
    196
Collapse, 25

Collective intelligence, 159
Collins, A., 153, 213
Colonization, 177
Comic books, 78
Commodore 64, 2
Communication role of art, 93
Community organization, 61–76, 194, 195–196
Community partnerships, 211–212
Competition, 142, 170–176
Compton-Lilly, C., 46
Computer Games magazine, xii
Connecting in-school and out-of-school lives, 177
Conner, R. F., 85
Constructionism, 21
Consumer to producer ramp, 33, 37
Context in media use, 84–85
Cook, T. D., 85
Cooldown, 146
Cooperative play, 38–39, 105, 169, 184, 196
Corpse retrieval, 40–41
Cosmos Chaos, xii
Cottage industries, 160
Counterstrike, 160
Crabtree, C., 111
Crawford, C., 28
Crayon Physics, 215
Creating game content. *See* Modding;
    Participatory culture
Crecente, B., 57
Credibility of media, 70
Critical literacy, 71
Csikszentmihalyi, M., 56, 147, 148
Cuban, L., 80
Cuckoo Time!, 86, 87f, 89
Culture flipping, 154
Cultures, 12–13, 118–122, 129

Daer, A. J., 94
Daily Kos, 14, 62, 64
Daily Radar, 62
Dance, Dance, Revolution, 63
Darii, the Godmother, 42
DARs, 152, 153–155
Davidson, D., 150, 214
Dean, A., 63
Death and Life of Great American Cities, The, 43
Dede, Chris, 196, 197
Design
    design literacy, 165–181
    design thinking, 155–158
    and entertainment, 148

and learning theory, 80–81, 89–90
and literacy, 175–176
and play, 83–84
principles of, 5–10
studies of, x
teams for, 105–106
Designing games for learning, 19–37, 56–57,
    77–108
Design-then-play rhythm, 88
Desktop Tower Defense, 215
Deus Ex, 61, 72, 73, 90, 140, 148, 149
DeVane, Ben, 165, 197
Devane, B., 189
Developing game expertise, 166–167
Dewey, John, 15, 74, 233
Diamond, J., 25, 112, 124
Dikkers, S., 41, 225
Digital Games Research Association, 62, 141
Digital literacy, 64
Digital media and learning, 14–15, 21
DiGRA, 62, 141
DimenxianM, xii
Diner Dash, 5, 6, 215
Direct X, 92
DiSessa, A., 92
Diversity of games, 3, 4
Doing vs. telling, 142–143
Donald Duck in Mathmagicland, 79
Doom, 61
Doonesbury's Election Game, 78
Dora the Explorer, 213
Dori, Y. J., 95
Douglas, Jim, 1
Dow Chemical Company, 185
Dow Day, 186
Dow Day, 106t, 185–188, 187f
Dueber, B, 193
Duffy, T. M., 89, 193
Dunn, R., 111
Dunn, R. E., 111, 112, 137
Durga, Shree, 165
During Action Reports, 152, 153–155
Dynamic feedback, 219

E3, 81, 83
East Asia, 83n
Ecologies in affinity spaces, 66–67
Economics learning, 134
Editor, 130, 168
Educational game development, 90–94, 100,
    106, 215, 216, 217

Educational games, xii, 56–57, 105, 215
Educational media, 79, 213–214
Education goals, xii
Education reform process, 197
Edwards, E. K., 64
Effectiveness of interventions, 228–234
Effects of teaching with games, 106–139
Egenfeldt-Nielsen, S., 177
Egozy, Eran, 91
Electromagnetism, 90, 91, 92
Electronic Arts, 8, 71, 160, 214
Electronic Entertainment Expo, 81, 83
E-Line Ventures, 217
Elitist Jerks, 13
Embedded assessment, 200–201
Embodied learning, ix–x
Emergent patterns in games, 126
Endogenous game play, 80
Engagement, 5, 15, 115, 138
Engineering, 214–215
Entertain Electronic Exposition, 78
Entertainment and educational media, 79
Entertainment Technology Program, 86
Entrainment, 145, 146
Environmental Detectives
   data analysis, 102f
   development, 100–101
   general, 222
   implementation, 99–104
   as linear action game, 106t
Environmental Protection Agency, 100, 102
EPA, 100, 102
Equity and affinity spaces, 68–69
Erikson, Erik, 48
ESPN, 69
Europa, 177
EverQuest, 81, 83, 160
Execution vs. ideas, 83
Experiential learning, ix, 88, 161
Expertise, 129–137, 142, 147, 150, 195
Externalizing play, 170
"Eye candy" notion, 86, 87, 93

Facebook, 220
Failure states, 142, 149
Fano, A., 140
Farside. See Avatar
Feynman, Richard, 79
Fez, 215
Figueroa, Rob, 92
Filament Games, 142, 215, 222

Final Fantasy: Crystal Chronicles, 38
Financial literacy, 197–198
Financial simulation, 17
Firaxis, 22, 159
Firefighter training, 87
Fire Hose Games, 215
First-Person Shooters, xi
Flash, 215
Fleicher, Max, 79
"Floor or ceiling" debate, 96
Flow, ix, 148
Flow, 215
Flower, 8, 148, 215
Flow theory, 147–148
Forbus, 95
Forbus, K., 92
Ford, Matt, 78
Forensic games, 206
Formal abstract design tools, 8
FPSs, xi
Frank, Anne, 48
FreQuency, 92
Friedman, T., 25
Friends of Lake Wingra, The, 207
From Barbie to Mortal Kombat, 62
Full Spectrum Warrior, 97, 106t, 107, 108
Fund for the Improvement of Postsecondary
   Education, 87n
"Fun factor", 5–10
Future of games for learning, 213–227

Game Boy Advance, 38
Gamecritics.com, 68
GameCube, 38, 142
Game Developers Conference, 67, 68, 71, 148, 215
GameLab, 146
Game On, 62
Game-playing cultures, 12–13, 118–122, 129
Game publishing, 216
Gamer mindset, 65
Games and learning field, x, xiii
Games as sites of learning, 1–15
Games + Learning + Society, 141
Games literacy, 83–85
Games research, 141
GameStar Mechanic, xii
Game statistics, 121, 122t
Games-to-Teach Project, 77, 83, 85–104, 206
Games-to-Teach Team, 90, 206
Game Studies, 80, 141
Games vs. simulations, 29

Game testing and communities, 159
Gaming communities, 12–13, 30–35, 61–75,
    119, 138, 159, 162. *See also* Affinity spaces;
    Apolyton University; *Civ*Camp
GarageBand, 14
Garfinkle, R. J., 197
Gates, Bill, 71
GDC, 68, 71
Gee, J. P., 5, 31, 44, 64, 68, 130, 140, 141, 142,
    148, 155, 194, 219
Gender and games, 97–98, 120–121, 166,
    171–172
Genres of games, 105, 106t
Geography learning, 3, 133
Gernsback, Hugo, 79
Gibson, J. J., 81, 94
Gillespie, Thom, 79
Giordano, A., 67
Giovanetto, Levi, 3, 151, 159, 165, 166, 169–
    170
Gladwell, M., 69
Global Positioning System, 100, 101
"Global Tanning: Anatomy of a Media Virus," 67
GLS, 141, 226, 227
Goals in gaming, 6–8, 36
"Gold standard" research, 228–230
Goodwin, Jon, 61, 68, 71
Google, 48
Gordon, B., 71
Gordon, Bing, 71, 160
GPS, 100, 101
Graham, Katherine, 48
Grand Theft Auto, 29, 30, 66, 96, 211
Grant, J., 95, 193
Gravemeijer, K., 119
Great Lakes Water Institute, 198
Great Pyrenees dogs, 46
Gredler, M. E., xiii
Greenbush, 188–192, 193
Greenbush, Wisconsin, 188–189, 190–194
"Greening up," 82
Green Monster Studios, 160
Grinding, 146
Gu, Sulvan, 209–210
Guardian, 68
Guitar Hero, 164
Guns, Germs, and Steel, 112

Hacking Video Game Consoles, 67
Half Life, 160
Halo, 3, 90

Halverson, R., 213
Halverson, Richard, 219
Harboe, Gunnar, 100, 101
Hardcore games, 142, 144
Harmonix, 91, 164
Harvest Moon, 3
Hayes, E., 31, 194
Health care model of research, 232–233
Heckendorn, B., 67
Heckendorn, Benjamin, 67
Hephaestus, 88, 106t
Herr-Stephenson, B., 47, 224
Herz, J. C., 21, 62, 72
Hidden Agenda, 80
Higgenbotham, T., 95
Hinrichs, Randy, 74, 77
Hip Hop Tycoon, 197–198
History learning, 3, 134
History on Trial, 111
Hmelo-Silver, C., 193
Hocking, Clint, 148
Holden, C., 189
Holden, Chris, 197
Holland, Walter, 91
"Horse and buggy problem," 101n
Horst, H., 47, 224
Hortus, 219
Houghton Mifflin, 218
Hulk Davidson, 143, 143f

ICampus, 77
Ico, 10
Idea vs. execution, 83
Identity, 10–12, 36, 61–62, 131–132
Ideological worlds, 28–35, 36
Immersion-to-investment process, 150
Immune Attack, 106t
IMovie, 14
Implementing games research in classes, 94–95
Inaccuracies, 23–24
Independent games, 214–219
Independent learning, 13n, 59
Indianapolis Depot, 18
Indiana University, 62, 63, 74
Informal learning contexts, 219–221
Inside Magazine, 72
Institute for Creative Technologies and
    Pandemic, 107
Institutions in a participatory age, 70
Integrated design teams, 105–106
Intellectual play, 4, 15

Interactive narratives, 149
Interactivity, 90, 149
Interdisciplinary connections, 132–133
Interest development, 15, 36, 177–179
Interest-driven learning, 19–22, 46–47, 59, 195, 225
Internal Review Board, 117n
IPhone, 224, 225, 227
IPod Touch, 224
IRB, 117n
IrrKlang, 215
Italian Workmen's Club, 190, 191f
Ito, M., 47, 224
Ivan Vasily, 182–183

Jack's Big Music Show, 213
Jacobs, J., 43
Jan, M., 184, 189
Jan, Mingfong, 184
Jenkins, H., 14, 62, 69, 92
Jenkins, Henry, xii, 38, 67, 68, 72, 74, 77, 107, 164
Jenkins, Henry IV, 78
Jenlink, P., 197
Jigsawing, 166, 184, 196, 200
Johnson, B. Z., 33
Johnson, C. I., xii
Johnson, S., 4, 13
Johnson, Soren, 150, 151, 158, 159
Jona, M., 140
Jones, Chuck, 79
Joystick Nation, 62
Joystick101.org, xii, 61, 63–69, 71, 75, 81
Just-in-time lectures, 116, 138

Kaplan, Jeffrey, 160
Karras, A. L., 24
Kilpatrick, W. H., 51, 56
King, E., 46
Kirschner, P. A., 56
Klopfer, E., 100
Klopfer, Eric, 38, 99, 196
Knowledge generation, 151, 153–154, 161
Knowledge sharing, 8, 129, 151
Knoxville Montessori School, 49
Kongregate, 215
Koster, Raph, 8, 35, 67, 82, 160
Kozma, R., 84
Kretschmer, J., 42
Kretschmer, Janet, 42–43, 46, 85n
Kucan, L., 203

Kurtz, Tina, 199, 200, 201, 211

Lake Mendota, 182
Lake Michigan, 198, 202
Lange, P. G., 47, 224
Lara Croft, 61
Laurel, B., 172
Laurel, Brenda, 72
Lea, ix
Learning
    communities of, 61–76
    and competition, 170–172
    and digital media, 14–15, 21
    and game design, 80–81
    and school-based gaming, 127–128
    through game play, 40–59
Learning Company, 218
Lebon, L. B., 95
Leeroy Jenkins, 4
Legos, 79
Lemke, J., 25, 204
Lenhart, A., 172
Levels and leveling, x, 82, 97, 148
Levin, D., 15
Levy, P., 159
Lewis, O., 172
Lexicon creation, 154
LGN, 217
Libcurl, 215
Librande, S., 215
Lies My Teacher Told Me, 111
LightSpan, 218
Linear action genre, 106t
Literacy and games, 140, 205–206
Loewen, J. W., 70, 110, 111
LOGO, 79
Lotka-Volterra equations, 28
Love, 215
"Ludic spirit," 195
Ludwig, J., 202

Mac, 83n
McCarthy, L., 10
Mad City Mystery, 182–185, 189, 194, 198, 222
Madden, 10, 11
Madison, Wisconsin, 141, 185–194, 208, 222, 224
Makinster, J., 218
Malaby, T., 94
Manning, P., 111
Manuals and rules, 130–131
Maraniss, D., 186

Mario Brothers, 146
Market research, 216
Marshall McLuhan, 137
Martin, J., 189
Martin, John, 189
Mary Lou Fulton Presidential Professor of
    Literacy Studies, x
Massachusetts Comprehensive Assessment
    System, 112
Massachusetts Institute of Technology. *See* MIT
Massively multiplayer games. *See* MMOs
Mastery. *See* Expertise
MATCH, 109, 112, 113–136, 137
Mathematica software, 88
Mathews, Jim, 185, 186, 188, 198, 202
Matthews, J., 189
Maus, 78
Maxis team, 32, 33
Mayer, R. E., xii
MCAS, 112
McCall, J. B., 177
McClain, K., 119
McGonigal, Jane, 68
McGuffey Foundation School, 40–58, 59, 85n
McKenzie, N., 160
McKenzie, Nathan, 94
McKeown, M. C., 203
McNeil, W. H., 111
McNeill, J. R., 24
Meaning-making in ideological worlds, 30–31
Media and Technology Charter School, 109,
    112, 113–136, 137
Media failures, 70
Media literacy, 67
Media vs. play debate, 30
Meier, Sid, 2, 17-22, 68, 161–162
Metroid, 94
Microsoft, 72, 73, 74, 77
Microworld genre, 106t
"Militainment," 108
Military Operations in Urban Terrain
    Simulation, 107
Miller, J. D., 220, 221
Milwaukee, Wisconsin, 200, 201, 202, 207
Misogyny in video games, 78n
Mister Rogers, 48
MIT
    and competition, 175
    educational games development, 39, 74, 77,
        185
    and TEAL, 94–95

MIT Teacher Education Program, 99–100
Mitchell, E., 109
Miyamoto, Shigeru, 68
MMOs, 4, 10, 12, 35, 81, 160–161, 170. *See
    also under World of Warcraft*
Mobile media, 224–227
Modding, 33, 34, 65, 155–156, 157, 174,
    175–176
Model-based reasoning, 104
Models, 23, 23n
Model UN, 85n
Modifications. *See* Modding
Moisl, David, 86
Montessori, M., 49, 52
Montessori, Maria, 15, 49
Montessori system, 48–58, 204
Moriarty, B., 145
Moriarty, Brian, 145
Morris, B. A., xii
Mortal Kombat, 61
Motivation in gaming, 150
Moulitsas, M. Z., 64
MOUT, 107
MUDding and MUDs, xi, 40–43, 44–45, 48, 63,
    83, 144
Multiplayer games, 9, 169–170, 179–180, 195.
    See also MMOs; *See also under World of
    Warcraft*
Multiplexer, 65
Multi-User Dungeons, xi
Mystery at the Museum, 39
Mythic Entertainment, 160

Narratives, 149, 180
NASA Exceptional Scientific Achievement
    Medal, 90
Nash, G., 111
National Academies of Science, 87 or National
    Academy of Sciences?
National Association of Home Builders, 217
National Endowment for the Arts, 47
National Public Radio, 68
National Science Foundation, 222
Nepf, Heidi, 100
.NET, 100
New London Group, 44, 175
Newman, S. E., 153
New York Times, 70
Ninja Gaiden, 142
Nintendo, 3, 109, 214
Nintendogs, 3

Nitsche, M., 31, 179
Niwa, F., 221
Normalization, 52
Norton, Dan, 142
Nova, 213

Obama, Barack, 70
Odyssey, xi
Okami, 148
Onassis, Jacqueline Bouvier Kennedy, 48
"One size fits all" education, 213
Online communities. *See* Affinity spaces;
    Apolyton University; MMOs
Open access, 48
Open Dynamics Engine, 215
Operation Frontal Lobe, 79
Operation Jelly-Filled Doughnuts, 45
Oregon Trail, xii, 3, 79
Orland, Kyle, 68
Overgeneralizing, 81–83
Overlapping goals, 7–8
Owens, Trevor, 147

Page, Larry, 48
Palincsar, A. S., 12
Palm Treo, 224
Pandora, 225
Papert, S., 21, 173
Papert, Seymour, 101n, 227
Pardo, R., 221
Parent participation in media use, 85
Participation and game aesthetics, 161–162
Participation trajectories, 34, 34f, 150–153,
    176–177
Participatory communities. *See* Affinity spaces;
    Apolyton University
Participatory culture, 12, 14, 15, 21, 68, 71, 75.
    See also Joystick101.org
Participatory learning, 61–76, 194–195
Patrician, 177
Patterns of change approach to history, 111–112
P Diddy, 48
PeaceMakers, xii
Pearce, C., 31, 32, 33
Peegs.com, 69
Pegram, Mike, 69
Perceptions about gamers, xiii
Perceptions about games, 3
Performance before mastery, 155
Performative game play, 164
Persistent-world genre, 106t

Personalized learning, 226
Physics, 90, 91, 92, 98. *See also*
    Electromagnetism
Physics-based games, 90–92, 214
Physics-first curriculum, 95
Physicus, 91
Piaget, Jean, 48
Pirates!, 1–3, 5, 6–7, 9, 74, 96, 177
Place-based gaming, 185–188
Place-based learning, 188–194
"Planes" of gaming, 31, 180
PLATO Learning Inc., 218
Play and designers, 83–84
Play concept, 162n
Players as designers, 180, 194, 208
Player to designer trajectory, 43–45
Playfulness of games, 163, 195
PlayStation, 67, 216, 218
Play styles, 96–99
Play vs. media debate, 30
Pokémon, 140
Pollan, M., 231
Polyrhythm, 146
Pong, xi, 146
Pontifex, 214
Poole, S., 148
Poole, Stephen, 68
PopCap Games Framework, 215
Portal, 160
Possibility spaces, 8–9
Pragmatic research models, 233–234
Predictive simulation, 91
Prensky, M., 80
Press Start, 68
Primary documents, 186
Prince of Persia, 150
Problem-based learning, ix
Problem-centered discussion, 204–205
Problem solving play, 4
Problems vs. puzzles, 90–91
Productive play, 160–161
"Professor Jenkins Goes to Washington," 78n
Prototyping, 92, 100, 106
"PS2 Launches! Word from the Street!", 67
Puzzlement, 89
Puzzle-solving games, 214
Puzzles vs. problems, 90–91

Quake, 63, 145–146
Quentin Tarantino's Star Wars, 78
Quest Atlantis, 106t

Railroad Tycoon games, 17–18, 177
Rainie, L., 172
Randel, J. M., xii
Randomized controlled trials, 228–230, 231
Rantings of Lumthemad, 160
Raphael, Jordan, 72
Rapid expansion, 153–154
Rathunde, K., 56
Raven Studios, 141
Reader Rabbit, 73, 74, 79
Realism/unrealism, 121–122, 122t
Recursive play, 116–117, 122–127
Reigeluth, C. M., 197
Rejeski, D., 78
Relevance motive for learning, 196
Replaying history, 115
Representativeness of a stimuli, 81n
Resilient Planet, xii
Resistance to technology integration, 201–202
Resnick, 53
Results of class game testing
    Civilization, 117–118, 124–126
    Environmental Detectives, 103–104
    Saving Lake Wingra, 208–209
    Supercharged!, 97–99, 99f
RevRaven, 68
REXing, 153–154
Reynolds, Brian, 22
Rez, 92
Rhythm, 145–146
Rieber, L. P., xiii, 80
Rigopoulos, Alex, 91
Rise of Nations, 219
River City, 106t
Riverdeep, 218
Rock Band, 3, 31, 82
Role-playing, 199–200
Role-playing games, 184, 186, 190, 196
Role-playing genre, 106t
Rome Total War, 177
Rules and manuals, 130–131
Runescape, 46

Sandbox genre, 106t
Savery, J. R., 89, 193
Saving Lake Wingra, 106t, 207–210, 222
Scaling, 67, 210–211
Schank, R., 140
Schilling, Curt, 160
Schneider, Edd, 63
Schultz, Ben, 4

Schut, K., 26
Schwartz, D. L., 136
Science fetish, 230–232
Science-learning games, 206
Science-mystery games, 101–103
Scientific citizenship, 207–210, 221–222
Scientific civil literacy, 221
SCOOP code, 62
Sea Dogs, 7, 96
Secret of Childhood, The, 49
Seixas, P., 110
Self-improvement games, 82, 87
Sensory experience, 148
Sesame Street, 85, 213
Shaffer, D., 231
Sick at South Beach, 198–206, 211, 222
Sidekick, 224
Sid Meier. *See* Meier, Sid
Silberman, L, 11
Silver, M., 11
Simmons, Bill, 47, 69
Simmons, W., 69, 195
Simple DirectMedia Layer, 215
Simplification, 23–24
Sims games
    general, 3, 31–33, 81
    SimCity, 21, 50, 58, 106t, 109
    Sims, The, ix, 3, 32, 33, 57, 97
    Sims Online, The, 81–82
Simulations vs. games, 29
Singapore-MIT GAMBIT Game Lab, 92
Sirlin, D., 142
Situated learning, ix–x, 182–212
Sizer, T., 53
Skill improvement, 122
Skills application, 195
Slashdot.org, 62, 63, 66, 67
Smarphone, 224
Social factor, 10–12, 36, 131–132, 150, 166, 180
Social networking, 225
Social order of schools and mobile media, 226
Social studies, 109–110, 133–135
"Soft modding," 194
Soglin, Paul, 186
Soloway, Eliot, 140
Sony, 81, 218
Spaulders, 13, 13n, 14
Spector, Warren, 72, 74
Spiegelman, A., 78
Splinter Cell, 148
Spore, 5, 31–32, 57

Spring, F., 219
Spring Harbor Middle School, 209
Square Enix, 38
Squire, K., 38, 41, 80, 92, 95, 100, 123, 151,
    164, 177, 184, 189, 193, 197, 199, 218,
    223f, 225
Standardization in research, 229–230
Standards, 110, 110n
Starcraft, 78, 83n
Starr, P., 130
Star Wars Galaxies, 81
States, 144
State University of New York, Binghamton, 63
Satwicz, T., 10
Stearns, P. N., 110
Steering student game play, 169–170
Steinkuehler, C. A., 4, 10, 33, 34, 41, 46, 66, 219
Steinmeyer, Phil, 17
Stephan, M., 119
Stephanopoulos, George, 70
Stevens, R., 10
Strategies for teaching with games, 138–139
Styles of play, 96–99
Success by design, 164
Supercharged!, 91–93, 93f, 94–99, 105, 106t,
    215
Super Mario Brothers Headquarters, 68
Super Mario Galaxies, xi
Super Why, 85
Surfing on the Internet, 21
Surge, 106t
Sustainability in schools, 206–207
Sutton-Smith, B., 162
Sweller, J., 56
Swiss Montessori Society, 48
Systemic thinking, 5, 11, 36, 138, 155, 193

Taking On the System, 64
Tan, P., 92
Tank function, 11
Teacher-designed games, 211
Teachers and Machines, 80
"Teacher's red pen," 45
Teaching with games, 40–59
TEAL, 94
Technical methods of research, 230–232
Technology Enabled Active Learning course, 94
Technology-enhanced learning companies, 218
Telling vs. doing, 142–143
Testing effectiveness of game-based education,
    228–230

Testing games, 106
Testing in schools, 204, 231
Text-based online cooperative game. *See*
    MUDding and MUDs
Textbook publishing, 217, 218
"The Great Video Game Crash of 2000," 68
Theory and design, 80–81
Theory building and testing, 169–170
Theory of Fun for Game Design, 8
Theseus, 151
The War at Home, 186
They Marched into Sunlight, 186
Thief, 90–91, 148
Thotbott, 160
Tigole, 160
Time orchestration, 6–7
Timing, 146
TinyXML, 215
Tom Clancy, 148
Torque Garage Games, 215
Trajectories of participation, 34, 34f, 150–153,
    176–177
Transgressive play, 119–120
Transparency, 130
Trigger Happy, 148
Truth in design, 156, 156n
Turkle, S., 130

UbiSoft, 148
Ultima, 61, 81, 83
UNICEF education rankings, 233
Uniformity, 229–230
Unity, 215
Universalis, 177
University of California, Irvine, 63
University of Southern California, 71, 107
University of Wisconsin—Madison, 3
Urban Ecology Center, 207
Urban renewal, 190–191, 190n
U.S. Department of Education, 196
User scenarios, 88

Valve, 160
Vietnam War, 186
Viewtiful Joe, 142–145, 143f, 147, 149, 160
Virtual University, 106t
Visual design, 86–87
Visual humor, 86
Vogel, Rich, 83
Wade, M., 163
Wagler, M., 188–192, 188f, 189, 194, 201, 210

Wallace, M., 83
Walt Disney, 79
"War college," 151
Warner, Jack, 79
Weiner, Eric, 44, 45, 46, 47, 59
Wertsch, J., 111
Wetzel, C. D., xii
What Video Games Have to Teach Us About Literacy and Learning, 141
When Commas Meet Kryptonite, 78
Whitehill, B. V., xii
Whyville, 106t
Wii Fit, 3, 82, 214
Wiley, D., 64
Williams, Brian, 70
Williams, D., 196
Will Wright. *See* Wright, Will
Wilware, 215
Win state, x, 150
Wineburg, S., xiii, 110
Wired.com, 67
Wisconsin Public Radio, 64
Wisconsin Youth Company, 212
Wolfe, C. R., 21
Wolfe, Christopher, 21, 58
WolfQuest, 106t
Woodrow Wilson Foundation, 78

World Health Organization, 233
World history education, 109–112
World of Goo, 8, 150, 214–215
World of Warcraft, 7–10
    affinity spaces, 65, 66
    balance, 35
    and communities, 11–14
    and cottage industries, 160
    development, 83
    and "fun factor," 7–10
    and hardcore gaming, 144
    influence on gaming, 4
    participatory gaming, 33, 195
    and rhythmic play, 146
WoW. See World of Warcraft
WPR, 64
Wright, Will, 5, 22, 31, 32, 33, 48, 57, 65, 68, 72, 74

Xbox game systems, 67, 71, 215
Xzins, 65

YouTube, 14

Zimmerman, E., 41
Zimmerman, Eric, 67, 72, 146
Zuckerman, O., 53